LIBERTY, EQUALITY, FRATERNITY

JAMES FITZJAMES STEPHEN

EDITED BY STUART D. WARNER

LIBERTY FUND

This book is published by Liberty Fund, Inc., a
foundation established to encourage study of the ideal of a society of
free and responsible individuals.

【✳】 ╣人≫

The cuneiform inscription that serves as our logo and as the design
motif for our endpapers is the earliest-known written appearance of the
word "freedom" (*amagi*), or "liberty." It is taken from a clay
document written about 2300 B.C. in the Sumerian city-state
of Lagash.

Frontispiece portrait from a photograph by Bassano, 1886.

Library of Congress Cataloging-in-Publication Data

Stephen, James Fitzjames, Sir, 1829–1894.
Liberty, equality, fraternity / James Fitzjames Stephen;
edited by Stuart D. Warner.
p. cm.
Includes bibliographical references and index.
ISBN 0-86597-110-2 (alk. paper). — ISBN 0-86597-111-0 (pbk.:
alk. paper)
1. Liberty.   2. Equality.   3. Mill, John Stuart, 1806–1873—
Contributions in political science.   I. Warner, Stuart D., 1955–
II. Title
JC571.S83   1993
323.44—dc20   93-12505

08 21 22 23 24 C 6 5 4 3 2
21 22 23 24 25 P 8 7 6 5 4

LIBERTY, EQUALITY, FRATERNITY

James Fitzjames Stephen

ἡδύ τι θαρσαλέαις
τὸν μακρὸν τείνειν βίου ἐλπίσι, φαγαῖξ
θυμὸν ἀλδαίνουσαν ἐν εὐφροσύναις,
φρίσσω δέ σε δερκομέγ'α
μυρίοιξ μόχθοιξ διακναιόμενου.
Ζῆνα γὰρ οὐ τρομέων
ἐν ἰδία γνώμη σέβει
θνατοὺξ ἄγαυ, Προμηθεῦ

PROM. VINCT. 535–542

Sweet is the life that lengthens,
While joyous hope still strengthens,
And glad, bright thought sustain;
But shuddering I behold thee,
The sorrows that enfold thee
And all thine endless pain.
For Zeus thou has despised;
Thy fearless heart misprized
All that his vengeance can,
The wayward will obeying,
Excess of honour paying,
Prometheus, unto man.

Prometheus Bound
(translated by G. M. Cookson)

CONTENTS

FOREWORD

James Fitzjames Stephen's *Liberty, Equality, Fraternity* figured prominently in the mid- to late nineteenth century Victorian debates on two concepts at the heart of politics in the modern world—liberty and equality. Understanding himself to be a defender of an older English Liberalism that he thought to be under assault and weakening at an ever-quickening pace, Stephen attempted in *Liberty, Equality, Fraternity* to offer a corrective to what he believed were the mistaken views of liberty, equality, *and* fraternity that were leading the charge. He found these views most fully and powerfully expressed in three of John Stuart Mill's works: *On Liberty, The Subjection of Women,* and *Utilitarianism*. Stephen thus subjected Mill's political philosophy to intense criticism in *Liberty, Equality, Fraternity*. Yet Stephen was no mere polemicist, and throughout *Liberty, Equality, Fraternity* we find Stephen's own understanding of liberty—as ordered liberty—equality—as equality under law—and fraternity—as a value incompatible with a free society—braided around his critique of Mill. And it is *this* understanding that is the most important feature of *Liberty, Equality, Fraternity*, and is eminently worthy of the attention of anyone concerned with the character of a free society.

We will be aided in our pursuit of Stephen's understanding of liberty, equality, and fraternity by first surveying certain features of his life and times and the influences upon his thought.

James Fitzjames Stephen was born in London on March 3, 1829. His father, Sir James Stephen, was for a time Regius Professor of Modern History at Cambridge, a position later held by Lord Acton. Stephen's father drafted the legislation abolishing the slave trade in the British Empire, and his grandfather too, James Stephen, labored to abolish slavery.[1] Stephen's education took him to Eton, Kings College (London), and Trinity College (Cambridge) where he was a student of Sir Henry Sumner Maine. After further study at the Inner Temple, he was called to the Bar in 1854. Stephen's pursuit of a career in law carried him to India in 1869 to serve for some two and a half years as Legal Member of the Viceroy's Council (succeeding Maine) and ultimately to a Judgeship on the Queen's Bench.

Stephen's legal career would surely have failed to provide sufficient support for his immediate family, so he took up a second career as a journalist. Stephen wrote often and on a wide range of intellectual matters. Many of his best pieces appeared in four periodicals in particular: *Cornhill Magazine*, *Fraser's Magazine*, *Pall Mall Gazette*, and *Saturday Review*. Eventually, 55 of the articles that Stephen published in *Saturday Review*, ones that he himself admired, were collected and published in three volumes in 1892, two years before his death, as *Horae Sabbaticae*.[2] Many of these have the outward appearance of book reviews and canvass in some detail the works of Thomas Hobbes, David Hume, Edward Gibbon, Edmund Burke, Jeremy Bentham, and Alexis de Tocqueville, among others. And although the intellectual influences upon Stephen were many, his understanding of things moral, social, and political perhaps owes most to Bentham and Hobbes.

Through Bentham, Stephen came to favor utilitarianism. Yet Stephen's utilitarianism was not the technical, philosophical doctrine that one finds represented in Bentham or presented in Henry Sidgwick's *The Methods of Ethics*. Rather, it was a certain disposition of mind that expressed itself by privileging observation and facts over abstract reason. Stephen's utilitarianism is most profoundly marked by a recognition that a calm and intelligent appraisal of moral and political life requires an understanding of the advantages and disadvantages of pursuing one course of conduct rather than another. Our starting point for appraising our moral and political lives demands that we begin from where we are—our time, place, and circum-

1. For more on the role of the Stephen family in the anti-slavery movement, see Frank J. Klingberg, *The Anti-Slavery Movement in England* (New Haven: Yale University Press, 1926).

2. See the bibliography on p. xxvii for a complete reference to this and other works by Stephen cited in this foreword.

stances—for the question we are addressing is what to do next, and that can only be answered by first discovering where we are. Stephen's utilitarianism, therefore, aims at the reform of current practices, not their elimination, and it is certainly not a morality and politics of uniformity.

Hobbes's influence on Stephen is more diffuse and perhaps for that reason greater. Stephen's admiration for Hobbes—"the greatest of English philosophers"[3]—is profound. Of *Leviathan*, Stephen writes, "Hardly any *magnum opus* of the speculative kind has been so maturely weighed, so completely thought out, and so deliberately fashioned to express in every point the whole mind of its author."[4] Stephen was particularly attracted to the idea that informs the whole of *Leviathan*, namely, that political philosophy rests upon a conception of human nature. It is not surprising, then, that Stephen's own conception of human nature animates *Liberty, Equality, Fraternity*, which should lead us to understand Stephen's work as a meditation upon human nature as applied to the practical world of political association.

Although it is the spirit of Hobbes more than any particular one of his theories that seems most to have affected Stephen, there are two distinct features of Hobbes's thought that penetrated deeply into Stephen's work. The first of these is the view that the interests of human beings conflict, and that this is an irremediable feature of the human condition; and insofar as the interests of individuals conflict, they may arrive at different conceptions of the good.

The second feature of Hobbes's thought that greatly influenced Stephen is the idea that social order depends upon the imposition of force. Social order, in this view, requires the restraint of morality, law, and religion; and these forms of restraint obtain their power to bring about social order from the intermediary of some human agency.

Liberty, Equality, Fraternity appeared first in periodical form—anonymously, although its author was no secret—in the *Pall Mall Gazette* from November of 1872 through January of 1873. It was published in book form in

---

3. From an autobiographical fragment cited in Leslie Stephen, *The Life of Sir James Fitzjames Stephen* (New York: G. P. Putnam's Sons, 1895), p. 116. Also, in a telling remark, Stephen says, "Of all men of his age [Hobbes] was most alive to the importance of treating all questions as questions of fact, and of not being led away by phrases." *Horae Sabbaticae*, vol. 2, p. 63.

4. *Horae Sabbaticae*, vol. 2, p. 20.

March of 1873 and followed a year later by a second edition which included
some minor substantive changes, a lengthy second preface, and additional
footnotes in the text responding to some of its critics. That the movement
from periodical to book form was not unusual at this time is evidenced by the
fact that works similar in some important respects to *Liberty, Equality, Fraternity* followed the same course: for example, Matthew Arnold's *Culture
and Anarchy*, Walter Bagehot's *The English Constitution*, and Maine's *Popular Government*.

A not insubstantial amount of Stephen's writing focused on the subject of
the law proper, and he produced several works on the criminal law that
earned him the highest praise. The best of these works is his three-volume *History of the Criminal Law* (1883), a work about which Maitland remarked, "I
am struck every time I take up the book with the thoroughness of his work
and the soundness of his judgments. . . . [A]nd — so I think, but it is imperti-
nent in me to say it — he almost always got hold of the true story."[5] Nevertheless, Stephen's enduring contribution to intellectual affairs is *Liberty,
Equality, Fraternity*.

The French Revolution gave birth to the creed "Liberty, Equality, Fraternity"; however, this creed outlasted the Revolution, finding expression in the
nineteenth century, both on the continent and in England. In offering a powerful polemic against this creed in *Liberty, Equality, Fraternity*, Stephen is
most emphatically not presenting himself as a defender of, as he puts it,
"Slavery, Caste, and Hatred." But he believed that many exponents of the
creed of liberty, equality, and fraternity exaggerated the advantages and ig-
nored the disadvantages of the political arrangements intended by this famed
triptych of values, thereby distorting a proper understanding of liberty,
equality, and fraternity along the way. In *Liberty, Equality, Fraternity*,
Stephen makes a point of revealing the character of these disadvantages. We
should not lose sight of the fact, however, that Stephen's criticisms are informed by his own understanding of these values, an understanding to which
we now turn.

5. Cited in Leslie Stephen, *The Life of Sir James Fitzjames Stephen*, p. 415.

Sir Isaiah Berlin directs us to the idea that a political philosophy is often presented by means of analogy to the more familiar: a contract, the family, an army on the march, a night watchman, or an umpire.[6] Stephen's understanding of liberty leads him to employ the metaphor of water running through pipes. In a passage that both makes use of this metaphor and stakes out other important features of his conception of liberty, Stephen remarks:

> Discussions about liberty are in truth discussions about a negation. Attempts to solve problems of government and society by such discussions are like attempts to discover the nature of light and heat by inquiries into darkness and cold. The phenomenon which requires and will repay study is the direction and nature of the various forces, individual and collective, which in their combination or collision with each other and with the outer world make up human life. If we want to know what ought to be the size and position of a hole in a water pipe, we must consider the nature of water, the nature of pipes, and the objects for which the water is wanted. . . .[7]

To understand this remark, we must explore two important features of Stephen's conception of liberty. First, Stephen recognizes liberty to be an instrumental value, not a value in and of itself; and the ultimate value that liberty principally serves is the well-being of society. We should be careful not to misunderstand this feature of Stephen's thought—as a common understanding of Stephen would have us do—as portraying either a disregard for liberty or an authoritarian bent, for *Liberty, Equality, Fraternity* does not support such a reading. Not to value liberty as an end in itself is not to treat it lightly or to shy away from its endorsement as central to a civilized world. It is rather, as Stephen would see it, an admission that liberty, along with all of the other social elements of human life, has its advantages and disadvantages; and, if we are primarily concerned with the well-being of society, then we should not blindly support any given liberty in those circumstances in which its disadvantages outweigh its advantages.

6. See Isaiah Berlin, "The Purpose of Philosophy," in *Concepts and Categories* (New York: Viking Press, 1978), pp. 9–10.

7. *Liberty, Equality, Fraternity*, p. 119. Three other analogies between water pipes and liberty are to be found on pp. 14–15, 23, and 118.

The second feature of Stephen's conception of liberty is that liberty is fundamentally a negative concept. Stephen understands liberty at its core to be an absence of restraint; however, liberty cannot be understood to involve an absence of *all* restraint; for Stephen, like Hobbes, recognizes that it is impossible for a society and, therefore, liberty to exist in the absence of all restraint. Restraints are required if there is to be any society at all, if only because the human condition is one in which the actions of some frequently and inevitably conflict with the actions of others. This understanding of the role of restraint in society is the basis for Stephen's distinguishing between liberty and license, and it encourages him to understand liberty as an "absence of *injurious* restraint."[8] In this conception of liberty, morality, law, and religion are understood to restrain an individual's actions, but not injuriously, and hence do not constitute an infringement of his liberty. In fact, in the deepest sense, it is these restraints that make liberty of action possible. And since these restraints constitute a realm of power, Stephen can maintain that, "Liberty, from the very nature of things, is dependent upon power. . . ."[9]

Now we can begin to understand Stephen's frequent appeals to a waterworks project to illuminate the nature of liberty. Just as the holes of water pipes are given their character and value by the nature of what bounds them, so liberty is given its character and value by what bounds and, hence, forms it; namely, the restraints of morality, religion, and law. A society's liberties are thus constituted by the restraints that allow for the possibility of choice. For Stephen, therefore, talk of liberty makes no sense outside of the context of the restraints of morality, law, and religion.

Stephen is promoting an understanding of *ordered liberty* or *liberty under morality and law*. Part of the value of liberty lies in its allowing individuals to pursue their own choices or, more exactly, *a certain set of choices* rather than others, for this contributes to the well-being of society. Importantly, some sets of choices must be excluded. Genuine options are possible for human beings only within the context of a web of restraint provided by the moral, political, legal, and religious institutions that form the social arrangements in which individuals can pursue their own ends in concert with one another.

8. *Liberty, Equality, Fraternity*, p. 122; my emphasis.
9. *Liberty, Equality, Fraternity*, p. 111.

Therefore, on Stephen's analysis, the character and value of liberty reside in the restraints that frame it: there is no liberty outside of restraint.

Morality is foremost among the restraints that shape society generally and a free society in particular. For Stephen, morality is constituted in some measure by the fear of disapprobation, the fear of the opinion of others, the fear of being ostracized. Thus, Stephen remarks that "the custom of looking upon certain courses of conduct with aversion is the essence of morality."[10] And this aversion or disapprobation Stephen understands as being coercive. Although morality on this account might therefore be considered a system of force, the force in question is the pressure imposed by others and not punishment (or the threat of punishment) inflicted by government. Here we must underscore the idea that, as Stephen sees it, the restraints imposed by morality are vastly more extensive and important than those of law in establishing the web of restraint in which liberty is formed and has value:

> Criminal legislation proper may be regarded as an engine of prohibition unimportant in comparison with morals and the forms of morality sanctioned by theology. For one act from which one person is restrained by the fear of the law of the land, many persons are restrained from innumerable acts by the fear of the disapprobation of their neighbors, which is the moral sanction; or by the fear of punishment in a future state of existence, which is the religious sanction; or by the fear of their own disapprobation, which may be called the conscientious sanction.[11]

Stephen's conception of morality as a web of restraint that shapes individual conduct is deeply influenced by his conception of the human condition. Forgoing a pollyannish understanding of human beings, Stephen embraces a position some—perhaps with cause—may consider a dark and foreboding one. It may be more accurate to see Stephen as offering a rather sober-minded understanding of human beings, one that captures the curse *and* blessing of the human condition. Without the discipline imposed by morality, individuals will tend to pursue a life of idleness, a life that is vapid, without high culture, a life lacking the motivation to achieve greatness of character. Stephen

10. *Liberty, Equality, Fraternity,* p. 13.
11. *Liberty, Equality, Fraternity,* pp. 8–9.

sees that the human condition involves greater ambiguity than a world of men and women possessing exclusively either greatness or meanness of character: We are a mixed lot. Unfortunately, the human spirit typically does not aim high; however, human beings do have social desires, Stephen suggests, which in conjunction with the restraints of morality help to sustain a social order in which greatness of character and liberty are possible and can flourish. And while rejecting an optimistic view of human beings, Stephen lovingly cradles the high culture of England that a few are able to produce. However, both the few who are capable of high culture and those who are not still greatly benefit from being subjected to an Augustinian or Calvinist tinged morality of self-restraint and discipline.

Given that liberty is of instrumental value for Stephen, it is easy to understand why he rejects any categorical, simple principle of liberty, one that would specify exactly which liberties should be protected, and where and when. "We must," Stephen writes, "proceed in a far more cautious way, and confine ourselves to such remarks as experience suggests about the advantages and disadvantages of compulsion and liberty respectively in particular cases."[12] However, there are certain liberties that Stephen highlights in *Liberty, Equality, Fraternity* and in other of his writings that he believes to be of paramount importance to civilized life. The first is property: "Of all items of liberty, none is either so important or so universally recognized as the liberty of acquiring property."[13] The second liberty of great importance to Stephen, perhaps surprisingly, is privacy: "Legislation and public opinion ought in all cases whatever scrupulously to respect privacy. . . . To try to regulate the internal affairs of a family, the relations of love or friendship, or many other things of the same sort, by law or by the coercion of public opinion, is like trying to pull an eyelash out of a man's eye with a pair of tongs. They may put out the eye, but they will never get hold of the eyelash."[14]

Essential to protecting these liberties and others is the rule of law. And so closely linked is the rule of law to various liberties that Stephen suggests the rule of law is itself a liberty; for in a significant way, the procedures afforded to individuals by the rule of law specify the liberties that an individual has.

12. *Liberty, Equality, Fraternity,* p. 35.
13. *Liberty, Equality, Fraternity,* p. 120.
14. *Liberty, Equality, Fraternity,* pp. 106, 107–8.

For Stephen, the rule of law is a remarkable moral conquest, a monumental achievement over despotism and the desires of some to enslave others for their own purposes. The rule of law both constitutes and vouchsafes liberties that Stephen, although holding them to be instrumentally valuable, embraces and understands to be of paramount importance to the civilized world he deeply valued.

Along with fellow Victorians such as Arnold, Maine, W. E. H. Lecky, and even J. S. Mill, Stephen was deeply troubled by what he saw as the debilitating consequences of an ever-expanding democracy. In part because of the Reform Bill of 1867 which doubled the electorate in England, by the time of his writing *Liberty, Equality, Fraternity*, Stephen reasoned that there was no turning back from an extensive democratic government; that is, no turning back from a regime resting upon universal suffrage. "If I am asked, What do you propose to substitute for universal suffrage? . . . I answer at once, Nothing. The whole current of thought and feeling, the whole stream of human affairs, is setting with irresistible force in that direction."[15] Stephen argued, however, that even if universal suffrage were achieved, the promissory note of *political equality* that defenders of universal suffrage advanced could not be fulfilled:

> Legislate how you will, establish universal suffrage, if you think proper, as a law which can never be broken. You are still as far as ever from equality. Political power has changed its shape but not its nature. The result of cutting it up into little bits is simply that the man who can sweep the greatest number of them into one heap will govern the rest. The strongest man in some form or other will always rule. If the government is a military one, the qualities which make a man a great soldier will make him a ruler. If the government is a monarchy, the qualities which kings value in counsellors, in generals, in administrators, will give power. In a pure democracy the ruling men will be the wirepullers and their friends. . . . Changes in the form of a government alter the conditions of superiority much more than its nature.[16]

15. *Liberty, Equality, Fraternity*, p. 155.
16. *Liberty, Equality, Fraternity*, pp. 154–55.

What is especially troubling to Stephen is that the plea for democracy or political equality frequently masquerades as a plea for liberty. This conflates democracy and universal suffrage—which are concerned with the distribution of political power—with liberty, which is another matter entirely.[17] A precondition of deliverance from the political and cultural predicament that will be spawned by growing democracy is the recognition of the evils that the so-called political equality will make manifest in the world. It is just this recognition that Stephen hopes to provide in *Liberty, Equality, Fraternity*.

Whatever may be the benefits of democracy, it also levies severe costs that render it a languid business. For the "wirepullers" need only satisfy an ignorant multitude, and this, Stephen feared, would ultimately lead to a debased and mediocre culture, one predicated on sordidness and vulgarity. In order to satisfy the unenlightened, these new rulers would extend government into the deepest recesses of the lives of individuals, willingly abandoning certain liberties along the way.

An appeal to *political* equality is only one form that the appeal to equality takes, and it is an appeal that Stephen finds to be suspect, as we have seen. What is more disturbing to Stephen is the appeal to equality *per se*, for this is a conception that is devoid of content. One needs to know, Equal in what respect? However, when equality is offered as a value without qualification, what is typically being offered is equality of property. Equality in this sense is especially antithetical to liberty: "If human experience proves anything at all, it proves that, if restraints are minimized, if the largest possible measure of liberty is accorded to all human beings, the result will not be equality but inequality. . . ."[18] As a result of industriousness, luck, skill, and a myriad of other factors, some will acquire and accumulate much more property than others: Liberty of action thus leads to inequality of results, an inequality that can be eliminated, if at all, only by constant governmental interference in the various liberties of individuals to pursue their own ends. For Stephen, equal-

17. In his essay "Hobbes on Government," Stephen writes, "It would tend considerably to clear up various matters connected with the question of extension of the suffrage, if we bore in mind the fact that the question is one, not of liberty, but of the distribution of political power." See *Horae Sabbaticae*, vol. 2, p. 12.

18. *Liberty, Equality, Fraternity*, p. 120.

ity of property is the death-knell of liberty, and this provides a powerful reason to eschew it.

The equality that Stephen does value is equality under the law, the equality vouchsafed by the rule of law: Treat like cases alike. As philosophers of law recognize, however, deciding what constitutes a like case is puzzling. Yet, however complicated this issue is, numerous contemporary readers of *Liberty, Equality, Fraternity* will find Stephen's understanding of what constitutes a like case in at least one area of life to be defective. Stephen holds that men are superior to women, not only in terms of physical strength, but also in terms of "greater intellectual force" and "greater vigour of character."[19] Men and women, not being equal in these respects, should not be treated the same by those "laws which affect their relations"[20]; for example, the law of military conscription and, most especially, the law of marriage. Indeed, Stephen presses the point that such inequality actually benefits women.

Central to the legacy bequeathed to us by the liberal tradition is the idea that there is no natural, political authority, an idea expressed with great clarity by two of the founders of the liberal tradition, Hobbes and Locke. Toward the end of the eighteenth century and the start of the nineteenth, an idea that had its home in the world of politics, begins to spread to a broader range of human relationships, including the various relationships between men and women. The dismissal of natural authority in political life in the seventeenth century begins to be extended, leading many to dismiss hierarchical relationships generally by the end of the nineteenth century. And it is within the context of this movement of ideas that one must locate Stephen's views on the relations between men and women; for certainly Stephen is attempting to hold on to a world in which hierarchical relations are possible and desirable.

Although the nineteenth century was replete with accounts of the first two frames of the triptych of political values—liberty and equality—fraternity, the last frame, received surprisingly little critical attention. Indeed, whatever the influence of the French Revolution, it was much more because of Auguste Comte's "Religion of Humanity"—and J. S. Mill's partial appropriation of

19. *Liberty, Equality, Fraternity*, p. 138.
20. *Liberty, Equality, Fraternity*, p. 143.

it—that reflection about fraternity became any part of the English intellectual landscape. And if only because substantial criticisms of the idea of fraternity were rare, Stephen's savage attack on the value of fraternity becomes quite noteworthy.

By fraternity, Stephen understands the idea of a universal brotherhood, the idea of a universal love of mankind; that is, the idea of individuals in a society associated with each other foremost by the love that they feel for one another. Support for the moral and political value of fraternity flows, Stephen believes, from two sources. The first source is a maudlin view of human nature that imagines a world without significant conflicts of interest among individuals and the hostility to which those lead. Few defenders of fraternity would suggest that this is the world of human beings as we find it. Thus, the second source is an appeal to the progress of which human beings are capable if only they are liberated from various restraints and treated as the equals that they are; and it is the human nature that is to be newly animated by the driving forces of progress which makes fraternity possible.

For Stephen, however, a more sober-minded reflection reveals human nature to be incompatible with fraternity. He declares:

> I believe that many men are bad, a vast majority of men indifferent . . . and [this] great mass . . . sway[s] this way or that according to circumstances. . . . I further believe that between all classes of men there are and always will be real occasions of enmity and strife, and that even good men may be and often are compelled to treat each other as enemies either by the existence of conflicting interests which bring them into collision, or by their different ways of conceiving goodness.[21]

Defenders of fraternity are sanguine about eliminating a good deal of the enmity and evil to be found in human existence; but, for Stephen, these elements of the human condition, although capable of being ameliorated to some degree by morality, religion, and law, stem from permanent features of human nature. Stephen claims that it is not only different interests that put individuals at odds with one another, but also differing conceptions of the good, both ineradicable features of human nature. And Stephen thought that

21. *Liberty, Equality, Fraternity*, p. 169.

the various conflicts of interest and value endemic to the human condition produce enmity not only among individuals, but also among groups. He suspected, for example, that Moslems and Christians would always feel hostility toward one another because of their disparate views of the good.

Stephen believes that those who impatiently hunger for fraternity will not only fail to find a place for it in the world, but are apt to produce corrupting results in the world of practical affairs.

> A man to whom this ideal [of fraternity] becomes so far a reality as to colour his thoughts, his feelings, his estimate of the present and his action towards it, is usually, as repeated experience has shown, perfectly ready to sacrifice that which living people do actually regard as constituting their happiness to his own notions of what will constitute the happiness of other generations.[22]

Love of humanity often becomes infected by fanaticism. The appeal to fraternity that on the surface bears the stamp of universal brotherhood, underneath has little concern for those in the present. For insofar as the advocates of fraternity recognize that human beings as we find them do not pass muster, it is convenient to discard them to the dustbin of concrete reality in favor of those who exist only in an ethereal, theoretical world: Neither the liberty nor happiness of those in the present matter when a vision of a world driven by fraternity is at stake.

As we have mentioned, Stephen elucidates his own positions in *Liberty, Equality, Fraternity* within the frame of a critique of John Stuart Mill that runs throughout the book. Stephen was a great admirer of the early Mill, the Mill of "The Spirit of the Age," "Civilization," "Bentham," Book VI of *A System of Logic* ("On the Logic of the Moral Sciences"), and the two essays on "De Tocqueville on Democracy in America." Indeed, Stephen admired *On Liberty* when it first appeared in 1859. However, the Reform Bill of 1867, his experience in India, the publication of Mill's *The Subjection of Women*, as well as further reflection, moved him to the conclusion that the later Mill had

---

22. *Liberty, Equality, Fraternity*, p. 181.

renounced what Stephen understood to be the principles of English Liberalism.

As Stephen has it, the faults of *On Liberty* are many: the human condition is too complicated for Mill's "simple principle of liberty" which holds that coercion is justified only to prevent harm to others; the distinction that provides the ground for Mill's principle of liberty, the distinction between self-regarding and other-regarding actions, cannot be articulated in a clear-cut fashion; Mill's principle of liberty is at loggerheads with his utilitarianism; Mill's principle of liberty requires the absence of almost all restraint in human affairs, a circumstance that will lead to idleness and wretchedness, and not the self-development that Mill (following Wilhelm von Humboldt) imagines; liberty without the restraints of morality backed by the sanction of public opinion is license and of no social value; freedom of thought does not tend to verisimilitude as Mill suggests; Mill's principle of liberty, vigorously applied, would be subversive of all morality, for morality is instantiated through the coercive opinions of others.

Stephen's litany of criticism of Mill's *The Subjection of Women* and *Utilitarianism* is briefer but no less severe: The former work misleads us as to the proper relationship between men and women and fosters a view of democracy that violates high culture and liberty; the latter work suggests the possibility of a brotherhood of mankind that is grossly false to the facts and destructive of liberty, as well.

It is fair to say that Stephen understands his view of liberty, equality, and fraternity to be contrary to Mill's in almost every important particular. For on his view, he stands for liberty and Mill stands for license; he stands for equality under law and Mill stands for a morose egalitarianism; he stands for a sober understanding of the conflicts in human affairs and Mill for a great illusion.

It cannot be denied that at least sometimes Stephen misconstrues Mill's doctrine, heedless of the nuances to be found there, and that some of the charges that he levels against Mill miss their intended mark. Nevertheless, it is just as true that Stephen sees in Mill what others have missed and that many of his shots are on target. However, more important than this is the character of Stephen's own teaching on liberty, equality, and fraternity, a teaching that has been unduly neglected and one that is unquestionably worthy of our attention.

The analytic tradition that reigned supreme over the Anglo-American philosophical world would now have us ask: Is Stephen's political philosophy best understood as a form of Liberalism or Conservatism? And, in fact, a considerable amount of intellectual energy has been spent on this question. Of course, any attempt to answer it would require a lengthy and careful analysis of what Liberalism and Conservatism are—a matter of incalculable difficulty at best—and it is unclear that the attempt to understand Stephen's political philosophy in terms of abstract, timeless, ahistorical categories would be helpful or important in any case.

What certainly is important, however, is Stephen's understanding of himself as a defender of an older English Liberalism. In Stephen's eyes, we should not conceive this Liberalism to be an abstract, philosophical category, but rather a term denoting a form of political life that historically was at home in mid-nineteenth century England. This was a form of political life that valued ordered liberty and dreaded license, one that despised despotism, yet trembled fearfully before universal suffrage. The English Liberalism that Stephen embraced valued "generous and high-minded sentiments upon political subjects, guided by a highly instructed, large minded, and impartial intellect,"[23] not the sordidness and vulgarity that Stephen believed to be forthcoming in a different vision of political life, one he thought was enunciated and implied in Mill's writings.

Like mid- to late nineteenth century Victorian England, our world is moved to reflect about liberty, equality, and fraternity. And all around— both in the domains of politics and philosophy—we see admiring portraits of this famed triptych. Yet many of these portraits are vague and hazy, and at times it is hard to make out, for example, whether we are looking at liberty or license. Surely which it is matters, and Stephen's *Liberty, Equality, Fraternity* is a fine work that can aid us in achieving clarity about what is being offered. And more broadly, in a world that continues to pamper fraternity and equal-

23. "Liberalism," in *Cornhill Magazine*, 5 (1862): 71.

ity of all kinds, Stephen's invocations against them might provide a salutary reminder that it is liberty—not license—for which they are being exchanged, and this might lead us to consider carefully the character of what we are getting in return.

PROFESSOR STUART D. WARNER

Thanksgiving, 1992   Roosevelt University

EDITOR'S NOTE

The copytext for this edition of *Liberty, Equality, Fraternity* is the second edition of 1874, published by Smith, Elder, & Co. In a small number of cases, I compared the second edition to the first edition of 1873.

I have made several changes in the text. I have moved Stephen's "Preface to the Second Edition" to follow the text. This preface is a lengthy reply to two critics of the first edition of *Liberty, Equality, Fraternity,* and, since the text of the second edition is virtually identical to that of the first, this preface is best positioned following the text itself.

Stephen quotes Mill some 125 times, and almost all of these quotations come from three of Mill's works: *On Liberty, The Subjection of Women,* and *Utilitarianism.* I have provided these references in brackets following the various quotations as follows. In the case of the first two of these works, I have provided citations to two editions of Mill's writings. The first citation is from Stefan Collini's edition of Mill's *On Liberty with the Subjection of Women and Chapters on Socialism;*[1] the second citation is from the appropriate volume of the University of Toronto Press edition of the *Collected Works of John Stuart Mill.*[2] Thus, for example, "78/278 L" is a reference to *On Liberty,* referring to p. 78 of the Collini edition and p. 278 of the

---

1. John Stuart Mill, *On Liberty with the Subjection of Women and Chapters on Socialism,* ed. Stefan Collini, Cambridge Texts in the History of Political Thought (Cambridge: Cambridge University Press, 1989).

2. John Stuart Mill, *Collected Works of John Stuart Mill,* ed. J. M. Robson, 33 vols. (Toronto: University of Toronto Press, 1963–1991), vol. 10, *Essays on Ethics, Religion, and Society* [*Utilitarianism*] (1969), vol. 18, *Essays on Politics and Society* [*On Liberty*] (1977), vol. 21, *Essays on Equality, Law, and Education* [*The Subjection of Women*] (1984).

University of Toronto Press edition; "119/261 *SW*" is a reference to *The Subjection of Women,* referring to p. 119 of the Collini edition and p. 261 of the University of Toronto Press edition. In the case of *Utilitarianism* (abbreviated by *U*), I have provided a citation only from the *Collected Works.* Quotations from others of Mill's writings are cited in footnotes.

Stephen's quotations from Mill are not always accurate. I have corrected these. I have silently made the change for punctuation and when Stephen has accidentally substituted a synonym; I have noted the cases in which there are more substantial differences.

All of Stephen's footnotes are indicated as in the 1874 edition by an asterisk; editor's footnotes are indicated by a number. These notes have been kept to a minimum, typically directing the reader to something else Stephen has written that illuminates the matter at hand. Material within brackets is in all cases my addition. Material within braces is Stephen's addition.

I have silently modernized Stephen's punctuation. In most cases this involved omitting one punctuation mark where two appeared together (for example, omitting a dash when it immediately followed a colon). Also, Stephen sometimes fails to place his *mention* of a word in single quotation marks, and I have silently added these marks (for example, I added single quotation marks in this phrase: "the words 'temporal' and 'spiritual'"). I have also modernized the language to a certain extent—for example, transforming "any one" to "anyone," "to-morrow" to "tomorrow," and so on.

I have been aided in this project by conversations with Timothy Fuller, Gilbert Goldman, Emilio Pacheco, and, most especially, Inger Thomsen. I dedicate this book, with incalculable gratitude, to Harold Trueman Walsh.

SELECTED BIBLIOGRAPHY

WORKS OF JAMES FITZJAMES STEPHEN

Essays by a Barrister. London: Smith, Elder & Co., 1862.

Defence of the Rev. Rowland Williams, D.D., in the Arches Court of Canterbury. London: Smith, Elder & Co., 1862.

A General View of the Criminal Law. London: Macmillan & Co., 1863; 2nd ed., 1890.

Liberty, Equality, Fraternity. London: Smith, Elder & Co., 1873; 2nd ed., 1874.

A Digest of the Law of Evidence. London: Macmillan and Co., 1874; 4th ed., 1893.

A Digest of the Criminal Law. London: Macmillan & Co., 1877; 5th ed., 1894.

A Digest of the Law of Criminal Procedure in Indictable Offences. London: Macmillan, 1883.

A History of the Criminal Law of England. 3 vols. London: Macmillan and Co., 1883.

The Story of Nuncomar and the Impeachment of Sir Elijah Impey. 2 vols. London: Macmillan & Co., 1885.

Horae Sabbaticae. 3 vols. London: Macmillan & Co., 1892.

SELECTED SECONDARY WRITINGS

Colaiaco, J. A. *James Fitzjames Stephen and the Crisis of Victorian Thought*. New York: St. Martin's Press, 1983.

Collini, Stefan. *Public Moralists: Political Thought and Intellectual Life in Britain 1850–1930*. Oxford: Clarendon Press, 1991.

Cranston, Maurice. *Political Dialogues*. New York: Basic Books, Inc., 1968.

Kirk, Russell. *The Conservative Mind: From Burke to Santayana*. Chicago: Henry Regnery & Co., 1953.

Lippincott, B. E. *Victorian Critics of Democracy*. Minneapolis: University of Minnesota Press, 1938.

Radzinowicz, Leon. *Sir James Fitzjames Stephen (1829–1894) and His Contribution to the Development of Criminal Law.* Seldon Society Lecture. London: Seldon Society, 1957.*

Roach, John. "Liberalism and the Victorian Intelligentsia." *The Cambridge Historical Journal* 13 (1957):58–81

Smith, K. J. M. *James Fitzjames Stephen: Portrait of a Victorian Rationalist.* Cambridge: Cambridge University Press, 1988.*

Stephen, Leslie. *The Life of Sir James Fitzjames Stephen.* New York: G. P. Putnam's Sons, 1895.

White, R. J., ed., Introduction to *Liberty, Equality, Fraternity,* by James Fitzjames Stephen. Cambridge: Cambridge University Press, 1967.

*These works should be consulted for an extensive bibliography of Stephen's periodical writings.

PREFACE TO
THE FIRST EDITION

TO SIR JOHN STRACHEY, K.C.S.I.
&c. &c. &c.

MY DEAR STRACHEY,

I dedicate this book to you for three reasons: First, as an expression of strong personal regard, and of deep gratitude for great kindness, all the more valuable because it resembled that which I received from everyone with whom I had any relations in India.

Secondly, in recollection of the month, after the arrival at Calcutta of the news of Lord Mayo's murder, when you acted as Governor-General. The sorrow which we both felt for a man whom each of us had so many grounds, both public and private, to love and honour, and the anxiety and responsibility which we shared during a very trying time, formed a tie between us which I am sure you feel as strongly as I do.

Thirdly, because you are one of the most distinguished of Indian civilians, and my Indian experience strongly confirmed the reflections which the book contains, and which had been taking shape gradually in my mind for many years. The commonplaces and the vein of sentiment at which it is levelled appeared peculiarly false and poor as I read the European newspapers of 1870–1 at the headquarters of the Government of India.

The book was planned in India, and partly written on my voyage home.

I am, my dear STRACHEY,

Your sincere friend and late colleague,

JAMES FITZJAMES STEPHEN.

24 Cornwall Gardens, South Kensington: *March 31, 1873.*

LIBERTY, EQUALITY, FRATERNITY

CHAPTER ONE

THE DOCTRINE
OF LIBERTY IN GENERAL

The object of this work is to examine the doctrines which are rather hinted at than expressed by the phrase 'Liberty, Equality, Fraternity.' This phrase has been the motto of more than one Republic. It is indeed something more than a motto. It is the creed of a religion, less definite than any one of the forms of Christianity, which are in part its rivals, in part its antagonists, and in part its associates, but not on that account the less powerful. It is, on the contrary, one of the most penetrating influences of the day. It shows itself now and then in definite forms, of which Positivism is the one best known to our generation, but its special manifestations give no adequate measure of its depth or width. It penetrates other creeds. It has often transformed Christianity into a system of optimism, which has in some cases retained and in others rejected Christian phraseology. It deeply influences politics and legislation. It has its solemn festivals, its sober adherents, its enthusiasts, its Anabaptists and Antinomians. The Religion of Humanity is perhaps as good a name as could be found for it, if the expression is used in a wider sense than the narrow and technical one associated with it by Comte. It is one of the commonest beliefs of the day that the human race collectively has before it splendid destinies of various kinds, and that the road to them is to be found in the removal of all restraints on human conduct, in the recognition of a substantial equality between all human creatures, and in fraternity or general love. These doctrines are in very many cases held as a religious faith. They are regarded not merely as truths, but as truths for which those who believe in them are ready to do battle, and for the establishment of which they are prepared to sacrifice all merely personal ends.

Such, stated of course in the most general terms, is the religion of which I take 'Liberty, Equality, Fraternity' to be the creed. I do not believe it.

I am not the advocate of Slavery, Caste, and Hatred, nor do I deny that a sense may be given to the words, Liberty, Equality, and Fraternity, in which they may be regarded as good. I wish to assert with respect to them two propositions.

First, that in the present day even those who use those words most rationally—that is to say, as the names of elements of social life which, like others, have their advantages and disadvantages according to time, place, and circumstance—have a great disposition to exaggerate their advantages and to deny the existence, or at any rate to underrate the importance, of their disadvantages.

Next, that whatever signification be attached to them, these words are ill-adapted to be the creed of a religion, that the things which they denote are not ends in themselves, and that when used collectively the words do not typify, however vaguely, any state of society which a reasonable man ought to regard with enthusiasm or self-devotion.

The truth of the first proposition as a mere general observation will not, in all probability, be disputed; but I attach to it a very much more specific meaning than is conveyed by a mere commonplace. I mean to assert that the most accredited current theories upon this subject, and those which have been elaborated with the greatest care, are unsound; and to give point to this, I say more specifically that the theories advanced upon the subject by Mr. John Mill in most of his later works are unsound. I have several reasons for referring specifically to him. In the first place, no writer of the present day has expressed himself upon these subjects with anything like the same amount either of system or of ability. In the second place, he is the only modern author who has handled the subject, with whom I agree sufficiently to differ from him profitably. Up to a certain point I should be proud to describe myself as his disciple, but there is a side of his teaching which is as repugnant as the rest of it is attractive to me, and this side has of late years become by far the most prominent. I do not say that the teaching of his works on Liberty, on Utilitarianism, and on the Subjection of Women is inconsistent with the teaching of

4

his works on Logic and Political Economy; but I wish to show the grounds on which it is possible to agree with the greater part of the contents of the two works last mentioned, and even to maintain principles which they rather imply than assert, and at the same time to dissent in the strongest way from the view of human nature and human affairs which pervades the works first mentioned.

No better statement of the popular view—I might, perhaps, say of the religious dogma of liberty—is to be found than that which is contained in Mr. Mill's essay on the subject. His works on Utilitarianism and the Subjection of Women afford excellent illustrations of the forms of the doctrines of equality and fraternity to which I object. Nothing is further from my wishes than to make a captious attack upon the writings of a great man to whom I am in every way deeply indebted; but in stating the grounds of one's dissent from wide-spread and influential opinions it is absolutely necessary to take some definite statement of those opinions as a starting point, and it is natural to take the ablest, the most reasonable, and the clearest.

To proceed, then. The following is, I think, a fair abridgment of the introductory chapter of the Essay on Liberty,[1] which is much the most important part of that work.

Civil or social liberty as distinguished from 'the so-called Liberty of the Will' [5/217 L] is its subject. The expression, Mr. Mill tells us, meant originally protection against the tyranny of political rulers. Their power was recognized as a necessary evil, and its limitation either by privilege or by constitutional checks was what was meant by liberty. People came in time to regard their rulers rather as their own agents and the depositaries of their own power than as antagonistic powers to be kept in check, and it did not occur to them that their own power exercised through their own agents might be just as oppressive as the power of their rulers confined within closer or wider limits. By degrees, however, experience showed that the whole might, and was by no means disinclined to, tyrannize over the part, and hence came the phrase 'tyranny of the majority.' [8/219 L] This tyranny of the majority has its root in 'the feeling in each person's mind that everybody should be required to act as he, and those with whom he sympathizes, would like them to act.' [9/221 L] After having illustrated this, Mr. Mill proceeds: 'Those who have been in

1. Stephen consistently refers to the title of Mill's On Liberty as Essay on Liberty. This was a common mistake made up through the first half of our century.

5

advance of society in thought and feeling have left this condition of things unassailed in principle, however they may have come into conflict with it in some of its details. They have occupied themselves rather in inquiring what things society ought to like and dislike, than in questioning whether its likings or dislikings should be a law to individuals.' [11/222 L] He then enunciates his own view in the following passage:

> The object of this essay is to assert one very simple principle, as entitled to govern absolutely the dealings of society with the individual in the way of compulsion or control, whether the means used be physical force in the form of legal penalties, or the moral coercion of public opinion. That principle is that the sole end for which mankind are warranted individually or collectively in interfering with the liberty of action of any of their number is self-protection; that the only purpose for which power can be rightfully exercised over any member of a civilized community against his will is to prevent harm to others. His own good, either physical or moral, is not a sufficient warrant. He cannot rightfully be compelled to do or forbear because it will be better for him to do so, because it will make him happier, because in the opinions of others to do so would be wise or even right. These are good reasons for remonstrating with him, or reasoning with him, or persuading him, or entreating him, but not for compelling him, or visiting him with any evil in case he do otherwise. To justify that, the conduct from which it is desired to deter him must be calculated to produce evil to some one else. The only part of the conduct of any one for which he is amenable to society is that which concerns others. In the part which merely concerns himself his independence is of right, absolute. Over himself, over his own body and mind, the individual is sovereign. [13/223–224 L]

He points out that 'this doctrine is meant to apply only to human beings in the maturity of their faculties,' [13/224 L] and that 'we may leave out of account those backward states of society in which the race itself may be considered as in its nonage.' [13/224 L] He then disclaims any advantage which could be derived to his 'argument from the idea of abstract right as a thing independent of utility.' He adds: 'I regard utility as the ultimate appeal on all ethical questions; but it must be utility in the largest sense grounded on the

6

permanent interests of a man as a progressive being.' [14/224 L] He concludes by specifying

> the appropriate region of human liberty. It comprises, first, the inward domain of consciousness; demanding liberty of conscience in the most comprehensive sense, liberty of thought and feeling; absolute freedom of opinion and sentiment on all subjects practical or speculative, scientific, moral, or theological. The liberty of expressing and publishing opinions may seem to fall under a different principle, since it belongs to that part of the conduct of an individual which concerns other people, but being almost of as much importance as the liberty of thought itself, and resting in great part on the same reasons, is practically inseparable from it. Secondly, the principle requires liberty of tastes and pursuits, of framing our plan of life to suit our own character, of doing as we like, subject to such consequences as may follow, without impediment from our fellow-creatures, so long as what we do does not harm them—even though they should think our conduct foolish, perverse, or wrong. Thirdly, from this liberty of each individual follows the liberty within the same limits of combination among individuals. [15–16/225–226 L]

This, I think, is the substance of the doctrine of the introductory chapter. It is the whole doctrine of the essay, and it is remarkable that, having thus fully and carefully enunciated his doctrine, Mr. Mill never attempts to prove it, as a whole. Probably the second, third, and fourth chapters are intended as separate proofs of distinct parts of it. Chapter II may thus be regarded as an argument meant to prove that absolute liberty of thought and discussion is good. Chapter III in the same way is an argument to show that individuality is an element of well-being, but it assumes instead of proving that liberty is a condition of individuality; a point on which much might be said. Chapter IV is entitled, "Of the Limits of the Authority of Society over the Individual."[2] It is little more than a restatement in detail of the general principles stated in the introductory chapter. It adds nothing to the argument, except this remark, which, no doubt, is entitled to great weight: 'The strongest of all the arguments against the interference of the public with purely personal conduct is that when it does interfere the odds are that it interferes wrongly and in the wrong place.' [83/283 L] Finally, Chapter V, entitled 'Applications,' con-

2. The correct title is "Of the Limits to the Authority of Society over the Individual."

7

sists, as might be expected from its title, of the application of the general principle to a certain number of specific cases.

There is hardly anything in the whole essay which can properly be called proof as distinguished from enunciation or assertion of the general principles quoted. I think, however, that it will not be difficult to show that the principle stands in much need of proof. In order to make this clear it will be desirable in the first place to point out the meaning of the word 'liberty' according to principles which I think are common to Mr. Mill and to myself. I do not think Mr. Mill would have disputed the following statement of the theory of human actions. All voluntary acts are caused by motives. All motives may be placed in one of two categories—hope and fear, pleasure and pain. Voluntary acts of which hope is the motive are said to be free. Voluntary acts of which fear is the motive are said to be done under compulsion, or omitted under restraint. A woman marries. This in every case is a voluntary action. If she regards the marriage with the ordinary feelings and acts from the ordinary motives, she is said to act freely. If she regards it as a necessity, to which she submits in order to avoid greater evil, she is said to act under compulsion and not freely.

If this is the true theory of liberty—and, though many persons would deny this, I think they would have been accepted by Mr. Mill—the propositions already stated will in a condensed form amount to this: 'No one is ever justified in trying to affect any one's conduct by exciting his fears, except for the sake of self-protection'; or, making another substitution which he would also approve—'It can never promote the general happiness of mankind that the conduct of any persons should be affected by an appeal to their fears, except in the cases excepted.'

Surely these are not assertions which can be regarded as self-evident, or even as otherwise than paradoxical. What is all morality, and what are all existing religions in so far as they aim at affecting human conduct, except an appeal either to hope or fear, and to fear far more commonly and far more emphatically than to hope? Criminal legislation proper may be regarded as an engine of prohibition unimportant in comparison with morals and the forms of morality sanctioned by theology. For one act from which one person is restrained by the fear of the law of the land, many persons are restrained from innumerable acts by the fear of the disapprobation of their neighbours, which is the moral sanction; or by the fear of punishment in a future state of exis-

tence, which is the religious sanction; or by the fear of their own disapprobation, which may be called the conscientious sanction, and may be regarded as
a compound case of the other two. Now, in the innumerable majority of
cases, disapprobation, or the moral sanction, has nothing whatever to do
with self-protection. The religious sanction is by its nature independent of it.
Whatever special forms it may assume, the fundamental condition of it is a
being intolerant of evil in the highest degree, and inexorably determined to
punish it wherever it exists, except upon certain terms. I do not say that this
doctrine is true, but I do say that no one is entitled to assume it without proof
to be essentially immoral and mischievous. Mr. Mill does not draw this inference, but I think his theory involves it, for I know not what can be a greater
infringement of his theory of liberty, a more complete and formal contradiction to it, than the doctrine that there are a court and a judge in which, and
before whom, every man must give an account of every work done in the
body, whether self-regarding or not. According to Mr. Mill's theory, it ought
to be a good plea in the day of judgment to say 'I pleased myself and hurt
nobody else.' Whether or not there will ever be a day of judgment is not the
question, but upon his principles the conception of a day of judgment is fundamentally immoral. A God who punished anyone at all, except for the purpose of protecting others, would, upon his principles, be a tyrant trampling
on liberty.

The application of the principle in question to the moral sanction would be
just as subversive of all that people commonly regard as morality. The only
moral system which would comply with the principle stated by Mr. Mill
would be one capable of being summed up as follows: 'Let every man please
himself without hurting his neighbour'; and every moral system which aimed
at more than this, either to obtain benefits for society at large other than protection against injury or to do good to the persons affected, would be wrong
in principle. This would condemn every existing system of morals. Positive
morality is nothing but a body of principles and rules more or less vaguely expressed, and more or less left to be understood, by which certain lines of conduct are forbidden under the penalty of general disapprobation, and that
quite irrespectively of self-protection. Mr. Mill himself admits this to a certain extent. In the early part of his fourth chapter he says that a man grossly
deficient in the qualities which conduce to his own good is 'necessarily and
properly a subject of distaste, or, in extreme cases, even of contempt,' [77/

9

278 L] and he enumerates various inconveniences to which this would expose such a person. He adds, however: 'The inconveniences which are strictly inseparable from the unfavourable judgment of others, are the only ones to which a person should ever be subjected for that portion of his conduct and character which concerns his own good, but which does not affect the interests of others in their relation with him.' [78/278–279 L] This no doubt weakens the effect of the admission; but be this how it may, the fact still remains that morality is and must be a prohibitive system, one of the main objects of which is to impose upon everyone a standard of conduct and of sentiment to which few persons would conform if it were not for the constraint thus put upon them. In nearly every instance the effects of such a system reach far beyond anything that can be described as the purposes of self-protection.

Mr. Mill's system is violated not only by every system of theology which concerns itself with morals, and by every known system of positive morality, but by the constitution of human nature itself. There is hardly a habit which men in general regard as good which is not acquired by a series of more or less painful and laborious acts. The condition of human life is such that we must of necessity be restrained and compelled by circumstances in nearly every action of our lives. Why, then, is liberty, defined as Mr. Mill defines it, to be regarded as so precious? What, after all, is done by the legislator or by the person who sets public opinion in motion to control conduct of which he disapproves—or, if the expression is preferred, which he dislikes—which is not done for us all at every instant of our lives by circumstances? The laws which punish murder or theft are substitutes for private vengeance, which, in the absence of law, would punish those crimes more severely, though in a less regular manner. If there were laws which punished incontinence, gluttony, or drunkenness, the same might be said of them. Mr. Mill admits in so many words that there are 'inconveniences which are strictly inseparable from the unfavourable judgment of others.' [78/278 L] What is the distinction in principle between such inconveniences and similar ones organized, defined, and inflicted upon proof that the circumstances which call for their infliction exist? This organization, definition, and procedure make all the difference between the restraints which Mr. Mill would permit and the restraints to which he objects. I cannot see on what the distinction rests. I cannot understand why it must always be wrong to punish habitual drunkenness by fine, imprisonment, or deprivation of civil rights, and always be right to punish it by the infliction of those consequences which are 'strictly inseparable from the unfavourable judgment of others.' [78/278 L] It may be said that these consequences follow, not because we think them desirable, but in the common order of nature. This answer only suggests the further question, whether nature is in this instance to be regarded as a friend or as an enemy? Every reasonable man would answer that the restraint which the fear of the disapprobation of others imposes on our conduct is the part of the constitution of nature which we could least afford to dispense with. But if this is so, why draw the line where Mr. Mill draws it? Why treat the penal consequences of disapprobation as things to be minimized and restrained within the narrowest limits? What 'inconvenience,' after all, is 'strictly inseparable from the unfavourable judgment of others'? [78/278 L] If society at large adopted fully Mr. Mill's theory of liberty, it would be easy to diminish very greatly the inconveniences in question. Strenuously preach and rigorously practise the doctrine that our neighbour's private character is nothing to us, and the number of unfavourable judgments formed, and therefore the number of inconveniences inflicted by them, can be reduced as much as we please, and the province of liberty can be enlarged in a corresponding ratio. Does any reasonable man wish for this? Could anyone desire gross licentiousness, monstrous extravagance, ridiculous vanity, or the like, to be unnoticed, or, being known, to inflict no inconveniences which can possibly be avoided?

If, however, the restraints on immorality are the main safeguards of society against influences which might be fatal to it, why treat them as if they were bad? Why draw so strongly marked a line between social and legal penalties? Mr. Mill asserts the existence of the distinction in every form of speech. He makes his meaning perfectly clear. Yet from one end of his essay to the other I find no proof and no attempt to give the proper and appropriate proof of it. His doctrine could have been proved if it had been true. It was not proved because it was not true.*

---

*Mr. Morley says of me, 'Mr. Stephen wishes to prove that social coercion would in many cases tend to make men virtuous. He does so by proving that the absence of coercion does not tend in such cases to make men virtuous. Of course, the latter proposition is no more equivalent to the former than the demonstration of the inefficacy of one way of treating disease is equal to, or demonstrative of, the efficacy of some other way.' Mr. Morley has overlooked this passage. In

Each of these propositions may, I think, be established by referring to the commonest and most important cases of coercion for other purposes than those of self-protection. The most important of them are:

1. Coercion for the purpose of establishing and maintaining religions.

2. Coercion for the purpose of establishing and practically maintaining morality.

3. Coercion for the purpose of making alterations in existing forms of government or social institutions.

None of these can in the common use of language be described as cases of self-protection or of the prevention of harm to persons other than those co-erced. Each is a case of coercion, for the sake of what the persons who exercise coercive power regard as the attainment of a good object, and each is accordingly condemned, and the first and second were no doubt intended to be condemned, by Mr. Mill's principle. Indeed, as he states it, the principle would go very much further. It would condemn, for instance, all taxation to which the party taxed did not consent, unless the money produced by it was laid out either upon military or upon police purposes or in the administration of justice; for these purposes only can be described as self-protective. To force an unwilling person to contribute to the support of the British Museum is as distinct a violation of Mr. Mill's principle as religious persecution. He does not, however, notice or insist upon this point, and I shall say no more of it than that it proves that his principle requires further limitations than he has thought it necessary to express.

Returning, then, to the three kinds of coercion mentioned, I say that it was Mr. Mill's business to show not merely that they had had bad effects—it would be as superfluous to show that surgical operations have bad effects—

---

this and in the following pages I argue that all organized religions, all moral systems, and all political institutions, are so many forms of coercion for purposes extending beyond self-protection, and that they have done great good. Of course, if Mr. Mill or his disciples can show that religion, law, and morals have in fact done more harm than good they answer me; but surely the burden of proof is on them. I say first (positively), the fact that law, morals, and religion are beneficial proves that coercion is beneficial; secondly (negatively), experience shows that in many cases the absence of coercion is not beneficial; and Mr. Morley charges me with proving the first proposition by the second. Each is, in fact, proved independently—the first here, and the second at p. 23.

but that the bad effects arose from the coercion itself, irrespectively of the objects for which it was employed, and of the mistakes and excesses of those who employed it. He had to show not that surgery is painful, or that the loss of a limb is a calamity, or that surgeons are often unskillful or rash, but that surgery is an art bad in itself, which ought to be suppressed. This, I say, he has never attempted to show from the beginning of the book to the end of it. If he had, he would have found his task an impossible one.

As regards coercion for the purpose of establishing and maintaining religions and systems of morality it would be a waste of time to insist upon the principle that both religion and morals are good on the whole, notwithstanding the evils of various kinds which have been connected with them. Nor need I repeat what I have already said on the point that both religion and morality are and always must be essentially coercive systems. Taking these matters for granted, however, it will be desirable to consider somewhat more fully the nature of moral and religious coercion, and the manner in which they operate. If Mr. Mill's view of liberty had always been adopted and acted upon to its full extent—if it had been the view of the first Christians or of the first Mahommedans—everyone can see that there would have been no such thing as organised Christianity or Mahommedanism in the world.* Even after such success as these and other religions have obtained, the morality of the vast mass of mankind is simply to do what they please up to the point at which custom puts a restraint upon them, arising from the fear of disapprobation. The custom of looking upon certain courses of conduct with aversion is the essence of morality, and the fact that this aversion may be felt by the very person whose conduct occasions it, and may be described as arising from the action of his own conscience, makes no difference which need be considered here. The important point is that such disapprobation could never have become customary unless it had been imposed upon mankind at large by persons who themselves felt it with exceptional energy, and who were in a position which enabled

*Mr. Morley says: 'To this one might reply by asking how we know that there might not have been something far better in their stead. We know what we get by effective intolerance, but we cannot ever know what possible benefactions we lose by it.'

Surely the region of the 'might have been' lies beyond the limits of sane speculation. If I show (and Mr. Morley has not attempted to deny it) that the agents by which in fact men have been improved have been mostly coercive I have proved my point. To ask what might have been if the world had had another history is like asking what might have been if men had had wings.

them to make other people adopt their principles and even their tastes and feelings.

Religion and morals, in a word, bear, even when they are at their calmest, the traces of having been established, as we know that in fact they were, by word of command. We have seen enough of the foundation of religions to know pretty well what is their usual course. A religion is first preached by a single person or a small body of persons. A certain number of disciples adopt it enthusiastically, and proceed to force their views upon the world by preaching, by persuasion, by the force of sympathy, until the new creed has become sufficiently influential and sufficiently well organised to exercise power both over its own members and beyond its own sphere. This power, in the case of a vigorous creed, assumes many forms. It may be military power, if the early converts are fighting men; it may be power derived from threats as to a future state—and this is the commonest and most distinctive form of religious power of which we have practical experience. It may be power derived from mere superior energy of will, or from organisations which those who possess that energy are able to set on foot by means of it. But, be the special form of religious power what it will, the principle is universally true that the growth of religions is in the nature of a conquest made by a small number of ardent believers over the lukewarmness, the indifference, and the conscious ignorance of the mass of mankind.* The life of the great mass of men, to a great extent the life of all men, is like a watercourse guided this way or that by a system of dams, sluices, weirs, and embankments. The volume and the quality of the different streams differ, and so do the plans of the works by which their flow is regulated, but it is by these works—that is to say, by their various

---

*One of the most famous passages in Gibbon exactly shows what I mean. 'The condemnation of the wisest and most virtuous of the pagans on account of their ignorance or disbelief of the divine truth seems to offend the reason and humanity of the present age. But the primitive Church, whose faith was of a much firmer consistence, delivered over without hesitation to eternal torture the far greater part of the human species.' . . . 'These rigid sentiments, which had been unknown to the ancient world, appear to have inspired a spirit of bitterness into a system of love and harmony, and the Christians who in this world found themselves oppressed by the power of the pagans, were sometimes reduced by resentment and spiritual pride to delight in the prospect of their future triumph'; and he proceeds to quote the famous passage from Tertullian. He then proceeds: 'The careless polytheist assailed by new and unexpected terrors, against which neither his priest nor his philosophers could afford him any certain protection, was very frequently terrified and subdued by the menace of eternal tortures. His fears might assist the

customs and institutions—that men's lives are regulated. Now these customs are not only in their very nature restraints, but they are restraints imposed by the will of an exceedingly small numerical minority and contentedly accepted by a majority to which they have become so natural that they do not recognise them as restraints.

As for the third set of cases in which coercion is habitually employed—I mean coercion for the purpose of making alterations in existing forms of government and social institutions—it surely needs no argument to show that all the great political changes which have been the principal subject of European history for the last three centuries have been cases of coercion in the most severe form, although a large proportion of them have been described as struggles for liberty by those who were, in fact, the most vigorous wielders of power.

Mr. Mill and his disciples would be the last persons in the world to say that the political and social changes which have taken place in the world since the sixteenth century have not on the whole been eminently beneficial to mankind; but nothing can be clearer than that they were brought about by force, and in many instances by the force of a minority numerically small, applied to the conduct of an ignorant or very partially informed and for the most part indifferent majority. It would surely be as absurd to say that the Reformation or the French Revolution was brought about freely and not by coercion as to say that Charles I walked freely to the block. Each of these and many other cases which might be mentioned were struggles for political power, efforts to

---

progress of his faith and reason, and if he could once persuade himself to suspect that the Christian religion might possibly be true, it became an easy task to convince him that it was the safest and most prudent party he could possibly embrace.'[3] In a note on this, Dr. Milman disclaims the 'fierce African' and his 'unchristian fanaticism.' I do not love him, but if Christianity had had no threats and used no intimidation, there would have been no metropolitan deans. Religions are not founded on mildness and benevolence. Talleyrand's speech to the the theophilanthropists has always been memorable to me. 'Gentlemen, when Jesus Christ wanted to found a religion he had to be crucified, dead, and buried, and to rise on the third day from the dead. If you want to convince mankind, go and do likewise.'

3. Edward Gibbon, *The History of the Decline and Fall of the Roman Empire*, ed. J. B. Bury, 7 vols. (London: Methuen, 1910), vol. 2, Chapter 15, sec. 2, pp. 26–28. Stephen reviewed Gibbon's *History:* see *Horae Sabbaticae*, vol. 2, pp. 387–401. (For a complete reference to *Horae Sabbaticae*, see the bibliography on p. xxvii.)

bring about a change in the existing state of things, which for various reasons appeared desirable to people who were able to carry out their designs more or less successfully.

To say that force was justifiable in none of these cases would be a paradox which Mr. Mill would probably be the last person to maintain. To say that it was justifiable only in so far as it was necessary for self-protection would not explain the facts. Take such a case as the establishment of a new religion and the reduction of an old one to the position of a permitted form of private opinion. Life has gone on for ages upon the supposition of the truth of the old religion. Laws and institutions of various kinds are founded upon it. The great mass of the population of a country have no particular wish to disturb the existing state of things even though they may be ceasing to believe in the creed which it implies. Innovators arise who attack corruptions and preach new doctrines. They are punished. They resist, sides are formed, and the results follow with which history is filled. In what sense can it be said that the acts of violence which take place on such occasions are acts done in self-defense and in order to prevent harm? They are acts of aggression upon an established system which is regarded as bad, and with a view to the substitution of a different system which it is supposed will be better. If anyone supposes that in regard to such transactions it is possible to draw a line between what ought to be done and what ought not; if anyone will undertake to say how the French Revolution or the Reformation ought to have been conducted so as to avoid all violence on both sides and yet to arrive at the desired conclusion, he will be able to give us a universal political constitution and a universal code of laws. People in such positions as those of Charles V, Philip II, Henry VIII, Queen Elizabeth, Louis XVI, and many others, must take a side, and must back it vigorously against its antagonists, unless they mean to be devoured themselves.

The only way by which this can be reconciled with Mr. Mill's principle is by describing such violence as a case of self-protection. Now if the word 'self-protection' is so construed as to include every act of violence done for the purpose of procuring improvements in the existing state of things it will follow that if men happen to be living under a political or social system with the principles or with the working of which they are not satisfied, they may fight out their difference, and the conqueror may determine the matter in dispute according to his own will, which reduces the principle to an absurdity. On the other hand, if no act of violence done for the purpose of improving the existing state of things is described as a case of self-protection, no such act is justifiable, unless it is necessary for the immediate protection of the agent. This again is an absurdity.

The truth is that the principle about self-protection and self-regarding acts is not one by which the right or wrong of revolutions can be measured, because the distinction upon which it depends is radically vicious. It assumes that some acts regard the agent only, and that some regard other people. In fact, by far the most important part of our conduct regards both ourselves and others, and revolutions are the clearest proof of this. Thus, Mr. Mill's principle cannot be applied to the very cases in which it is most needed. Indeed, it assumes the existence of an ideal state of things in which everyone has precisely the position which, with a view to the general happiness of the world, he ought to hold. If such a state of things existed there would be some plausibility in saying that no one ought to interfere with anyone else except for the sake of protecting himself against attack, by maintaining the existing state of things. But as no such state of things exists or ever yet existed in any age or country, the principle has at present no *locus standi*.*

Not only is an appeal to facts and experience opposed to Mr. Mill's principle, but his essay contains exceptions and qualifications which are really inconsistent with it. He says that his principle 'is meant to apply only to human beings in the maturity of their faculties,' and, he adds, 'we may leave out of consideration those backward states of society in which the race itself may be considered in its nonage.' [13–14/224 L] Despotism, he says,

> is a legitimate mode of government in dealing with barbarians, provided the end be their improvement, and the means justified by actually effecting that end. Liberty, as a principle, has no application to any state of things anterior to the time when mankind have become capable of being improved

*This passage is somewhat expanded, as it appeared from a criticism of Mr. Morley's that he had failed to understand it. He seems to have thought that I meant to say that in a revolution every sort of intolerance and fanaticism was right. I meant only to show that Mr. Mill's fundamental distinction about self-regarding acts is shown by the case of revolutions to be quite unequal to the weight which he lays upon it, though of course there are cases in which as a mere practical rule, it would be useful in revolutions as well as at other times.

by free and equal discussion. Until then there is nothing for them but implicit obedience to an Akbar or a Charlemagne if they are so fortunate as to find one. But as soon as mankind have attained the capacity of being guided to their own improvement by conviction or persuasion (a period long since reached in all nations with whom we need here concern ourselves), compulsion is no longer admissible as a means to their own good, and is justifiable only for the security of others. [13–14/224 L]

It seems to me that this qualification either reduces the doctrine qualified to an empty commonplace which no one would care to dispute, or makes an incredible assertion about the state of human society. No one, I suppose, ever denied either in theory or in practice that there is a sphere within which the tastes of people of mature age ought not to be interfered with, and within which differences must be regarded as natural and inevitable—in which better or worse means that which the individual prefers or dislikes. On the other hand, no one ever suggested that it was or could be good for anyone to be compelled to do what he did not like, unless the person compelling was not only stronger but wiser than the person compelled, at all events in reference to the matter to which the compulsion applied.

Either, then, the exception means only that superior wisdom is not in every case a reason why one man should control another—which is a mere commonplace—or else it means that in all the countries which we are accustomed to call civilised the mass of adults are so well acquainted with their own interests and so much disposed to pursue them that no compulsion or restraint put upon any of them by any others for the purpose of promoting their interests can really promote them.

No one can doubt the importance of this assertion, but where is the proof of it? Let us consider how it ought to have and would have been proved if it had been capable of proof. Mr. Mill might have specified the different classes of which some considerable nation—our own, for instance—is composed. Then he might have stated what are the objects which, if attained, would constitute the happiness of each of those classes. Then he might have shown that a knowledge of those interests, a knowledge of the means by which they must be attained, and a disposition to make use of the means proper to obtain them, was so generally diffused among each class that no compulsion put by the other classes upon any one class as a whole, or by any part of any class

upon any other part of it, could increase the happiness of the persons compelled to such an extent as to overbalance the pain of the compulsion itself.
Before he affirmed that in Western Europe and America the compulsion of
adults for their own good is unjustifiable, Mr. Mill ought to have proved that
there are among us no considerable differences in point of wisdom, or that if
there are, the wiser part of the community does not wish for the welfare of the
less wise.*

It seems to me quite impossible to stop short of this principle if compulsion
in the case of children and 'backward' races is admitted to be justifiable; for,
after all, maturity and civilisation are matters of degree. One person may be
more mature at fifteen than another at thirty. A nation or a particular part of
a nation may make such an advance in the arts of life in half a century that
other nations, or other parts of the same nation, which were equally civilised
at the beginning of the period, may be relatively barbarous at the end of it.

I do not overlook the qualification contained in the passages quoted above.
It fixes the limit up to which compulsion is justifiable at the 'time when mankind have become capable of being improved by free and equal discussion.'
[14/224 L] This expression may imply that compulsion is always or never
justifiable, according to the manner in which it is construed. I am not quite
sure that I know what Mr. Mill means by 'equal' discussion, but was there
ever a time or place at which no men could be improved on any point by free
discussion? The wildest savages, the most immature youths, capable of any
sort of education, are capable of being improved by free discussion upon a

*Mr. Morley says upon this passage: 'Why so? Mr. Mill's very proposition is that though
there is a wiser part, and though the wiser part may wish well to the less wise, *yet* even then the
disadvantages of having a wise course forced upon the members of civilised societies exceed the
disadvantages of following an unwise course freely. Mr. Stephen's allegation of the points
which Mr. Mill should have proved rests on the assumption of the very matter at issue—namely,
whether freedom is not in itself so valuable an element in social life (in civilised communities),
that for the sake of it we should be content to let the unwiser part have their own way in what
concerns themselves only.'

Mr. Morley quotes only a part of my argument, which is this: 'You admit that children and
human beings in "backward states of society" may be coerced for their own good. You would
let Charlemagne coerce the Saxons, and Akbar the Hindoos. Why then may not educated men
coerce the ignorant. What is there in the character of a very commonplace ignorant peasant or
petty shopkeeper in these days which makes him a less fit subject for coercion on Mr. Mill's principle than the Hindoo nobles and princes who were coerced by Akbar?'

great variety of subjects. Compulsion, therefore, in their own interests would, at least in relation to these subjects, be unjustifiable as regards them. If boys in a school can be convinced of the importance of industry, you must never punish them for idleness. Such an interpretation of the rule would practically exclude compulsion altogether.

A narrower interpretation would be as follows. There is a period, now generally reached all over Europe and America, at which discussion takes the place of compulsion, and in which people when they know what is good for them generally do it. When this period is reached, compulsion may be laid aside. To this I should say that no such period has as yet been reached anywhere, and that there is no prospect of its being reached anywhere within any assignable time.

Where, in the very most advanced and civilised communities, will you find any class of persons whose views or whose conduct on subjects on which they are interested are regulated even in the main by the results of free discussion? What proportion of human misconduct in any department in life is due to ignorance, and what to wickedness or weakness? Of ten thousand people who get drunk, is there one who could say with truth that he did so because he had been brought to think on full deliberation and after free discussion that it was wise to get drunk? Would not every one of the ten thousand, if he told the real truth, say in some dialect or other—'I got drunk because I was weak and a fool, because I could not resist the immediate pleasure for the sake of future and indefinite advantage'? If we look at the conduct of bodies of men as expressed in their laws and institutions, we shall find that, though compulsion and persuasion go hand in hand, from the most immature and the roughest ages and societies up to the most civilised, the lion's share of the results obtained is due to compulsion, and that discussion is at most an appeal to the motives by which the strong man is likely to be actuated in using his strength. Look at our own time and country, and mention any single great change which has been effected by mere discussion. Can a single case be mentioned in which the passions of men were interested where the change was not carried by force—that is to say, ultimately by the fear of revolution? Is it in any degree true that when the brains are out a question dies? Look at small matters which involve more or less of a principle, but do not affect many men's passions, and see how much reasoning has to do with their settlement. Such questions as the admission of Jews into Parliament and the legalisation of marriage between brothers and sisters-in-law drag on and on after the argument has been exhausted, till in course of time those who take one view or the other grow into a decided majority, and settle the matter their own way. Parliamentary government is simply a mild and disguised form of compulsion. We agree to try strength by counting heads instead of breaking heads, but the principle is exactly the same. It is not the wisest side which wins, but the one which for the time being shows its superior strength (of which no doubt wisdom is one element) by enlisting the largest amount of active sympathy in its support. The minority gives way not because it is convinced that it is wrong, but because it is convinced that it is a minority.

This again suggests an observation on a different part of the passage quoted from Mr. Mill. In rough states of society he admits of Charlemagnes and Akbars, if the world is so fortunate as to have them at hand. What reason is there to suppose that Charlemagnes or Akbars owe their power to enlightenment superior to that of the persons whom they coerce? They owe it to greater force of character and to the possession of power. What they did was to suppress anarchy—to substitute the vigorous rule of one Sovereign for the jarring pretensions of a crowd of petty rulers. No doubt powerful men are generally comparatively enlightened men, as were both Charlemagne and Akbar, for knowledge is a high form of power, as light implies intense force. But power in whatever form is the essential thing. Anarchy may be mischievous in civilised as well as in uncivilised life, and the only way out of it is by coercion. To direct that power aright is, I think, the principal object of political argument. The difference between a rough and a civilised society is not that force is used in the one case and persuasion in the other, but that force is (or ought to be) guided with greater care in the second case than in the first. President Lincoln attained his objects by the use of a degree of force which would have crushed Charlemagne and his paladins and peers like so many eggshells.

The correctness of the assertion that 'in all nations with whom we need here concern ourselves,' the period at which 'mankind have become capable of being improved by free and equal discussion has long since arrived,' [14/224 L] may be estimated by reference to two familiar points:

1. Upon all the subjects which mainly interest men as men—religion, morals, government—mankind at large are in a state of ignorance which in

favourable cases is just beginning to be conscious that it is ignorance. How far will free discussion carry such knowledge as we have on these subjects? The very most that can be hoped for—men being what they are—is to popularise, more or less, a certain set of commonplaces, which, by the condition of their existence, cannot possibly be more than half-truths. Discussion produces plenty of effects, no doubt. People hunger and thirst after theories to such a degree that whatever puts their own wishes into a compact and intelligible form will obtain from them a degree of allegiance which may be called either touching or terrible. Look at the great popular movements which discussion has provoked, and consider what approach any one of them made to the real truth. Innumerable creeds, religious and political, have swept across the world, arguing, preaching, gesticulating, and fighting. Compare the amount of recognition which the worst of them has obtained and the devotion which it has called forth with the degree of really intelligent appreciation which has been awarded to science. Millions upon millions of men, women, and children believe in Mahommed to the point of regulating their whole life by his law. How many people have understood Adam Smith? Did anybody, except perhaps Mr. Buckle, ever feel any enthusiasm about him?

If we wish to test the capacity of mankind at large for any sort of abstract discussion, we ought to consider the case of the minor branches of human knowledge which have been invested with some approach to a systematic character. How many people are capable of understanding the fundamental principles of either political economy or jurisprudence? How many people can understand the distinction between making the fundamental assumptions of political economy for the purpose of calculating the results of the unrestrained action of the desire to get rich, and regarding those assumptions as being true in fact and capable of serving as the foundations of human society? One would have thought that it was easy to distinguish between the proposition, 'If your only object in trade is to make the largest possible profit, you ought always to buy in the cheapest market and sell in the dearest,' and the proposition, 'All men ought, under all circumstances, to buy all things in the cheapest and sell them in the dearest market.' Yet how many people do in fact distinguish them? How many recognise in the faintest degree the importance of the distinction?

2. Men are so constructed that whatever theory as to goodness and badness we choose to adopt, there are and always will be in the world an enormous mass of bad and indifferent people—people who deliberately do all sorts of things which they ought not to do, and leave undone all sorts of things which they ought to do. Estimate the proportion of men and women who are selfish, sensual, frivolous, idle, absolutely commonplace and wrapped up in the smallest of petty routines, and consider how far the freest of free discussion is likely to improve them. The only way by which it is practically possible to act upon them at all is by compulsion or restraint. Whether it is worth while to apply to them both or either I do not now inquire; I confine myself to saying that the utmost conceivable liberty which could be bestowed upon them would not in the least degree tend to improve them. It would be as wise to say to the water of a stagnant marsh, 'Why in the world do not you run into the sea? you are perfectly free. There is not a single hydraulic work within a mile of you. There are no pumps to suck you up, no defined channel down which you are compelled to run, no harsh banks and mounds to confine you to any particular course, no dams and no floodgates; and yet there you lie, putrefying and breeding fever, frogs, and gnats, just as if you were a mere slave!' The water might probably answer, if it knew how, 'If you want me to turn mills and carry boats, you must dig proper channels and provide proper water-works for me.'

CHAPTER TWO

ON THE LIBERTY OF
THOUGHT AND DISCUSSION

Though, as I pointed out in my last chapter, Mr. Mill rather asserts than proves his doctrines about liberty, the second chapter of his essay on the Liberty of Thought and Discussion, and the third chapter on Individuality as one of the Elements of Well-being—may be regarded as arguments to prove certain parts or applications of the general principle asserted in his Introduction; and as such I will consider them. I object rather to Mr. Mill's theory than to his practical conclusions. I hope to show hereafter how far the practical difference between us extends. The objection which I make to most of his statements on the subject is that in order to justify in practice what might be justified on narrow and special grounds, he lays down a theory incorrect in itself and tending to confirm views which might become practically mischievous.

The result of his chapter on Liberty of Thought and Discussion is summed up, with characteristic point and brevity, by himself in the following words:

> We have now recognized the necessity to the mental well-being of mankind (on which all their other well-being depends) of freedom of opinion and freedom of the expression of opinion on four distinct grounds.
>
> First, if any opinion is compelled to silence, that opinion may, for aught we can certainly know, be true. To deny this is to assume our own infallibility.
>
> Secondly, though the silenced opinion be an error, it may, and very commonly does, contain a portion of truth; and since the general or pre-

24

vailing opinion is rarely or never the whole truth, it is only by the collision of adverse opinions that the remainder of the truth has any chance of being supplied.

Thirdly, even if the received opinion be not only true, but the whole truth, unless it is suffered to be and actually is vigorously and earnestly contested, it will by most of those who receive it be held in the manner of a prejudice, with little comprehension or feeling of its rational grounds.

Fourthly,[1] the meaning of the doctrine itself will be in danger of being lost or enfeebled and deprived of its vital effect on the character and conduct; the dogma becoming a mere formal profession inefficacious for good, but cumbering the ground, and preventing the growth of any real and heartfelt conviction from reason or personal experience. [53–54/ 257–58 L]

The chapter in question is, I think, one of the most eloquent to be found in its author's writings, and it contains, as is not unfrequently the case with him, illustrations which are even more valuable for what they suggest than for what they say.

These illustrations are no doubt the part of this chapter which made the deepest impression when it was first published, and which have been most vividly remembered by its readers. I think that for the sake of them most readers forget the logical framework in which they were set, and read the chapter as a plea for greater freedom of discussion on moral and theological subjects. If Mr. Mill had limited himself to the proposition that in our own time and country it is highly important that the great questions of morals and theology should be discussed openly and with complete freedom from all legal restraints, I should agree with him. But the impression which the whole chapter leaves upon me is that for the sake of establishing this limited practical consequence, Mr. Mill has stated a theory which is very far indeed from the truth, and which, if generally accepted, might hereafter become a serious embarrassment to rational legislation.

His first reason in favour of unlimited freedom of opinion on all subjects is this: 'If any opinion is compelled to silence, that opinion may, for aught we can certainly tell, be true. To deny this is to assume our own infallibility.' [53/258 L]

1. In *On Liberty,* this paragraph actually begins with: "And not only this, but, fourthly, . . ."

He states fairly and fully the obvious objection to this—that 'there is no greater assumption of infallibility in forbidding the propagation of error, than in any other thing which is done by public authority on its own judgment and responsibility.' [22/230 L] In other words, the assumption is not that the persecutor is infallible, but that in this particular case he is right. To this objection he replies as follows: 'There is the greatest difference between presuming an opinion to be true because, with every opportunity for contesting it, it has not been refuted, and assuming its truth for the purpose of not permitting its refutation. Complete liberty of contradicting our opinion is the very condition which justifies us in assuming its truth for purposes of action; and on no other terms can a being with human faculties have any rational assurance of being right.' [22–23/231 L]

This reply does not appear to me satisfactory. It is not very easy to disentangle the argument on which it rests, and to put it into a perfectly distinct shape, but I think it will be found on examination to involve the following propositions:

1. No one can have a rational assurance of the truth of any opinion whatever, unless he is infallible, or unless all persons are absolutely free to contradict it.

2. Whoever prevents the expression of any opinion asserts by that act that he has a rational assurance of the falsehood of that opinion.

3. At the same time he destroys one of the conditions of a rational assurance of the truth of the assertions which he makes, namely, the freedom of others to contradict him.

4. Therefore he claims infallibility, which is the only other ground on which such an assurance of the truth of those assertions can rest.

The first and second of these propositions appear to me to be incorrect.

As to the first, I think that there are innumerable propositions on which a man may have a rational assurance that he is right whether others are or are not at liberty to contradict him, and that although he does not claim infallibility. Every proposition of which we are assured by our own senses, or by evidence which for all practical purposes is as strong as that of our own senses, falls under this head. There are plenty of reasons for not forbidding people to deny the existence of London Bridge and the river Thames, but the fear that the proof of those propositions would be weakened or that the person making the law would claim infallibility is not among the number.*

A asserts the opinion that B is a thief. B sues A for libel. A justifies. The jury give a verdict for the plaintiff, with £1,000 damages. This is nearly equivalent to a law forbidding everyone, under the penalty of a heavy fine, to express the opinion that in respect of the matters discussed B is a thief. Does this weaken the belief of the world at large in the opinion that in respect of those matters B is not a thief? According to Mr. Mill, no one can have a rational assurance upon the subject unless everyone is absolutely free to contradict the orthodox opinion. Surely this cannot be so.

The solution seems to be this. The fact that people are forbidden to deny a proposition weakens the force of the inference in its favour to be drawn from their acquiescence in it; but the value of their acquiescence considered as evidence may be very small, and the weight of other evidence, independent of public opinion, may not only be overwhelming, but the circumstances of the case may be such as to be inconsistent with the supposition that any further evidence will ever be forthcoming.

Again, an opinion may be silenced without any assertion on the part of the person who silences it that it is false. It may be suppressed because it is true, or because it is doubtful whether it is true or false, and because it is not considered desirable that it should be discussed. In these cases there is obviously no assumption of infallibility in suppressing it. The old maxim, 'the greater the

---

*Mr. Morley says: 'Were not men assured by their own senses that the earth is a plain, and that the sun revolves around the earth?'

No; men were not assured of any such thing. They were assured by their senses of the appearance of the sun in the morning in the East, at noon in the South, and in the evening in the West, and they are still assured of the same fact by the same means. Whether that appearance is to be accounted for by the motion of the sun or the motion of the earth was a question on which their senses could tell them nothing. Mr. Morley adds, 'It may be said that before Copernicus they had a rational assurance that they were right in thinking that the sun moved round the earth. The belief was not correct, but it was a rational assurance. Precisely, and people would have lived to this day with their erroneous rational assurances uncorrected unless Copernicus had been at liberty to contradict them.' Do I say they would not? or that Copernicus's liberty was bad? Not at all. I say only that persecution does not of necessity involve a claim to infallibility, which Mr. Mill asserts. Mr. Morley never distinguishes between the denial of a proposition and the denial of an argument in its favour.

truth the greater the libel,' has a true side to it, and when it applies it is obvious that an opinion is silenced without any assumption of infallibility. The opinion that a respectable man of mature years led an immoral life in his youth may be perfectly true, and yet the expression of that opinion may be a crime, if it is not for the public good that it should be expressed.

In cases in which it is obvious that no conclusion at all can be established beyond the reach of doubt, and that men must be contented with probabilities, it may be foolish to prevent discussion and prohibit the expression of any opinion but one, but no assumption of infallibility is involved in so doing. When Henry VIII and Queen Elizabeth silenced to a certain extent both Catholics and Puritans, and sought to confine religious controversy within limits fixed by law, they did not assume themselves to be infallible. What they thought—and it is by no means clear that they were wrong—was that unless religious controversy was kept within bounds there would be a civil war, and they muzzled the disputants accordingly.

There are, in short, two classes of cases to which, as it appears to me, Mr. Mill's argument does not apply—cases in which moral certainty is attainable on the evidence, and cases in which it is not attainable on the evidence.

Where moral certainty is attainable on the evidence the suppression of opinion involves no claim to infallibility, but at most a claim to be right in the particular case.

Where moral certainty is not attainable on the evidence the suppression of opinion involves no claim to infallibility, because it does not assert the falsehood of the opinion suppressed.

The three remaining arguments in favour of unlimited liberty of thought and discussion are: 1. That the silenced opinion may be partially true and that this partial truth can be brought out by discussion only. 2. That a true opinion when established is not believed to be true unless it is vigorously and earnestly contested. 3. That it comes to be held in a dead conventional way unless it is discussed.

These arguments go to show not that the suppression of opinion can never be right, but that it may sometimes be wrong, which no one denies. None of them show—as the first argument would if it were well founded—that persecution in all cases proceeds on a theory involving distinct intellectual error. As to the first argument, it is obvious that if people are prepared to take the chance of persecuting a proposition which may be wholly true as if it were wholly false, they will be prepared to treat it in the same manner though it is only partially true. The second and third arguments, to which I shall have to return hereafter, apply exclusively to that small class of persons whose opinions depend principally upon the consciousness that they have reached them by intellectual processes correctly performed. The incalculable majority of mankind form their opinions in quite a different way, and are attached to them because they suit their temper and meet their wishes, and not because and in so far as they think themselves warranted by evidence in believing them to be true. The notorious result of unlimited freedom of thought and discussion is to produce general scepticism on many subjects in the vast majority of minds. If you want zealous belief, set people to fight. Few things give men such a keen perception of the importance of their own opinions and the vileness of the opinions of others as the fact that they have inflicted and suffered persecution for them. Unlimited freedom of opinion may be a very good thing, but it does not tend to zeal, or even to a distinct appreciation of the bearings of the opinions which are entertained. Nothing will give either but a deep interest in the subject to which those opinions relate, and this is so personal and deeply seated a matter that it is scarcely capable of being affected by external restraints, unless, indeed, it is irritated and so stimulated by them.

I pass over for the present the illustrations of this chapter, which, as I have already said, are by far the most important part of it; and I proceed to the chapter on Individuality as one of the Elements of Well-being.

The substance of the doctrine eloquently expounded in it is that freedom is essential to originality and individuality of character. It consists, however, almost entirely of eulogies upon individuality, to which Mr. Mill thinks the world is indifferent. He accordingly sets forth at length the advantage of having vigorous impulses and plenty of them, of trying experiments in life, of leaving every man of genius free, not indeed 'to seize on the government of the world and make it do his bidding in spite of itself,' but to 'point out the way,'[2] This individuality and energy of character, he thinks, is dying out under various depressing influences. 'The Calvinistic theory' regards 'the crushing out the human faculties, capacities, and susceptibilities, as 'no evil,'

2. This is a paraphrase of 67/269 L.

inasmuch as 'man needs no capacity, but that of surrendering himself to the will of God: and if he uses any of his faculties for any other purpose but to do that supposed will more effectually, he is better without them.' [62/265 L] Apart, however, from this, 'society has now fairly got the better of individuality.' [61/264 L] All of us are enslaved to custom. 'Energetic characters on any large scale are becoming merely traditional. There is now scarcely any outlet for energy in this country except business.' 'The only unfailing and permanent source of improvement is Liberty, since by it there are as many possible independent centres of improvement as there are individuals.' [70/272 L] Individuality, however, is at a discount with us, and we are on the way to a Chinese uniformity.

Much of what I had to say on this subject has been anticipated by an article in 'Fraser's Magazine.'* It expands and illustrates with great vigour the following propositions, which appear to me to be unanswerable:

1. The growth of liberty in the sense of democracy tends to diminish, not to increase, originality and individuality. 'Make all men equal so far as laws can make them equal, and what does that mean but that each unit is to be rendered hopelessly feeble in presence of an overwhelming majority?' The existence of such a state of society reduces individuals to impotence, and to tell them to be powerful, original, and independent is to mock them. It is like plucking a bird's feathers in order to put it on a level with beasts, and then telling it to fly.

2. 'The hope that people are to be rendered more vigorous by simply removing restrictions seems to be as fallacious as the hope that a bush planted in an open field would naturally develope into a forest tree. It is the intrinsic force which requires strengthening, and it may even happen in some cases that force will produce all the more effect for not being allowed to scatter itself.'

3. Though goodness is various, variety is not in itself good. 'A nation in which everybody was sober would be a happier, better, and more progressive, though a less diversified, nation than one of which half the members were sober and the other half habitual drunkards.'

I might borrow many other points from the excellent essay in question, but I prefer to deal with the matter in my own way, and I will therefore add some

*On 'Social Macadamisation,' by L. S.,[3] in *Fraser's Magazine* for August 1872.
3. L. S. refers to Leslie Stephen, the younger brother of Fitzjames Stephen.

There is one more point in this curious chapter which I must notice in conclusion. Nothing can exceed Mr. Mill's enthusiasm for individual greatness. The mass, he says, in all countries constitute collective mediocrity. They never think at all, and never rise above mediocrity, 'except in so far as the sovereign many have let themselves be guided and influenced (which in their best times they always have done) by the counsels and influence of a more highly gifted or instructed one or few. The initiation of all wise or noble things, comes and must come from individuals; generally at first from some one individual.' [66/269 L] The natural inference would be that these individuals are the born rulers of the world, and that the world should acknowledge and obey them as such. Mr. Mill will not admit this. All that the man of genius can claim is 'freedom to point out the way. The power of compelling others into it, is not only inconsistent with the freedom and development of all the rest, but corrupting to the strong man himself.' [67/269 L] This would be perfectly true if the compulsion consisted in a simple exertion of blind force, like striking a nail with a hammer; but who ever acted so on others to any extent worth mentioning? The way in which the man of genius rules is by persuading an efficient minority to coerce an indifferent and self-indulgent majority, which is quite a different process.

The odd manner in which Mr. Mill worships mere variety, and confounds the proposition that variety is good with the proposition that goodness is various, is well illustrated by the lines which follow this passage: 'Exceptional individuals . . . should be encouraged in acting differently from the mass'—in order that there may be enough of them to 'point out the way.' [67/269 L] Eccentricity is much required in these days. Precisely because the tyranny of opinion is such as to make eccentricity a reproach, it is desirable, in order to break through that tyranny, that people should be eccentric. Eccentricity has always abounded when and where strength of character has abounded, and the amount of eccentricity in a society has generally been proportioned to the amount of genius, mental vigour, and moral courage it contained. That so few now dare to be eccentric makes the chief danger of the time.

If this advice were followed, we should have as many little oddities in manner and behaviour as we have people who wish to pass for men of genius. Eccentricity is far more often a mark of weakness than a mark of strength. Weakness wishes, as a rule, to attract attention by trifling distinctions, and strength wishes to avoid it. Originality consists in thinking for yourself, not in thinking differently from other people.*

Thus much as to Mr. Mill's view of this subject. I will now attempt to explain my own views on liberty in general, and in particular on liberty of thought.

To me this question whether liberty is a good or a bad thing appears as irrational as the question whether fire is a good or a bad thing. It is both good

---

*Upon this Mr. Morley observes: 'Mr. Mill deliberately held that variety is good on the ground that it is the essential condition of the appearance and growth of those new ideas, new practices, new sentiments, some of which must contain the germs of all future improvements in the arts of existence. It shows an incapacity to understand the essence of the doctrine to deal with it by such statements as that it involves "a worship of mere variety." It plainly does no such thing. Mr. Mill prizes variety, not at all as mere variety, but because it furnishes most chances of new forms of good presenting themselves and acquiring a permanent place. He prized that eccentricity which Mr. Stephen so heartily dislikes because he perceived that all new truth and new ways of living must from the nature of things always appear eccentric to persons accustomed to old opinions and old ways of living; because he saw that most of the personages to whom mankind owes its chief steps in moral and spiritual advance were looked upon by contemporaries as eccentrics, and very often cruelly ill treated by them (on Mr. Stephen's principles) for eccentricity, which was in truth the very deliverance of humanity from error or imperfection. Not all novelties are improvements, but all improvements are novel, and you can only, therefore, be sure of improvements by giving eccentricity a fair hearing, and free room for as much active manifestation as does no near, positive, recognisable, harm to other people.'

This seems to me like saying 'genuine banknotes are so valuable that for their sake forged banknotes ought to be encouraged.' To regard mere variety as furnishing most chances of new forms of good presenting themselves and acquiring a permanent place is to assume that people cannot be trusted to judge any variety or alteration upon its merits. This appears to me altogether unjust. The truth appears to be that in this, as in other parts of his writings, Mr. Mill assumed that the common standards of good and evil were so thoroughly wrong that if men exercised any discretion as to the varieties which they would encourage or discourage, they would do more harm than good, and that, therefore, in the present bad state of affairs the best thing to do was to encourage all varieties. This view is quite intelligible, though I do not agree with it.

As to eccentricity, surely the common use of language confines the word to affected oddity of behaviour. No one, I should suppose, would have called Mr. Mill 'eccentric' for his peculiar views about women. If he had worn a strange dress, or kept different hours from everyone else, or indulged in any other apparently unreasonable whim, he would have been eccentric. The eccentricity which, as Mr. Morley says, I 'heartily dislike,' is merely affectation. It would, I think, be hard to show that the great reformers of the world have been persecuted for 'eccentricity.' They were persecuted because their doctrines were disliked, rightly or wrongly as the case might be. The difference between Mr. Mill's views and mine is that he instinctively assumes that whatever is is wrong. I say, try each case on its own merits.

and bad according to time, place, and circumstance, and a complete answer to the question, In what cases is liberty good and in what cases is it bad? would involve not merely a universal history of mankind, but a complete solution of the problems which such a history would offer. I do not believe that the state of our knowledge is such as to enable us to enunciate any 'very simple principle as entitled to govern absolutely the dealings of society with the individual in the way of compulsion and control.' [13/223 L] We must proceed in a far more cautious way, and confine ourselves to such remarks as experience suggests about the advantages and disadvantages of compulsion and liberty respectively in particular cases.

The following way of stating the matter is not and does not pretend to be a solution of the question, In what cases is liberty good? but it will serve to show how the question ought to be discussed when it arises. I do not see how Mr. Mill could deny its correctness consistently with the general principles of the ethical theory which is to a certain extent common to us both.

Compulsion is bad:

1. When the object aimed at is bad.

2. When the object aimed at is good, but the compulsion employed is not calculated to obtain it.

3. When the object aimed at is good, and the compulsion employed is calculated to obtain it, but at too great an expense.

Thus to compel a man to commit murder is bad, because the object is bad.

To inflict a punishment sufficient to irritate but not sufficient to deter or to destroy for holding particular religious opinions is bad, because such compulsion is not calculated to effect its purpose, assuming it to be good.

To compel people not to trespass by shooting them with spring-guns is bad, because the harm done is out of all proportion to the harm avoided.

If, however, the object aimed at is good, if the compulsion employed such as to attain it, and if the good obtained overbalances the inconvenience of the compulsion itself I do not understand how, upon utilitarian principles, the compulsion can be bad. I may add that this way of stating the case shows that Mr. Mill's 'simple principle' is really a paradox. It can be justified only by showing as a fact that, self-protection apart, compulsion must always be a greater evil in itself than the absence of any object which can possibly be obtained by it.

I will now proceed to apply the principles stated to the case of compulsion applied to thought and discussion. This Mr. Mill condemns in all cases. I should condemn it in those cases only in which the object itself is bad, or in which the means used are not suited to its attainment, or in which, though suited to its attainment, they involve too great an expense. Compare the results of these two ways of thinking. Few persons would be found, I suppose, in these days to deny the paramount expediency, the utility in the highest sense, of having true opinions; and by true I mean not merely honest, but correct, opinions. To believe true statements, to disbelieve false statements, to give to probable or improbable statements a degree of credit proportioned to their apparent probability or improbability, would be the greatest of intellectual blessings. Such a state of mind is the ideal state which a perfectly reasonable human being would regard as the one at which he ought to aim as we aim at all ideals—that is to say, with a consciousness that we can never fully attain them. The most active-minded, the most sagacious, and those who are most favourably situated for the purpose, are in practice altogether unable to make more than an approximation to such a result, in regard to some few of the innumerable subjects which interest them. I am, of course, aware that this view is not universally admitted, but I need not argue at present with those who deny it.

Assuming it to be true, it will follow that all coercion which has the effect of falsifying the opinions of those who are coerced is coercion for an object bad in itself; and this at once condemns all cases of direct coercion in favour of opinions which are not, to say the least, so probable that a reasonable man would act upon the supposition of their truth. The second condition—namely, that coercion must be effective—and the third condition, that it must not inflict greater evils than it avoids, condemn, when taken together, many other cases of coercion, even when the object aimed at is good. For instance, they condemn all coercion applied directly to thought and unexpressed opinion, and all coercion which must be carried to the point of extermination or general paralysis of the thinking powers in order to be effective. In the first case the end is not attained. In the second it is attained at too great an expense. These two considerations are sufficient to condemn all the coarser forms of persecution. I have nothing to add to the well-known commonplaces which bear upon this part of the subject.

This being allowed, let us turn to the consideration of the other side of the question, and enquire whether there are no cases in which a degree of coercion, affecting, though not directly applied to, thought and the expression of opinion, and not in itself involving an evil greater than the evil avoided, may attain desirable ends. I think that such cases exist and are highly important. In general terms I think that the legal establishment and disestablishment of various forms of opinion, religious, political, and moral, their encouragement and recognition by law and public opinion as being true and useful, or their discouragement by law and public opinion as being false and mischievous, fall within this principle. I think, that is, that they are cases of coercion of which the object is or may be good, and in which the coercion is likely to be effective, and is not an evil great enough to counterbalance the evil which is avoided or the good which is attained. I think, in short, that Governments ought to take the responsibility of acting upon such principles, religious, political, and moral, as they may from time to time regard as most likely to be true, and this they cannot do without exercising a very considerable degree of coercion. The difference between, I do not say keeping up an Established Church at the public expense, but between paying a single shilling of public money to a single school in which any opinion is taught of which any single taxpayer disapproves, and the maintenance of the Spanish Inquisition, is a question of degree. As the first cannot be justified without infringing the principle of liberty as stated by Mr. Mill, so the last can be condemned on my principles only by showing that the doctrines favoured by the Inquisition were not true, that the means used to promote them were ineffective, or that their employment was too high a price to pay for the object gained; issues which I should be quite ready to accept.

In order to show more distinctly what I mean by coercion in favour of religious opinions, it is necessary to point out that I include under the head of religious opinions all opinions about religion, and in particular the opinion that a given religious creed is false, and the opinion that no religious creed is absolutely true, as well as the opinions which collectively form any one of the many confessions of faith adopted by religious bodies.

There are many subjects of legislation which directly and vitally interest all the members of religious bodies as such. Of these marriage, education, and the laws relating to religious endowments are the most prominent. Suppose, now, that the rulers of a nation were opposed to all religion, and were prepared to and did consistently legislate upon the principle that all religions are false. Suppose that in harmony with this view they insisted in every case on a civil marriage, and regarded it as the only one legally binding, although the addition of religious ceremonies was not forbidden; suppose that they confiscated all endowments for religious purposes, making provision for the life interests of the actual incumbents. Suppose that they legislated in such a way as to forbid all such endowments for the future, so as to render the maintenance of religious services entirely dependent on the temper of the existing generation. Suppose that, in addition to this, they were to organize a system of national education, complete in all its parts, from universities and special colleges for particular professions down to village day schools. Suppose that in all of these the education was absolutely secular, and that not a single shilling was allowed to be appropriated out of the public purse to the teaching of religion in any form whatever, or to the education of persons intended to be its ministers. No one, I think, will deny either that this would be coercion, or that it would be coercion likely to effect its purpose to a greater or less extent by means not in themselves productive of any other evil than the suppression of religion, which the adoption of these means assumes to be a good. Here, then, is a case in which coercion, likely to be effective at a not inadequate expense, is directed towards an end the goodness or badness of which depends upon the question whether religion is true or false. Is this coercion good or bad? I say good if and in so far as religion is false; bad if and in so far as religion is true. Mr. Mill ought, I think, to say that in every case it is bad, irrespectively of the truth or falsehood of religion, for it is coercion, and it is not self-protective.

That this is not an impossible case is proved by the action of the British Empire in India, which governs, not indeed on the principle that no religion is true, but distinctly on the principle that no native religion is true. The English have done, and are doing, the following things in that country:

1. They have forced upon the people, utterly against the will of many of them, the principle that people of different religions are to live at peace with each other, that there is to be no fighting and no oppression as between Mahommedans and Hindoos, or between different sects of Mahommedans.

2. They have also forced upon the people the principle that change of religion is not to involve civil disabilities. The Act* by which this rule was laid down utterly changed the legal position of one of the oldest and most widespread religions in the world. It deprived Brahminism of its principal coercive sanction.

3. They have set up a system of education all over the country which assumes the falsehood of the creed of the Hindoos and—less pointedly, but not less effectually—of the Mahommedans.

4. Whenever religious practices violate European ideas of public morality up to a certain point, they have, as in the cases of Suttee and human sacrifices, been punished as crimes.

5. They compel the natives to permit the presence among them of missionaries whose one object it is to substitute their own for the native religions, and who do, in fact, greatly weaken the native religions.

In these and in some other ways the English Government keeps up a steady and powerful pressure upon their Indian subjects in the direction of those moral and religious changes which are incidental to, and form a part of what we understand by, civilisation. It is remarkable that this pressure is exerted, as it were, involuntarily. No act which can in the ordinary use of language be described as remotely resembling persecution can be laid to the charge of the Government of India. The most solemn pledges to maintain complete impartiality between different religious persuasions have been given on the most memorable occasions, and they have been observed with the most scrupulous fidelity. Every civilian, every person of influence and authority, is full of a sincere wish to treat the native religions with respect. It would be difficult to find a body of men less disposed on the whole to proselytize, or more keenly aware of the weak side of the proselytizing spirit. Whatever faults the English in India have committed, the fault of being too ecclesiastically minded, of being too much led by missionaries, is certainly not one of them. For many years the bare presence of missionaries in British India was not tolerated by the Indian Government. The force of circumstances, however, was too strong for them, and has put them, against their will, at the head of a revolution. Little by

*Act xxi. of 1850. Commonly, though not very correctly, called the 'Lex Loci Act.'

little they were forced to become the direct rulers of the whole country, and to provide it with a set of laws and institutions. They found, as everyone who has to do with legislation must find, that laws must be based upon principles, and that it is impossible to lay down any principles of legislation at all unless you are prepared to say, I am right, and you are wrong, and your view shall give way to mine, quietly, gradually, and peaceably; but one of us two must rule and the other must obey, and I mean to rule.

I might multiply to any conceivable extent illustrations of the propositions that all government has and must of necessity have a moral basis, and that the connection between morals and religion is so intimate that this implies a religious basis as well. I do not mean by a religious basis a complete agreement in religious opinion among either the governors or the persons governed, but such an amount of agreement as is sufficient to determine the attitude of legislation towards religion. I think if these illustrations were fully stated and properly studied they would establish some such general inference as this:

There are three relations and no more in which legislation can stand towards religion in general, and towards each particular religious opinion or form of religion:

1. It may proceed on the assumption that some one religion is true and all others false.

2. It may proceed on the assumption that more than one religion is, so to speak, respectable, and it may favour them in the same or different degrees.

3. It may proceed on the assumption that all religions or that some religions are false.

I believe it to be simply impossible that legislation should be really neutral as to any religion which is professed by any large number of the persons legislated for. He that is not for such a religion is against it. Real neutrality is possible only with regard to forms of religion which are not professed at all by the subjects of legislation, or which are professed by so few of them that their opinions can be regarded as unimportant by the rest. English legislation in England is neutral as to Mahommedanism and Brahminism. English legislation in India proceeds on the assumption that both are false. If it did not, it would have to be founded on the Koran or the Institutes of Menu. If this is so, it is practically certain that coercion will be exercised in favour of some religious opinions and against others, and the question whether such coercion is

40

good or bad will depend upon the view of religion which is taken by different people.

The real opinion of most legislators in the present day, the opinion in favour of which they do, in fact, exercise coercion, is the opinion that no religion is absolutely true, but that all contain a mixture of truth and falsehood, and that the same is the case with ethical and political systems. One inference from this is that direct legislation against any religion as a whole is wrong, and this is one great objection to persecution. When you persecute a religion as a whole, you must generally persecute truth and goodness as well as falsehood. Coercion as to religion will therefore chiefly occur in the indirect form, in the shape of treating certain parts—vital parts, it may be—of particular systems as mischievous and possibly even as criminal falsehoods when they come in the legislator's way. When priests, of whatever creed, claim to hold the keys of heaven and hell and to work invisible miracles, it will practically become necessary for many purposes to decide whether they really are the representatives of God upon earth, or whether consciously or not they are impostors, for there is no way of avoiding the question, and it admits of no other solutions.

Many, perhaps most, of the extravagant theories which have been and are maintained about liberty and in particular about the division between the temporal and spiritual powers, have been devised by persons who, holding this view and not choosing to avow it, wished to discover some means of leaving uncontested the claims of various religious systems to divine authority, and of showing that an admission of the truth of those claims would not involve the consequences which those who believed in them wished to draw from it. It is for immediate practical purposes highly convenient to say, Your creed is, no doubt, divine, and you are the agents of God for the purpose of teaching it, but liberty of opinion is also more or less divine, and the civil ruler has his own rights and duties as well as the successors of the Apostles. But, convenient as this is, it is a mere compromise. The theory is untrue, and no one really believes more than that half of it which suits him. If spiritual means that which relates to thought and feeling, every act of life is spiritual, for in every act there is a mental element which gives it its moral character. If temporal means outward and visible, then every act is temporal, for every thought and feeling tends towards and is embodied in action. In fact every human action is both temporal and spiritual. The attempt to distinguish between temporal and spiritual, between Church and State, is like the attempt to distinguish between substance and form. Formless matter or unsubstantial form are expressions which have no meaning, and in the same way things temporal and things spiritual presuppose and run into each other at every point. Human life is one and indivisible, and is or ought to be regulated by one set of principles and not by a multitude. This subject, however, is too large and important to be disposed of parenthetically. I propose to discuss it separately.* With these preliminary observations, I proceed to say a few words on each of the three relations in which legislation may stand to religion. It will be found that the consideration of them will throw a strong light upon many of the illustrations of this subject discussed by Mr. Mill and others.

First, legislation may proceed on the assumption that one religion is true and all others false. This is the assumption which pervades nearly all early Christian legislation. It is made so unconsciously by Mahommedans and Hindoos that their law and their religion are to a great extent one and the same thing. Our own minds have become so much sophisticated by commonplaces about liberty and toleration, and about the division between the temporal and spiritual power, that we have almost ceased to think of the attainment of truth in religion as desirable if it were possible. It appears to me that, if it were possible, the attainment of religious truth and its recognition as such by legislation would be of all conceivable blessings the greatest. If we were all of one mind, and that upon reasonable grounds, about the nature of men and their relation to the world or worlds in which they live, we should have in our hands an important instrument for the solution of all the great moral and political questions which at present distract and divide the world, and cause much waste of strength in unfruitful though inevitable contests.

Even when a religion is only partially true, the effect of a general and perfectly sincere belief in it is to give unity and vigour and a distinct and original turn to the life of those who really believe it. Such a belief is the root out of which grow laws, institutions, moral principles, tastes, and arts innumerable. The phrases about our common Christianity are vague enough, but it was in religious beliefs common to great masses of people that the foundations of

*See Chap. III, p. 70.

much that we justly prize were laid. If from the fall of the Roman Empire to the revival of learning there had been no moral and spiritual unity in the world, we should still, in all probability, have been little better than barbarians. If the divided forces of mankind could now be based upon one foundation of moral and spiritual truth, and directed towards a set of ends forming one harmonious whole, our descendants would probably surpass us quite as decisively as we surpass the contemporaries of Alfred or Gregory the Great. Progress has its drawbacks, and they are great and serious; but whatever its value may be, unity in religious belief would further it in so far as the belief was true and was based upon reasonable grounds.*

The question how such a state of things is to be produced is one which it is impossible not to ask and equally impossible to answer, except by the words, 'the wind bloweth where it listeth, and ye know not whence it cometh nor whither it goeth.'[6] The sources of religion lie hid from us. All that we know is that now and again in the course of ages someone sets to music the tune which is haunting millions of ears. It is caught up here and there, and repeated till the chorus is thundered out by a body of singers able to drown all discords and to force the vast unmusical mass to listen to them. Such results as these come not by observation, but when they do come they carry away as with a flood and hurry in their own direction all the laws and customs of those whom they affect. To oppose Mr. Mill's 'simple principle' about liberty to such powers as

---

*I have added the concluding words of this paragraph, and altered an inaccurate expression on the preceding page, because Mr. Morley appears to have thought that I meant to say that mere unity of belief was good apart from the truth of the matter believed. Mr. Morley adds: 'It is no doubt true that unity in religious belief as in other things will slowly draw nearer as the results of the gradual acceptance by an increasing number of men of common methods of observing and interpreting experience. . . . but all the consequences of this quasi-unity may not prove to be beneficial or favourable to progress, nor is it at all clear . . . that unity of religious belief would further progress unless you replaced the discussion to which such unity would put an end by some other equally dividing subject of equal interest to an equal number of people.'

This is exactly in Mr. Mill's vein, and I must own that the nervous fear that a time may possibly come when there will be nothing left to argue about appears to me about as reasonable as the 'thought of the exhaustibility of musical combinations of the seven tones and semitones which make up the octave,' by which Mr. Mill tells us (Autobiography, p. 145) he was 'seriously tormented' at one time of his life. [John Stuart Mill, Collected Works of John Stuart Mill, ed. J. Robson, 33 vols (Toronto: University of Toronto Press, 1963–1991), vol. 1, Autobiography (1981), p. 149.]

6. John 3:8.

these is like blowing against a hurricane with a pair of bellows. To take any such principle as a rule by which such powers may be measured and may be declared to be good or bad is like valuing a painting by adding together the price of the colours, the canvas, and so much a day calculated on his average earnings for the value of the artist's labour.

When the hearts of men are deeply stirred by what they regard as a gospel or new revelation, they do as a fact not only believe it themselves, but compel others to accept it, and this compulsion for ages to come determines the belief and practice of enormous multitudes of people who care very little about the matter. Earth resembles heaven in one respect at least. Its kingdom suffereth violence, and the violent take it by force. That such violence is or under circumstances may be highly beneficial to the world, is, I think, abundantly proved by history. The evil and good done by it must in all cases be measured by the principles laid down above. Was the object good? Did the means conduce to it? Did they conduce to it at an excessive price? Apply this to the case of the establishment of Christianity as a State religion first in the Roman Empire and afterwards in modern Europe. It is obvious that we have before us the most intricate of all conceivable problems, a problem which no single and simple principle can possibly solve. Its solution would require answers to the following, amongst other questions: 1. What is Christianity? 2. How far is it true and useful? 3. How far was it and how far was each part of it promoted by coercion? 4. What kinds of coercion promoted the different parts of it? 5. What was the comparative importance of the coercion applied and the results obtained? Most of these questions are obviously insoluble.

The second case is that in which the Legislature regards various creeds as respectable, and favours them more or less according to circumstances, and either equally or unequally. This is the present state of things throughout the greater part of the civilised world. It is carried out to its fullest development in this country and in the United States, though in this country two State Churches are especially favored, while in America all Churches stand upon the same footing as lawful associations based upon voluntary contracts. The way in which this arrangement is accepted as a final result which is to last indefinitely has always seemed to me to afford a strong illustration of the manner in which people are disposed to accept as final the temporary solutions of great questions which are in fashion in their own days. The fatal

44

defect in the arrangement, which must sooner or later break it up, is that it tends to emasculate both Church and State. It cuts human life in two. It cuts off religion from active life, and it reduces the State to a matter of police. Moreover, it is but a temporary and not a very honest device. To turn Churches into mere voluntary associations, and to sever the connection between them and the State, is on the part of the State an act not of neutrality but of covert unbelief. On the part of the Churches which accept it, it is a tacit admission of failure, a tacit admission that they have no distinct authoritative message from God to man, and that they do not venture to expect to be recognised as institutions to which such a message has been confided. But if this is not their character, there is no other character for them to hold than that of human institutions, like the old schools of philosophy, based upon various theories as to the nature, the destiny, and the duties of men.

If this is the light in which Churches are to be regarded, the division between Church and State, the maxim of a free Church in a free State, will mean that men in their political capacity are to have no opinions upon the topics which interest them most deeply; and, on the other hand, that men of a speculative turn are never to try to reduce their speculations to practice on a large scale, by making or attempting to make them the basis of legislation. If this principle is adopted and adhered to, one of two results must sooner or later inevitably follow. In so far as the principle is accepted and acted upon with real good faith, the State will be degraded, and reduced to mere police functions. Associations of various kinds will take its place and push it on one side, and completely new forms of society may be the result. Mormonism is one illustration of this, but the strong tendency which has shown itself on many occasions both in France and America on the part of enthusiastic persons to 'try experiments in living,'[7] by erecting some entirely new form of society, has supplied many minor illustrations of the same principle. St. Simonianism, families of love by whatever name they are called, are straws showing the set of a wind which some day or other might take rank among the fiercest of storms. Such experiments as these have nothing whatever to do with liberty. They are embryo governments, little States which in course of time may well come to be dangerous antagonists of the old one.

7. This important expression, one of which Stephen makes some use, is never found neat in Mill. See, however, 57/260–61 L and 81/281 L.

Another possible result is that the State, finding itself confronted by Churches at all sorts of points, may at last renounce the notion that it is debarred from forming an opinion upon moral and religious problems, and from legislating in accordance with the opinions so formed. If and in so far as the State—that is to say, a number of influential people sufficient to dispose of the public force—arrives at distinct views upon these points, it must of necessity revert from the provisional and neutral attitude to a belligerent attitude. It must assume the truth of some religious opinions, and as a necessary consequence the falsehood of others, and as to these last it will take up a position of hostility. Cases may occur, as the state of our own time shows, in which it is extremely difficult to say what is true, but comparatively easy to say what is false, and I do not see why conscious ignorance upon some points should interfere with or excuse people from acting upon a distinct negative conviction upon others.

Such a course necessarily encounters the most virulent and passionate resistance. Unwelcome, however, and thorny as this path is, I believe that it ought, when necessary, to be taken; that it is desirable that legislators and their advisers should not legislate on the supposition that all sorts of conflicting creeds have an equal chance of being true, but should consider the question of the truth and falsehood of religious opinions; that legislation should when necessary proceed on distinct principles in this matter, and that such a degree of coercion as is necessary to obtain its end should be applied. What I have already said shows that in fact this is always done, though people are not always aware of it.*

As I have observed more than once, Mr. Mill's illustrations of his principles are in some respects the most attractive and effective parts of his book. By far the most important passage of his 'Essay on Liberty' is the well-known one in which he argues that people should be at perfect liberty to express any opinions whatever about the existence of God and a future state, and that for

---

*It is perhaps necessary to observe that I am speaking in this place with no reference to the actual state of affairs in this country. The questions which I have in my mind will not arise at all until the great change in religious belief, of which we now witness the beginning, has gone much further and assumed a much more decided character than can be expected, say for a generation to come. It seems probable that in this country, and in most others, the next step will be the adoption of the principle of free churches, as they are called. It is a petty expedient, and will not, I think, last as long as the older ones.

doing so they should neither be punished by law nor censured by public opinion. In the practical result I agree nearly, though not quite; but in order to set in as clear a light as possible the difference between his way of treating the subject and my own, I will deal with it in my own way, noticing his arguments in what I take to be their proper places.

The object of forbidding men to deny the existence of God and a future life would be to cause those doctrines to be universally believed, and upon my principles this raises three questions: 1. Is the object good? 2. Are the means proposed likely to be effective? 3. What is the comparative importance of the object secured and of the means by which it is secured? That the object is good if the doctrines are true admits, in my opinion, of no doubt whatever. I entirely agree with the commonplaces about the importance of these doctrines. If these beliefs are mere dreams, life is a very much poorer and pettier thing; men are beings of much less importance; trouble, danger, and physical pain are much greater evils, and the prudence of virtue is much more questionable than has hitherto been supposed to be the case. If men follow the advice so often pressed upon them, to cease to think of these subjects otherwise than as insoluble riddles, all the existing conceptions of morality will have to be changed, all social tendencies will be weakened. Merely personal inclinations will be greatly strengthened. Men who say 'tomorrow we die,' will add 'let us eat and drink.' It would be not merely difficult but impossible in such a state of society to address any argument save that of criminal law (which Mr. Mill's doctrine about liberty would reduce to a minimum) to a man who had avowed to himself that he was consistently bad. A few people love virtue for its own sake. Many have no particular objection to a mild but useful form of it if they are trained to believe that it will answer in the long run; but probably a majority of these persons would like it dashed with a liberal allowance of vice if they thought that no risk would be run by making the mixture. A strong minority, again, are so viciously disposed that all the considerations which can be drawn from any world, present or future, certain or possible, do not avail to hold them in. Many a man too stupid for speculative doubt or for thought of any kind says, 'I've no doubt at all I shall be damned for it, but I must, and I will.' In short, all experience shows that almost all men require at times both the spur of hope and the bridle of fear, and that religious hope and fear are an effective spur and bridle, though some people are too hard-mouthed and thick-skinned to care much for either, and though others will now and then take the bit in their teeth and rush where passion carries them, notwithstanding both. If, then, virtue is good, it seems to me clear that to promote the belief of the fundamental doctrines of religion is good also, for I am convinced that in Europe at least the two must stand or fall together.

It is sometimes argued that these beliefs are rather unimportant than either good or bad. It is said that great masses of the human race have done without any or with negative beliefs on these subjects. Interesting sketches are given of the creeds or no creeds of savage tribes, of educated men in classical times, of Buddhists, and others. Here, it is said, are cases of people living without reference to a God or a future state. Why cannot you do the same? A strong social impulse, a religion of humanity will fill your sails as well as the old wind which is dying away; and you will then think of these questions which now seem to you all-important as of insoluble riddles, mere exercises of ingenuity with which you have nothing to do.

This argument falls wide of the mark at which it seems to be aimed. Its object is to prove that the fundamental problems of religion may and ought to be laid aside as insoluble riddles on which it is a waste of time to think. The evidence to prove this is that solutions of these problems, widely differing from those which are established in this part of the world, have been accepted in other countries and by other races of men. No doubt this is true, but what does it prove? Taken in connection with other facts equally notorious, it proves that as a man's religion is, so will his morals be. The Buddhists have a religion and a morality which closely correspond. How does this show that European morality is not founded on Christianity, and that you can destroy the one without affecting the other? It proves the reverse. If Buddhists became Christians or Christians became Buddhists, a corresponding moral change would soon make itself felt. The difference between Hindoo and Mahommedan morals closely follows the difference between their creeds. Whether Christianity is true or false, and whether European morality is good or bad, European morality is in fact founded upon religion, and the destruction of the one must of necessity involve the reconstruction of the other. Many persons in these days wish to retain the morality which they like, after getting rid of the religion which they disbelieve. Whether they are right or wrong in disturbing the foundation, they are inconsistent in wishing to save the superstructure. If we are to think as Cæsar thought of God and a future state, we cannot avoid considering the question whether Cæsar's morals and principles of action were not superior to the common moral standards. Jesus Christ believed in God and a future state, and preached the Sermon on the Mount. Julius Cæsar believed the questions about God and a future state to be mere idle curiosities. He also preached impressive sermons by example and otherwise. Many persons in these days appear to me to think that they can reconcile the morals of Jesus Christ with the theology of Julius Cæsar by masquerading in the Pope's old clothes and asking the world at large to take their word of honour that all is well.

To return to Mr. Mill. One of his arguments tends to show that the object of promoting these beliefs is bad. He considers that rulers ought not to decide religious questions for others without allowing them to hear what can be said on the contrary side. I am not, I own, much moved by this argument. It is what everyone does and must of necessity be continually doing in nearly every department of life. What is all education except a strenuous and systematic effort to give the whole character a certain turn and bias which appears on the whole desirable to the person who gives it?* A man who did not, as far as he could, 'undertake to decide' for his children the questions whether they should be truthful, industrious, sober, respectful, and chaste, and that 'without allowing them to hear what was to be said on the contrary side,' would be a contemptible pedant. Legislators and the founders of great institutions must to a very considerable extent perform precisely the same task for the world at large. Surely it is an idle dream to say that one man in a thousand really exercises much individual choice as to his religious or moral principles, and I doubt whether it is not an exaggeration to say that one man in a million is capable of making any very material addition to what is already known or plausibly conjectured on these matters. I repeat, then, that the object of causing these doctrines to be believed appears to me to be clearly good if and in so far as the doctrines themselves are true.

*Mr. Mill's account of the education which he received from his father shows that Mr. James Mill, at all events, did not shrink from the responsibility of deciding religious questions for his son. It leaves open, however, the question whether the son thanked his father for it. [John Stuart Mill, *Collected Works of John Stuart Mill*, ed. J. Robson, 33 vols (Toronto: University of Toronto Press, 1963–1991), vol. 1, *Autobiography* (1981), pp. 41, 43, 47, 49.]

It may perhaps be suggested, on the other hand, that the object is good whether the doctrines are true or false, and no doubt the necessity for compulsion is greater if they are false; but the suggestion itself may be disposed of very shortly. It is a suggestion which it is childish to discuss in public, because no one could avow it without contradicting himself, and so defeating his own object. No one can publicly and avowedly ask people to believe a lie on the ground of its being good for them. Such a request is like asking a man to lift himself off the ground by pulling at his knees with his hands. The harder he tries to lift his feet from the ground, the harder he has to press his feet on the ground to get a purchase. The more you try to believe a lie because it will do you good, the more you impress on your mind the fact that it is a lie and that you cannot believe it. A man who wishes to persuade his neighbours to believe a lie must lie to them—he must say that the lie is true; and practically he must lie to himself in the first instance, or he will not have the heart to go on with his lie. There are ways of doing this so very far below the surface that an ingenious person may manage it with little or, perhaps, no consciousness of the fact that he is lying. The favourite way of doing it is by weaving metaphysical webs by which it may be made to appear that the common tests of truth, falsehood, and probability do not apply to matters of this sort. But I need not pursue this subject. We are brought back, then, to the question, Are these doctrines true?

This is the vital question of all. It is the true centre, not only of Mr. Mill's book upon liberty, but of all the great discussions of our generation. Upon this hang all religion, all morals, all politics, all legislation—everything which interests men as men. Is there or not a God and a future state? Is this world all?

I do not pretend to have anything to add to this tremendous controversy. It is a matter on which very few human beings have a right to be heard.

I confine myself to asserting that the attitude of the law and of public authority generally towards the discussion of this question will and ought to depend upon the nature of the view which happens to be dominant for the time being on the question itself, modified in its practical application by considerations drawn from the other two points above stated—namely, the adaptation of the means employed to the object in view, and the comparative importance of the measure of success which can be reasonably expected, and of the expense of the means necessary to its attainment. This, I say, is the only principle which can either serve as a guide in reference to any practical question, or enable us to do anything like justice to the historical problems of which Mr. Mill refers to one or two, and to which I propose to return immediately; and so much for the goodness of the object.

The next questions are as to the effectiveness and expense of the means, and these I will consider together. It is needless to discuss the question of legal prosecution in reference to these opinions.* Everyone must admit that it is quite out of the question. In the first place, it is impossible; and in the next place, to be effective, it would have to be absolutely destructive and paralysing, and it would produce at last no result for which anyone really wishes. I need not insist upon this point.

The real question is as to social intolerance. Has a man who believes in God and a future state a moral right to disapprove of those who do not, and to try by the expression of that disapproval to deter them from publishing, and to deter others from adopting, their views? I think that he has if and in so far as his opinions are true. Mr. Mill thinks otherwise. He draws a picture of social intolerance and of its effects which nothing but considerations of space prevent me from extracting in full. It is one of the most eloquent and powerful passages he ever wrote. The following is its key-note:

> Our merely social intolerance kills no one, roots out no opinions, but induces men to disguise them, or to abstain from any active effort for their diffusion. With us heretical opinions do not perceptibly gain or even lose ground in each decade or generation; they never blaze out far and wide, but continue to smoulder in the narrow circles of thinking and studious persons among whom they originate without ever lighting up the general affairs of mankind with either a true or a deceptive light. And thus is kept up a state of things very satisfactory to some minds, because, without the unpleasant process of fining or imprisoning anybody, it maintains all prevailing opinions outwardly undisturbed, while it does not absolutely

---

*There is a statute, 9 Will. III. c. 35, which inflicts severe penalties on persons 'who assert, or maintain, that there are more Gods than one, or deny the Christian religion to be true, or the Holy Scriptures of the Old and New Testament to be of divine authority'; and blasphemy is an offence at common law. I believe the statute has never been enforced in modern times, and it ought to be repealed. The common law upon blasphemy has a curious history, which this is not the place to relate. It is singular that the statute does not punish the profession of Atheism.

interdict the exercise of reason by dissentients afflicted with the malady of thought. A convenient plan for having peace in the intellectual world and keeping all things going on therein very much as they do already. But the price paid for this sort of intellectual pacification is the sacrifice of the entire moral courage of the human mind. [34–35/241–42 L]

The heretics, says Mr. Mill, are grievously injured by this, and are much to be pitied, but 'the greatest harm is done to those who are not heretics, and whose whole mental development is cramped, and their reason cowed, by the fear of heresy. Who can compute what the world loses in the multitude of promising intellects combined with timid characters, who dare not follow out any bold, vigorous, independent train of thought lest it should land them in something which would admit of being considered irreligious or immoral?' [35/242 L]

On this point I am utterly unable to agree with Mr. Mill. It seems to me that to publish opinions upon morals, politics, and religion is an act as important as any which any man can possibly do; that to attack opinions on which the framework of society rests is a proceeding which both is and ought to be dangerous. I do not say that it ought not to be done in many cases, but it should be done sword in hand, and a man who does it has no more right to be surprised at being fiercely resisted than a soldier who attacks a breach. Mr. Mill's whole charge against social intolerance is that it makes timid people afraid to express unpopular opinions. An old ballad tells how a man, losing his way on a hillside, strayed into a chamber full of enchanted knights, each lying motionless in complete armour, with his war-horse standing motionless beside him. On a rock lay a sword and a horn, and the intruder was told that if he wanted to lead the army, he must choose between them. He chose the horn and blew a loud blast, upon which the knights and their horses vanished in a whirlwind and their visitor was blown back into common life, these words sounding after him on the wind:

> Cursed be the coward that ever he was born
> Who did not draw the sword before he blew the horn.

No man has a right to give the signal for such a battle by blowing the horn, unless he has first drawn the sword and knows how to make his hands guard his head with it. Then let him blow as loud and long as he likes, and if his tune is worth hearing he will not want followers. Till a man has carefully formed his opinions on these subjects, thought them out, assured himself of their value, and decided to take the risk of proclaiming them, the strong probability is that they are not much worth having. Speculation on government, morals, and religion is a matter of vital practical importance, and not mere food for curiosity. Curiosity, no doubt, is generally the motive which leads a man to study them; but, till he has formed opinions on them for which he is prepared to fight, there is no hardship in his being compelled by social intolerance to keep them to himself and to those who sympathise with him. It should never be forgotten that opinions have a moral side to them. The opinions of a bad and a good man, the opinions of an honest and a dishonest man, upon these subjects are very unlikely to be the same.

It is the secret consciousness of this which gives its strange bitterness to controversies which might at first sight appear as unlikely to interest the passions as questions of mathematics or philology. What question can appear to be more purely scientific than the question whether people have or have not innate ideas? Yet it is constantly debated with a persistent consciousness on the part of the disputants that their argument is like a trumpery dispute made the pretext for a deadly duel, the real grounds of which are too delicate to be stated. The advocate of innate ideas often thinks or says more or less distinctly that his antagonist's real object is to get all the mysteries of religion submitted to the common processes of the understanding. The advocate of experience often thinks or says of his antagonist, 'You are a liar; and the object of your lie is to protect from exposure what you ought to know to be nonsense.' As opinions become better marked and more distinctly connected with action, the truth that decided dissent from them implies more or less of a reproach upon those who hold them decidedly becomes so obvious that everyone perceives it. The fact is that we all more or less condemn and blame each other, and this truth is so unpleasant that oceans of sophistry have been poured out for the purpose of evading or concealing it. It is true, nevertheless. I cannot understand how a man who is not a Roman Catholic can regard a real Roman Catholic with absolute neutrality. A man who really thinks that a wafer is God Almighty, and who really believes that rational men owe any sort of allegiance to any kind of priest, is either right—in which case the man who differs from him ought to repent in sackcloth and ashes—or else he is

53

wrong, in which case he is the partizan of a monstrous imposture. How the question of whether he is right or wrong can be regarded as one indifferent to his general character and to the moral estimate which persons of a different way of thinking must form of him is to me quite inconceivable. The converse is equally true. I do not see how a man who deliberately rejects the Roman Catholic religion can, in the eyes of those who earnestly believe it, be other than a rebel against God. Plaster them over as thick as you will, controversies of this sort go to the very core and root of life, and as long as they express the deepest convictions of men, those who really differ are and must be enemies to a certain extent, though they may keep their enmity within bounds. When religious differences come to be and are regarded as mere differences of opinion, it is because the controversy is really decided in the sceptical sense, though people may not like to acknowledge it formally.

Let anyone who doubts this try to frame an argument which could have been addressed with any chance of success to Philip II against the persecution of the Protestants, or to Danton and his associates against the persecution of Catholicism and the French aristocracy and Monarchy. Concede the first principle that unfeigned belief in the Roman Catholic creed is indispensably necessary to salvation, or the first principle that the whole Roman Catholic system is a pernicious falsehood and fraud, and it will be found impossible to stop short in theory of the practical inferences of the Inquisition and the Reign of Terror, though of course circumstances may render their application to any given state of facts inexpedient. Every conclusive* argument against these practical inferences is an argument to show either that we cannot be sure as to the conditions of salvation, or that the Roman Catholic religion is not a pernicious falsehood and fraud. A man who cannot be brought to see this will persecute, and ought to persecute (unless the balance of special expediencies is the other way) in the same sense of the word 'ought' in which we say that a man who believes that twice two make five *ought* to believe that two and three make six. The attainment or approximate attainment of truth, and

---

*In the first edition I employed the word 'real,' but Mr. Morley objected to it on the ground that 'arguments resting on a balance of expediencies, as shown through the experience of mankind, are real.' The word 'conclusive,' no doubt, expresses my meaning better than 'real.' I did not use it in the first edition simply because I used the word 'conclusions' in the preceding and following lines.

particularly the attainment of a true conception of the amount and nature of our own ignorance on religious subjects, is indispensable to the settlement of religious disputes. You can no more evade in politics the question, What is true in religion? than you can do sums right without prejudice to a difference of opinion upon the multiplication table. The only road to peace leads through truth, and when a powerful and energetic minority, sufficiently vigorous to impose their will on their neighbours, have made up their minds as to what is true, they will no more tolerate error for the sake of abstract principles about freedom than any one of us tolerates a nest of wasps in his garden.

Upon the question of the expense of persecution Mr. Mill argues at great length that perfect freedom of discussion is essential to give a person a living interest in an opinion and a full appreciation of its various bearings. This, I think, is an excellent illustration of the manner in which the most acute intellect may be deceived by generalising upon its own peculiar experience. That Mr. Mill should have felt what he described is not, perhaps, unnatural, but his intellect was enormously developed in proportion to his other faculties.[8] I should say that doctrines come home to people in general, not if and in so far as they are free to discuss all their applications, but if and in so far as they happen to interest them and appear to illustrate and interpret their own experience. One remarkable proof of this is taken from the whole history of religious controversy, and can hardly be better exemplified than by Mr. Mill's own words. He remarks that 'all ethical doctrines and religious creeds . . . are full of meaning to those who originate them and to the direct disciples of their originators; their meaning continues to be felt in undiminished strength, and is perhaps brought out with even fuller consciousness so long as the struggle lasts to give the doctrine or creed an ascendency over other creeds.' [41/247 L] When the struggle is over the doctrine takes its place as a received opinion; 'from this time may usually be dated the decline in its living power.' [41/247 L]

I do not agree with this. A doctrine which really goes to the hearts of men never loses its power if true, and never even if it is false until it is suspected or known to be false. There are in this day innumerable persons to whom the worship of the Virgin Mary and all the doctrines connected with it have as

8. John Stuart Mill, *Collected Works of John Stuart Mill*, ed. J. Robson, 33 vols (Toronto: University of Toronto Press, 1963–1991), vol. 1, *Autobiography* (1981), p. 147.

much life and freshness as they ever had to anyone—a life and freshness from which the freest and fullest discussion would rub off all the gloss, even if it left the doctrine unimpaired. Millions of men hold with the most living perception of their truth the doctrine that Honesty is the best policy, and the doctrine, Speak truth, and shame the devil. Experience and not discussion enforces maxims like these. Every racy popular proverb is a proof of it. If a dear friend, a man whom you have loved and honoured, and who is a well-wisher and benefactor to a large section of mankind, is stabbed to the heart by an assassin, it will give a very keen edge and profound truth to the maxim that murder is one of the most detestable of crimes, though I do not know that it admits of much discussion.

But whatever may be thought of the truth of Mr. Mill's statement, its logic is defective. The facts that whilst a doctrine is struggling for ascendency it is full of meaning, and that when it has become a received opinion its living power begins to decline, surely prove that coercion and not liberty is favourable to its appreciation. A 'struggle for ascendency' does not mean mere argument. It means reiterated and varied assertion persisted in, in the face of the wheel, the stake, and the gallows, as well as in the face of contradiction. If the Protestants and Catholics or the Christians and the Pagans had confined themselves to argument, they might have argued forever, and the world at large would not have cared. It was when it came to preaching and fighting, to 'Believe, and be saved,' 'Disbelieve, and be damned,' 'Be silent, or be burned alive,' 'I would rather be burned than be silent,' that the world at large listened, sympathized, and took one side or the other. The discussion became free just in proportion as the subjects discussed lost their interest.

Upon the whole, it appears to me quite certain that if our notions of moral good and evil are substantially true, and if the doctrines of God and a future state are true, the object of causing people to believe in them is good, and that social intolerance on the behalf of those who do towards those who do not believe in them cannot be regarded as involving evils of any great importance in comparison with the results at which it aims. I am quite aware that this is not a pleasant doctrine, and that it is liable to great abuse. The only way of guarding against its abuse is by pointing out that people should not talk about what they do not understand. No one has a right to be morally intolerant of doctrines which he has not carefully studied. It is one thing to say, as I do, that after careful consideration and mature study a man has a right to say such and such opinions are dishonest, cowardly, feeble, ferocious, or absurd, and that the person who holds them deserves censure for having shown dishonesty or cowardice in adopting them, and quite another thing to say that everyone has a right to throw stones at everybody who differs from himself on religious questions. The true ground of moral tolerance in the common sense of the words appears to me to lie in this—that most people have no right to any opinions whatever upon these questions, except in so far as they are necessary for the regulation of their own affairs. When some ignorant preacher calls his betters atheists and the like, his fault is not intolerance, but impudence and rudeness. If this principle were properly carried out, it would leave little room for moral intolerance in most cases; but I think it highly important that men who really study these matters should feel themselves at liberty not merely to dissent from but to disapprove of opinions which appear to them to require it, and should express that disapprobation.*

I will now proceed to compare Mr. Mill's principles and my own by contrasting the ways in which our respective methods apply to the appreciation of the celebrated passages of history. He, as I understand him, condemns absolutely all interference with the expression of opinion. The judges of Socrates, Pontius Pilate, Marcus Aurelius, Philip II, and the rest are, when tried by his standard, simple wrong-doers. Allowances may be made for them in consideration of the temper of the times, but the verdict is guilty, with or without, and generally without, a recommendation to mercy. Their guilt and shame is necessary in order to condemn the principle on which they acted. They interfered with liberty otherwise than for purposes of self-protection, and they thus incurred such penalties as can be inflicted on the memory of the

---

*This is one of the points on which I think that there was not really much difference between Mr. Mill and myself. I ground this opinion on a striking passage in Mr. Mill's Autobiography, in which he describes his father's feelings towards those with whom he disagreed. I have italicised the passages in which he does his best to distinguish his father's sentiments from intolerance, and I would appeal to everyone's experience of life on the question whether they are a more substantial barrier against it than a sheet of silver paper held before a blazing fire.

'His (Mr. James Mill's) aversion to many intellectual errors, or what he regarded as such, partook, in a certain sense, of the character of a moral feeling. All this is merely saying that he, in a degree once common, but now very unusual, threw his feelings into his opinions; which truly it is difficult to understand how any one who possesses much of both, can fail to do. None but

dead, however honest they may have been, and whatever may have been the plausibility of their opinions at the time. The law must be vindicated, and the law—Mr. Mill's law—is that nothing but self-protection can ever justify coercion. Once give up this, and where will you stop?

Mr. Mill says, 'Aware of the impossibility of defending the use of punishment for restraining irreligious opinions by any arguments which will not justify Marcus [Aurelius] Antoninus, the enemies of religious freedom when hard pressed occasionally accept this consequence, and say with Dr. Johnson that the persecutors of Christianity were in the right; that persecution is an ordeal through which truth ought to pass, and always passes successfully.' [30/237 L] This argument, says Mr. Mill, is ungenerous, but it also involves distinct error. That 'truth always triumphs over persecution' is a 'pleasant falsehood.' [30/238 L] Truth does not triumph; on the contrary, a very little very gentle persecution is often quite enough to put it out. Choose, says Mr. Mill in substance, between a principle which will condemn Aurelius and a principle which will justify Pontius Pilate. I will try to meet this challenge.

Was Pilate right in crucifying Christ? I reply, Pilate's paramount duty was to preserve the peace in Palestine, to form the best judgment he could as to the means required for that purpose, and to act upon it when it was formed. Therefore, if and in so far as he believed, in good faith and on reasonable grounds, that what he did was necessary for the preservation of the peace of Palestine, he was right. It was his duty to run the risk of being mistaken, notwithstanding Mr. Mill's principle as to liberty, and particularly as to liberty

---

those who do not care about opinions, will confound this with intolerance. Those, who having opinions which they hold to be immensely important, and their contraries to be prodigiously hurtful, have any deep regard for the general good, will necessarily dislike, *as a class and in the abstract,* those who think wrong what they think right, and right what they think wrong: though they need not therefore be insensible to good qualities in an opponent, nor governed in their estimation of individuals by one general presumption, instead of by the whole of their character. I grant that an earnest person, being no more infallible than other men, is liable to dislike people on account of opinions which do not merit dislike: *but if he neither himself does them any ill office, nor connives at its being done by others, he is not intolerant:* and the forbearance which flows from a conscientious sense of the importance to mankind of the equal freedom of all opinions, is the only tolerance which is commendable, or, to the highest moral order of minds, possible.' [John Stuart Mill, *Collected Works of John Stuart Mill,* ed. J. Robson, 33 vols (Toronto: University of Toronto Press, 1963–1991), vol. 1, *Autobiography* (1981), pp. 51, 53.]

in the expression of opinion. He was in the position of a judge whose duty it is to try persons duly brought before him for trial at the risk of error.

In order to justify this view I must first consider the question, In what sense can such words as 'right' and 'ought' be applied to questions of politics and government? If in criticising human history we are to proceed on the assumption that every act and every course of policy was wrong which would not have been chosen by an omnipotent, omniscient, and perfectly benevolent man, if such a being is conceivable, I suppose no course of policy and no action of importance and on a large scale can be said to have been right; but, in order to take a step towards the application of this method, it is necessary to know what the history of mankind ought to have been from the earliest ages to the present time. Even this is not enough. We ought to know what it ought to have been after each successive deviation from the highest possible standard. We ought to know not only what would have happened if Eve had not eaten the apple, but what would have happened if, Eve having eaten the apple, Adam had refused to eat, or had eaten of the tree of life; how it would have been if, when Adam and Eve were expelled from Paradise, Cain had not killed Abel, and so on. To take such a standard of right and wrong is obviously absurd.

The words 'ought' and 'right' must then be applied on a far more limited scale, and must in all cases be interpreted with reference to the fact that men inevitably are and always will be weak and ignorant, and that their apparent and possibly their real interests clash. If 'ought' and 'right' are construed with reference to this consideration, it will follow that duty will frequently bring individuals, nations, and creeds into conflict with each other. There is no absurdity in the conclusion that it may be my duty to kill you if I can and your duty to kill me if you can, that the persecutors and the Christians, Luther and Charles V, Philip II and William of Orange, may each have been right, or may each have been partly right and partly wrong. When Hobbes taught that the state of nature is a state of war, he threw an unpopular truth into a shape liable to be misunderstood; but can anyone seriously doubt that war and conflict are inevitable so long as men are what they are, except at the price of evils which are even worse than war and conflict?[9] that is to say, at the price of

9. For Stephen's relation to Hobbes, see editor's foreword, pp. x–xi.

absolute submission to all existing institutions, good or bad, or absolute want of resistance to all proposed changes, wise or foolish. Struggles there must and always will be, unless men stick like limpets or spin like weathercocks.

I proceed to consider the case of the Romans and the Christians, and more particularly the case of Pilate.

It is for obvious reasons unnecessary to develope the Christian side of the question. No one in these days will deny that, taking the only view which it is fitting to take here, the purely human view of the subject, Christ and his disciples were right in preaching their religion at all risks. Apart from its supernatural claims, its history is their justification; the great majority of rational men now agree* that Christianity, taken as a whole and speaking broadly, has been a blessing to men. From it not all, but most of, the things which we value most highly have been derived.

Upon this it is needless to dwell. The Roman view of the subject from the time of Pontius Pilate to that of Diocletian requires more illustration. The substance of what the Romans did was to treat Christianity by fits and starts as a crime. As to the brutality of the punishments inflicted—crucifixion, burning, and judicial tortures—all that need be said is that it was the habit of the day. There does not seem to have been any particular difference made between the treatment of the three persons who were crucified on Calvary. What, then, was the position of the Roman authorities when they had to consider whether Christianity should be treated as a crime?

*In the first edition this sentence ran: 'no rational man can doubt.' I have made the alteration to satisfy the following characteristic criticism of Mr. Morley's.

'Personally I am of Mr. Stephen's opinion, that, &c., but I should think twice before feeling myself entitled on the strength of this opinion to deny the title of rational man' to Gibbon, Voltaire, D'Alembert and Condorcet, James Mill and Mr. Grote. 'Mr. Stephen makes too much play with his rational man and reasonable people. The phrase does not really come to much more than the majority of the males of a generation engaged in the pleasing exercise of "that hidebound humour which they call their judgment."' Certainly nothing was further from my intention than to 'deny the title of rational man' to anyone at all. Mr. Morley is always in an attitude of watchful jealousy as regards the rights of the non-Christian world, and sees an implied affront to them in the most harmless remark. His little outburst of temper at such a very small overstatement reminds me of his trick of printing God with a 'g' as a sort of typographical intimation of his disagreement with common opinions on that subject. Every little bit helps, I suppose.

It has been often and truly pointed out that, humanly speaking, the establishment of the Roman Empire rendered Christianity possible, and brought about the 'fulness of time' at which it occurred. The Pax Romana gave to all the nations which surrounded the Mediterranean and to those which are bounded by the Rhine and the Danube benefits closely resembling those which British rule has conferred upon the enormous quadrangle which lies between the mountains on the northeast and northwest, and the Indian Ocean on the southeast and southwest. Peace reigned in the days of Pilate from York to Jerusalem, which are about as far from each other as Peshawur and Point de Galle, and from Alexandria to Antwerp, which are about the same distance as Kurrachee and the extreme east of Assam. This peace actually was, and the more highly educated Romans must have seen that it was about to become, the mother of laws, arts, institutions of all kinds, under which our own characters have been moulded. The Roman law, at that period as clumsy as English law is at present, but nearly as rich, sagacious, and vigorous, was taking root in all parts of the world under the protection of Roman armed force, and all the arts of life, literature, philosophy, and art were growing by its side. An Englishman must have a cold heart and a dull imagination who cannot understand how the consciousness of this must have affected a Roman governor. I do not envy the Englishman whose heart does not beat high as he looks at the scarred and shattered walls of Delhi or at the union jack flying from the fort at Lahore. Such sights irresistibly recall lines which no familiarity can vulgarize:

> Tu regere imperio populos, Romane, memento:
> Hæ tibi erunt artes; pacisque imponere morem,
> Parcere subjectis et debellare superbos.[10]

Think how such words, when as new and fresh as the best of Mr. Tennyson's poems to us, must have come home to a Roman as he saw his sentries keeping guard on the Temple. The position of Pilate was not very unlike that of an English Lieutenant-Governor of the Punjab. The resemblance would be still closer if for a lieutenant-governor we substitute a Resident with a strong

---

10. "Remember thou, O Roman, to rule nations with thy sway—these shall be thine arts—to crown Peace with Law, to spare the humbled, and to tame in war the proud." Virgil, *Aeneid*, trans. H. R. Fairclough, 2 vols. Loeb Classical Library (Cambridge: Harvard University Press, 1935), vol. 1, bk. 6, lines 851–53.

armed force under his orders and Runjeet Singh by his side. At all events Pilate, more or less closely associated with a native ruler, was answerable for the peace probably of the most dangerous and important province of the empire. The history of the Jews shows what a nation they were. 'A people terrible from the beginning,' and most terrible of all in matters of religion. It would not be difficult, nor would it be altogether fanciful, to trace a resemblance between the manner in which they would strike Pilate and the manner in which the Afghans or the Sikhs strike us; and it may help us to appreciate Pilate's position if we remember that, as we now look back upon the Indian mutiny, he, if he was observant and well informed, must have looked forward to that awful episode in Roman history which closed with the siege of Jerusalem and the destruction of the last vestiges of Jewish national independence. We may be very sure that the predictions that not one stone of the Temple should be left upon another, that the eagles should be gathered together, that there should be fire and blood and vapour of smoke, were not isolated. Pilate and his successors must have known that they sat on a volcano long before the explosion came.*

It was in such a state of things that Pilate learned that a prophet who for some years had been preaching in various parts of the province had entered Jerusalem with some of the circumstances which denote a powerful popular movement. Further he received from the priests, from the head of the established religion, complaints against the new religious reformer curiously like those which orthodox Mahommedans make against Wahabee preachers, or orthodox Sikhs against Kookas. As to the detail of the conduct which he pursued under these circumstances, we have not, I think, the materials for criticism. We know only one side of the story, and that side is told by men whose view of their position obviously is that they ought to submit with patient resignation to the deepest of all conceivable wrongs. Pilate's reports to his superiors and copies of the information on which he acted, with descriptions by impartial observers of the state of feeling in Palestine at the time, would be absolutely essential to anything like a real judgment on what he did.

---

*Upon this passage Mr. Harrison founds this remark—'Its rulers' (*i.e.*, the rulers of the Indian Empire) 'feel, as Mr. Stephen complacently says, that they sit on a volcano,'—and on being remonstrated with, he justified his statement as being substantially, or, at all events, constructively true.

It may be true that he sacrificed one whom he believed to be an innocent man to pacify the priests. It may be that he was perfectly convinced that the step taken was necessary to the peace of the country, and he may have formed that opinion more or less rashly. On these points we are and shall forever continue to be as much in the dark as on the merits of the quarrel which he is said to have made up with Herod. We know nothing whatever about it, nor is it material to the present subject.

The point to which I wish to direct attention is that Pilate's duty was to maintain peace and order in Judea and to uphold the Roman power. It is surely impossible to contend seriously that it was his duty, or that it could be the duty of anyone in his position, to recognise in the person brought to his judgment seat, I do not say God Incarnate, but the teacher and preacher of a higher form of morals and a more enduring form of social order than that of which he was himself the representative. To a man in Pilate's position the morals and the social order which he represents are for all practical purposes final and absolute standards. If, in order to evade the obvious inference from this, it is said that Pilate ought to have respected the principle of religious liberty as propounded by Mr. Mill, the answer is that if he had done so he would have run the risk of setting the whole province in a blaze.* It is only in very modern times, and under the influence of modern sophisms, that belief and action have come to be so much separated in these parts of the world that the distinction between the temporal and spiritual department of affairs even appears to be tenable; but this is a point for future discussion.

If this should appear harsh, I would appeal again to Indian experience. Suppose that some great religious reformer—say, for instance, someone claiming to be the Guru of the Sikhs, or the Imam in whose advent many

*Mr. Morley says upon this that I do not understand Mr. Mill. 'Mr. Mill expressly lays down the limitation proper to the matter in a passage to which Mr. Stephen appears not to have paid attention. "Even opinions lose their immunity when the circumstances in which they are expressed are such as to constitute a positive investigation to the mischievous act." ' I think it is Mr. Morley, in this case, who misunderstands my argument, or rather does not think it worth while to understand it. The passage quoted from Mr. Mill is in substance only a way of saying that you may throw the abetment of a crime into the form of the expression of an opinion. No doubt you may do so. You may also throw it into the form of the statement of a fact, as was done by the courtier of Ahasuerus, who, when Haman got into disgrace, casually observed, 'Behold, also, the gallows which Haman has set up.' My argument upon Pilate's case is that the

Mahommedans devoutly believe—were to make his appearance in the Punjab or the North-West Provinces. Suppose that there was good reason to believe—and nothing is more probable—that whatever might be the preacher's own personal intentions, his preaching was calculated to disturb the public peace and produce mutiny and rebellion: and suppose further (though the supposition is one which it is hardly possible to make even in imagination), that a British officer, instead of doing whatever might be necessary, or executing whatever orders he might receive, for the maintenance of British authority, were to consider whether he ought not to become a disciple of the Guru or Imam. What course would be taken towards him? He would be instantly dismissed with ignominy from the service which he would disgrace, and if he acted up to his convictions, and preferred his religion to his Queen and country, he would be hanged as a rebel and a traitor.

But let us pass from Pilate to his successors, the various persecutors who at intervals opposed the progress of Christianity during the first three centuries of its history. The charge against them is that they interfered with liberty, that they exercised coercion otherwise than for the purpose of self-protection, that they ought to have acted with absolute indifference and complete toleration. That is certainly not the lesson which I should be inclined to draw from the history in question. It is, I think, altogether unjust to blame them for maintaining and defending their own view. The true charge is that they acted as if they had no such view to maintain; that, instead of offering an intelligent opposition to Christianity in so far as they deliberately thought it wrong, they inflicted on it occasional brutalities, proceeding from a blind instinct of fear and hatred, and unaccompanied by any sort of appreciation of the existence of the problems which Christianity was trying to solve. I should say that they were to blame quite as much for what they left undone as for what they did.

---

mere preaching of a religion which relates principally to matters of belief and self-regarding acts may, under circumstances, tend to disturb the existing social order. If in that case the representatives of the existing social order persecute the religion it appears to me that the question whether they are right or wrong depends on the comparative merits of the religion which is persecuted and the social order which persecutes. Whether Pilate was right in thinking that what took place in Judea threatened social order directly or indirectly we cannot tell, but it was his business by all means to protect social order. This is directly opposed to the whole of Mr. Mill's chapter about the liberty of discussion.

Neither Marcus Aurelius nor his successors were wrong in seeing that the Christian and the Roman ideas of life differed widely, that there was not room for both, and that the two systems must of necessity struggle. Their faults were these among others. In the first place, their treatment of Christianity was, as far as we can now judge, brutal and clumsy. They persecuted just enough to irritate their antagonists, to give them a series of moral victories, and not enough to crush and exterminate. Atrocious as an exterminating policy would have been, it would probably have succeeded, in the same miserable sense in which the Spanish Inquisition succeeded, but it would at all events have been intelligible. The guilt incurred would not have been incurred for nothing. It would not have defeated itself.

In the second place, they are to blame for not having recognised the patent fact that Christianity had an intensely strong hold on men, and for being debarred by their pride and other evil tempers from trying to discover its source. I do not say that the Roman emperors and governors ought all to have become Christians, but men worthy to be regarded as rulers of men ought to have studied Christianity with deep attention. If it appeared to them to be false, or to be true in part only, they ought to have treated it as false, or partially true, and to have made public and put on record the grounds on which they regarded other parts of it as false. It may sometimes be necessary for Governments to legislate directly against religions. It may often be necessary for them to adopt a policy indirectly unfavourable to them, but it never can be right or wise to trust in such matters to sheer brute force producing bodily fear. Governments ought not only to threaten, but to persuade and to instruct. The Romans ought to have had a great deal more faith in themselves and in their own principles of conduct than they ever showed. They ought not to have left the whole management of the human heart and soul in the hands of devotional passion. They should have stood forward as competitors with Christianity in the task of improving the world which they had conquered. They should have admitted fully and at once the truth of one most important side of the Christian religion, a side which has been far too much forgotten—I mean its negative side. They should have owned that idolatry had had its day, that the Gods of their Pantheon, whatever they might once have represented, were mere dead idols, lies in marble and gold. They should have dethroned Jupiter and his fellows, and stood forward frankly and honourably to meet the new creed upon its merits, resolved to learn, and no less resolved to teach, for they had much to teach. If they had met as enemies in this spirit, would they not have been generous enemies? If there had been strife, would it not have been a noble strife? Would the Christian priests and bishops, full of religious emotions, and ready, as the event showed, to degrade the human race by wild asceticism and to bewilder it with metaphysical dreams, have had nothing to learn from the greatest masters of every form of organised human effort, of law, of government, of war, and of morals that the world has ever seen? In point of fact we know that the Church did learn much from ancient Rome. It might have learned much more, it might have unlearned much, if the two great powers of the world had stood to each other in the attitude of generous opponents, each working its way to the truth from a different side, and not in the attitudes of a touching though slightly hysterical victim mauled from time to time by a sleepy tyrant in his intervals of fury. In short, the indifference of the Empire to the whole subject of religion, which had grown out of its plethora of wealth and power, was its real reproach.

This illustration of the way in which I look at the history of religious struggles is enough for my purpose. If it were thrown, as it easily might be, into a logical shape, it would show that the merits of the attitude of the Empire towards Christianity depend upon our estimate of the object in view, and the efficiency and expense of the means adopted to obtain it; but this is of little importance. The main fact to bear in mind is that there are and there must be struggles between creeds and political systems, just as there are struggles between different nations and classes if and in so far as their interests do not coincide. If Roman and Christian, Trinitarian and Arian, Catholic and Protestant, Church and State, both want the allegiance of mankind, they must fight for it. No peace is possible for men except upon one of two conditions. You may purchase absolute freedom by the destruction of all power, or you may measure the relative powers of the opposing forces by which men act and are acted upon, and conduct yourself accordingly. The first of these courses is death. The second is harmonious and well-regulated life; but the essence of life is force, the exertion of force implies a conflict of forces, and the conflict of forces is the negation of liberty in so far as either force restrains the other.*

---

*In the first edition this was expressed obscurely, and in terms which were rather too wide. I have to thank a critic in the *Spectator* for pointing this out, though I do not think his criticisms were just.

It may very naturally be asked upon this, Do you then oppose yourself to the whole current of civilised opinion for three hundred years at least? Do you wish to go back to the Inquisition and the war which desolated the Netherlands and Germany for about eighty years? Is the whole theory and practice of English Liberalism a complete mistake, and are writers like de Maistre[11] and his modern disciples and imitators our true guides?

To this I should answer most emphatically, No. I do not object to the practice of modern Liberals. Under great difficulties they have contrived to bring about highly creditable results, but their theories have presented those defects which are inseparable from the theories of a weak and unpopular party making its way towards power. They could persuade those whom they had to persuade only by discovering arguments to show how toleration could be reconciled with the admission of the absolute truth of religious dogmas. They had to disconnect religious liberty from scepticism, and it is pretty clear that they were not aware of the degree in which they really are connected. At all events, they avoided the admission of the fact by resting their case principally on the three following points, each of which would have its due weight upon the theory which I have stated:

The first point was that, though persecution silences, it does not convince, and that what is wanted is conviction and not acquiescence. This is an argument to show that persecution does not effect its purpose, and is answered, or at least greatly diminished in weight, by the consideration that, though by silencing A you do not convince A, you make it very much easier to convince B, and you protect B's existing convictions against A's influence.

The second point was that people will not be damned for *bona-fide* errors of opinion. This is an argument to show that a severe and bloody persecution is too high a price to pay for the absence of religious error.

The third point, which I am inclined to think was in practice the most powerful of all with the class who feel more than they think, was that to support religion by persecution is alien to the sentiment of most religions, and especially to that of the Christian religion, which is regarded as peculiarly humane. In so far as Christianity recognises and is founded on hell, this has always appeared to me to be an inconsistency, not in all cases unamiable when

11. Stephen had an interest in modern French political thought generally and in Joseph de Maistre (1753–1821) in particular. See Stephen's reviews of several of de Maistre's works in *Horae Sabbaticae*, vol. 3, pp. 250–324.

genuine, but weak and often hypocritical. Whatever its value may be, it falls under the same head as the second point. It is an argument to show that persecution is an excessive price to pay for religious uniformity.

The true inference from the commonplaces about the doubtfulness of religious theories, and the inefficacy of persecution as a means of obtaining the object desired except at a ruinous price, is to moderate the passions of the combatants, not to put an end to the fight. Make people understand that there are other objects in life than the attainment of religious truth; that they are so ignorant and so likely to be mistaken in their religious opinions that if they persecute at all they are as likely to persecute truth as falsehood; that in order to be effectual a persecution must be so powerful, so systematic, and so vigorously sustained as to crush, paralyse, and destroy; and that the result when obtained will probably be of exceedingly small importance, and perhaps mischievous as far as it goes, and you teach people not to live at peace, but to strive with moderation, and with a better appreciation of the character and importance of the contest, its intricacy, its uncertainty, and the difficulty of distinguishing friends from enemies, than is possible in simple times. Sceptical arguments in favour of moderation about religion are the only conclusive ones.

If it should be supposed that moderation would render controversy uninteresting or ineffective, it should be remembered that there is a confusion in common thought and language between brutality and efficiency. There is a notion that the severest, the most effectual contest is that in which the greatest amount of bodily injury is done by the side which wins to the side which loses; but this is not the case. When you want a fair and full trial of strength, elaborate precautions are taken to make the test real and to let the best man win. If prize-fighters were allowed to give foul blows and hit or kick a man when he is down, they would hurt each other more than they do, but their relative strength and endurance would be less effectually tested. So with religions; what is wanted is not peace, but fair play.

De Maistre somewhere says that the persecution which the Church had suffered from the syllogism was infinitely worse than all that racks and crosses could inflict; and the remark, though odd, is perfectly true. Modern religious struggles—conducted by discussion, by legislation, by social intolerance—are to the religious persecutions of earlier times what modern war is to ancient war. Ancient war meant to the defeated at best death, at worst slavery, exile, and personal degradation. Modern war is more effective, though the procedure is less brutal and degrading. Either the German or the French army in 1870–71 would have crushed the hordes which fought at Châlons or Tours as a steam-engine cracks a nut. The French armies were just as effectually defeated and disabled by the Germans as if the prisoners had been sold for slaves.

It is the same with controversy. Civil war, legal persecution, the Inquisition, with all their train of horrors, form a less searching and effective conflict than that intellectual warfare from which no institution, no family, no individual man is free when discussion is free from legal punishment. Argument, ridicule, the expression of contempt for cherished feelings, the exposure of cherished fallacies, chilled or wounded affection, injury to prospects public or private, have their terrors as well as more material weapons and more definite wounds. The result of such a warfare is that the weaker opinion—the less robust and deeply seated feeling—is rooted out to the last fibre, the place where it grew being seared as with a hot iron; whereas the prison, the stake, and the sword only strike it down, and leave it to grow again in better circumstances. A blow bruises, and discolours for a time. Nitrate of silver does not bruise, but it changes the colour of the whole body for its whole life. It is impossible to draw any definite line at which the sensation of pressure becomes painful. It may be a touch just sufficient to attract attention. It may inflict the most agonising pain in many different ways. It is the same with respect to the pain occasioned by treating a man's opinions as false. The disagreement may be pleasant, it may be of trifling importance, it may cause intense pain, and this may be of many different kinds, the immediate causes of which are very various. Every mode of differing from a man which causes him pain infringes his liberty of thought to some extent. It makes it artificially painful for him to think in a certain way, and so violates Mr. Mill's canon about liberty, unless it is done for self-protection, which is seldom the case. Mr. Mill's doctrines about liberty of opinion and discussion appear to me to be a kind of Quakerism. They are like teaching that all revenge whatever, even in its mildest form, is wrong, because revenge carried to an extreme is destructive of society.

CHAPTER THREE

ON THE DISTINCTION
BETWEEN THE TEMPORAL AND
SPIRITUAL POWER

In the last chapter I more than once had to refer to the question of the distinction between the spiritual and the temporal power, or the spiritual and temporal order. It plays so large a part in discussions on this subject that it will be worthwhile to examine it with some degree of attention.[1]

I think it would not be unfair to state the common view upon the subject somewhat as follows: Life may be divided into two provinces, the temporal and the spiritual. In the temporal province are included all common affairs—war, commerce, inheritance; all that relates to a man's body and goods. Thought, feeling, opinion, religion, and the like form the spiritual province. These two provinces have usually been placed under separate governments. Kings, parliaments, lawyers, soldiers bear rule in the one; some sort of priests bear rule in the other. The recognition of this distinction and the practice of attaching great importance to it is one of the curious bonds of union between Positivists and Roman Catholics. It is also one of the favourite commonplaces of a large number of French political writers, and in particular it is the very foundation of the theories of Liberal Catholics, of those who try to reconcile the doctrines of the Roman Catholic Church with modern notions about liberty.

---

1. Stephen also treats of the relation between temporal and spiritual powers in "The Temporal and Spiritual Powers," in *Horae Sabbaticae*, vol. 3, pp. 343–358.

If I understand them rightly, the Ultramontane party do not adopt this view, but take what to me at least appears a far more rational one. It might, I think, be expressed as follows: The spiritual and temporal power differ not in the province which they rule, but in the sanctions by which they rule it. Spiritual power means the power of the keys; power to open and shut; power in heaven, purgatory, and hell; possibly in some cases power to interfere in a supernatural manner with the common course of nature. Temporal power means power to deal with life and limb, goods, liberty, and reputation—all the hopes and fears of this visible world. Each of these may be so used as to affect both opinions and actions. A man may be excommunicated or may be imprisoned, either for theft or for heresy. The two powers exercise a concurrent jurisdiction over men's conduct. In a healthy state of things they ought to act in the same direction. In an unhealthy state of things, they will come into collision, and when they do so the stronger of the two forces will overcome the other. They proceed to say that the penalties which the spiritual power can inflict are infinitely heavier than those which the temporal power can inflict, which, if they are real, is obviously true. The final inference is that the Pope and his clergy are the rightful king and rulers of the whole world.

This argument is surely altogether unanswerable if its fundamental assumption is true; and the attempts of the Liberal Catholics to evade it by drawing a line, not between the sanctions of which the two powers dispose, but between the provinces over which they reign, are excusable only on the ground of their practical utility in the case of people who want an excuse for civilly ousting the priests from their position, and have not the moral courage to look them straight in the face and tell them the plain truth in plain words that their claims are unfounded.

That this is so is obvious from the following considerations. In the first place, human life forms a whole. Thought, motive, wish, intention each run into, and cannot be distinguished from, each other. Whatever the spirit or soul may be, it is not only one, but the ultimate type of unity from which we get the idea. It is the man himself as distinguished from his organs through which it acts; and the stream (so to speak) of its operations is uninterrupted from the first conception of a thought down to the outward act in which it culminates. Every act is spiritual. Every power is spiritual. Whether a man is saying his prayers or buying an estate, it is he the spirit or soul, whatever that may be, which prays or buys. Whether he hopes for heaven or for sensual pleasure, whether he fears hell hereafter or bodily pain here, it is he the spirit or soul which hopes or fears, and it is thus impossible to find either centre or circumference for the two spheres of which his life is said to consist, though it is easy to imagine any number of classes of hopes and fears by which the whole of it may be acted upon.

If we approach the matter from the other end and examine the attempts which have been made to draw the line between the two provinces, we are led back to the same result. No one has ever been able to draw the line upon any intelligible principle, or to decide who ought to draw it. To take prominent concrete cases, who can say whether laws about marriage, education, and ecclesiastical property belong to the spiritual or to the temporal province? They obviously belong to each. They go down to the very depths of the human soul. They affect the most important outward actions of every-day life. Again, if the two provinces exist, and if the temporal and spiritual powers are independent, it is obvious that the line between their territories must either be drawn by one of them, or must be settled by agreement between them. If either has the power of drawing it, that one is the superior of the other, and the other has only to take what its superior leaves to it. The result of this will be either that the Church will be the ruler of the world, and the State dependent on and subordinate to it, or that the State will be the ruler and the Church a voluntary association bound together by contracts dependent upon the laws of the State. In other words, the powers cannot be independent if either of them is to define its own limits. If the limits are settled by agreement (which has never yet been done in any part of the world), you have no longer two provinces divided by a natural boundary, but two conflicting powers making a bargain. You have not a Church and a State each with a province naturally its own, but two States or two Churches—call them which you please—of rather different characters coming into collision and making a treaty. This is a merely conventional and accidental arrangement, and does not answer, as according to the theory it ought, to a distinction founded on the nature of things.

For these reasons it appears to me that the Ultramontane view of the relation between Church and State is the true one; that the distinction is one of sanctions and not of provinces. If this is so, it is obvious that the distinction will not affect the question whether opinion is to be subject to coercion, but only the question as to the sort of coercion to which it is to be subject. The object, or one of the principal objects, for which the distinction between the temporal and spiritual province is attempted to be set up, is to secure a region for liberty. In the spiritual province it is argued there should be no temporal coercion. But opinion is in the spiritual province. Therefore, there should be no temporal coercion of opinion. If the whole of human life falls within each province, it is obvious that this argument cannot be applied.

The distinction of which I have thus denied the existence has a very prominent place in the writings of Positivists, and the attention which they have attracted in this country makes it desirable to examine their views on the subject. I ought to say that my notions as to their opinions are derived mainly from the writings of the English members of that body. I have read, I think, most of them, and have found in them, among other things, many statements about Comte's views on this and other matters. They have never persuaded me to go very deep into Comte himself. More reasons than I can even glance at here have led me to the conclusion that it would be an unprofitable investment of time to study his writings.* What the value of his speculations on

---

*I will give one reason as a specimen. In Comte's 'General View of Positivism' (translated by Dr. Bridges) there occurs the following cardinal statement: 'The great problem, then, is to raise social feeling by artificial effort to the position which in the natural condition is held by selfish feeling' ('Gen. View,' p. 98). To me this is like saying, The great object of mechanics is to alter the laws of gravitation. The following passages in the work quoted bear on the relation of the spiritual and temporal powers, but I find no definition of the words spiritual and temporal— pp. 81–4, 122–7, 144–8, 378–85. [Auguste Comte, A General View of Positivism, trans. J. H. Bridges (London: Trübner, 1865).]

This passage and the pages which follow contain the only allusions to Comte in the whole of this book, though his name is mentioned at p. 3. Mr. Harrison, however, observes that I am under an impression, 'exhibited in a running fire of allusion, that' my book 'is an answer to Comte as well as Mr. Mill.' He says that if I had read Comte I should have discovered that I agree with him on many points; but 'it is a pity that Mr. Stephen, before assailing Comte with every weapon in the armoury of letters, did not learn more about him than he could gather from conversation and reviews.' He describes me as 'talking positivism with the amusing unconsciousness of a famous prosaist';—(is not M. Jourdain's talking prose without knowing it as stale as Lord Macaulay's New Zealander?)—and ends with 'No one is forced to study Comte, but then no one is forced to write about him.'

Though I never like to criticise people on hearsay evidence, and have therefore carefully abstained from any reference whatever to Comte, except upon this one isolated subject, I am by no means so ill informed about his views as Mr. Harrison supposes. I could hardly have read all that

natural science may have been I do not pretend to guess, but the writings of his disciples, still more the exposition given by them of his opinions, and perhaps, above all, their accounts of his life, give me a strong impression that his social and moral speculations will not ultimately turn out to be of much real value. I mention this because it is very possible that in discussing his views to a great extent at second hand I may not do them justice.

The writings, then, of his English disciples are full of discourse on the relations of the spiritual and the temporal power, which, as far as my experience goes, tend in every case to lower the importance of the latter and exalt the importance of the former. I think, too, that the distinction is used for the purpose of enforcing the universal duty of toleration on the grounds just stated. These views coming from Positivists are unembarrassed by a difficulty, which to me makes them unintelligible. I cannot understand what, thinking as they think, is the nature of the distinction.

What a believer in a future state of existence means by a spiritual power as distinguished from the temporal power is, as I have already shown, perfectly plain. The difficulty arises when we find the distinction insisted on by people whose leading doctrines are that there is no future state at all, or that, if there is, we know nothing about it and have nothing to do with it; that such words as 'spirit,' 'soul,' and the like are the names of figments proper to what they describe as the metaphysical stage of thought.* To find persons who think thus insisting on the distinction between spiritual and temporal power as

---

has been written about him of late years, and have read his own summary of his own creed without being well aware that his views and mine resemble each other in the points mentioned by Mr. Harrison, though they differ widely in other respects. But Mr. Harrison is as thin-skinned about Comte as Mr. Morley is about 'rational men.' He smells blasphemous allusions to his prophet in passages which had not the smallest reference to him. See *post*, p. 192.

*"There is no magic in the word "spiritual," ' says Mr. Harrison, 'and Comte may surely use it while holding his tongue about Hell. Spiritual with him includes all that concerns the intellectual, moral, and religious life of men, as distinct from the material.' It seems to me that there is magic in the word 'spiritual'—the magic which enables men to wear a religious mask to which they are not entitled. If it had not been for his misappropriation of this word, Mr. Harrison and Comte would hardly have been led into the assertion of the monstrous doctrine that a power which has to make laws about contracts, wrongs, marriage, personal liberty, and inheritance, which has to declare peace and war, which exercises the right of life and death, and has to organize public education, has nothing to do with the intellectual or moral life of man. Try to express the distinction which I am discussing without the use of the word 'spiritual,' and you will find it to be impossible to do so, and this impossibility proves what I say.

inherent in the nature of things, is as if an atheist were to make the love of God the foundation of a system of morals, or as if a disciple of Locke were to found his philosophy upon a set of principles which he declared to be innate.[2]

The nearest approach to a meaning which I can put upon the words as used by them is one which would make spiritual and temporal power correspond respectively to persuasion and force. The spiritual power is the power of those who appeal to and regulate public opinion. The temporal power is the power of those who make laws by which people are punished in body, goods, and reputation. If my knowledge of Comte is correct as far as it goes, his theory as to the spiritual power was that a certain class of specially well-instructed persons were to speak with the same sort of authority upon all the great questions of morals and politics as scientific bodies now speak with as to such subjects as astronomy, and that legislation and government, as we at present understand them, were to be carried on by an inferior class of persons in obedience to the principles so laid down for their guidance. I believe that he called these two classes respectively the spiritual and temporal powers, and justified his use of the expression by asserting that the real power of the clergy over men's minds when at its highest lay in the fact that they appealed to and represented public opinion as it then was, and not in the fact that they were supposed to have power over the future prospects of mankind, and even some degree of supernatural influence over their ordinary concerns.

I do not think this was true in fact, but, however that may be, the distinction thus expressed seems to me to be altogether groundless and misleading. To set up the temporal and spiritual powers thus understood as two distinct agents by which mankind are to be governed, each of which is to have its own sphere of action, and is entitled to be respected by the other so long as it keeps within that sphere, involves several errors, each of which separately is fatal to anything like an accurate view of the subject.

The first error is that the theory entirely misconceives the relation to each other of persuasion and force.* They are neither opposed to nor really altogether distinct from each other. They are alternative means of influencing

2. Stephen is referring to Book I of John Locke's *Essay concerning Human Understanding,* a work which he reviewed, praising Locke's critique of the theory of innate ideas. See Stephen's *Horae Sabbaticae,* vol. 2, p. 114.

*Mr. Harrison upon this charges me with denying that there is any difference between persuasion and force; and, after a diffuse caricature of part of this passage, he sums it up thus:

mankind, which may be, constantly are, and obviously ought to be exercised by and upon the very same persons in respect of the very same matter. To confine anyone who has to influence others in any capacity to the use of one of them to the exclusion of the other would be equivalent to destroying his influence. The old proverb which forbids the spurring of willing horses is of universal application. No one applies force when persuasion will do, and no sensible person applies force till persuasion has failed. Persuasion, indeed, is an indispensable condition to the application of force on any large scale. It is essential to the direction of force; nor is it possible for any practical purpose to separate the two. Whatever our spiritual power may be, nobody would deny that Parliament is in these islands the temporal power. It is only by and with the consent of Parliament that anybody can apply force in the ultimate form of legal punishment to anyone else for any purpose. How much persuasion of every kind has to be employed before that consent can be obtained it is needless to say. Force, therefore, is dependent upon persuasion, and cannot move without it. Under a system of parliamentary government this is a little more obvious than under other systems, but the same is true in all cases. No one ever yet ruled his fellow-men unless he had first, by some means or other, persuaded others to put their force at his disposal. No one ever yet used his force for any considerable time, or on any considerable scale, without more or less consultation as to the direction in which and the purposes for which it should be used.

Force thus implies persuasion acting in immediate conjunction with it. Persuasion, indeed, is a kind of force. It consists in showing a person the consequences of his actions. It is, in a word, force applied through the mind. Force, on the other hand, is a kind of persuasion. When a man is compelled to act in

---

'Most people, however, will agree that ordinary language is right in making a distinction between force and persuasion, between the arm of the law and counsel, between the action of government and the influence of opinion. Mr. Stephen, of course, like any other sensible person, when not trying to prove Comte a blockhead, draws the distinction very plainly,' and he refers to p. 171. Now I have carefully avoided saying that persuasion and force do not differ from each other; what I have said is that they do, and that the difference between them does not correspond to the difference between the spiritual and the temporal power, for both priests and legislators have to employ both persuasion and force, and that in reference to the very same subjects. I have no doubt said that they run into each other at certain points, as light, heat, and motion do; but this is a minor point.

a particular way by the fear of legal punishment, he is persuaded by the argument, 'If you do not act thus, you will be punished.' The argument is extremely simple, and can be made intelligible by gestures even to some animals; but still it is an argument. On the other hand, when a priest says, 'Vote as I tell you or you will be damned,' he employs force just as much as if he held a pistol to his parishioner's head, though the arguments through which the force is applied are more elaborate than in the other case. A surgeon tells a patient that he will die unless he submits to a painful operation. Is this persuasion or force? No man would lose a limb if he were not forced to do so by the fear of losing what he values even more, but the surgeon would usually be said to persuade his patient, and not to compel him.

Take again this consideration. In almost every instance in which force and persuasion are employed, some persons are persuaded and others are forced to the very same line of conduct by the very same act. A father has two sons who will not learn their lessons. He points out to both the importance of industry, and tells both that if they are idle he will punish them. One works and is not punished, the other is idle and is punished. Each has been exposed to the same motives, and they may be said to have persuaded the one and forced the other. This is only an example in a single instance of the action of civil society upon individuals. It presents to everyone a series of alternatives. On the one side, health, wealth, honour, all the enjoyments of life; on the other, poverty, disgrace, and, in extreme cases, legal punishment extending to death itself. This is the net result of the whole working of social institutions. They persuade in some directions, and they threaten in others. Some of those who are addressed listen to the persuasions; others do not listen to the threats, and have to take the consequences in their various degrees. But every man who lives in society is both persuaded and threatened by society in every action of his life.

Now, if the spiritual power is the power which works by persuasion, and the temporal power the power which works by force, it will follow that every society in the world is both spiritual and temporal; in other words, it will follow that the distinction is unfounded. Every law and every institution in the world will serve as an illustration of this. Take, for instance, the great institution of private property. Persuasion and force upon this matter cannot be divorced from each other. The laws by which property is secured both persuade and threaten. They enable the owner of the property to enjoy it, and so persuade people to acquire property. They threaten those who infringe the rights of property, and operate against them in the shape of force; but they are persuasion or force, they appeal to hope or to fear, according to the point of view from which they are regarded.

If the attempt to make the spiritual and the temporal power correspond with persuasion and force breaks down, the only other common distinction to which it can be assimilated is the distinction between theory and practice. There is no particular reason why this familiar distinction should not be called by its own name; but if the common distinction between matter and spirit is to be given up as exploded and unmeaning, there is no other meaning which can be assigned to the words 'temporal' and 'spiritual.' There is no doubt a certain sort of uniformity with common usage in speaking of general principles as spiritual and of their practical application to details as temporal, and if it gives people who do not believe in the distinction between spirit and matter great pleasure to use the words spiritual power and temporal power, this is, perhaps, the least fallacious way of doing it. The objection to such a mode of using language is that it is peculiarly likely to be misunderstood. To speak of theoretical and practical men as two powers opposed to, or at all events independent of, each other, is to revive all the old fallacies which are written in Bentham's book of fallacies about the opposition between theory and practice. The construction of theories and their application to practice ought to go hand in hand; they ought to check and correct each other, and ought never on any account to be permitted to be long or widely separated. The result of doing so is that practical men construct for themselves crude, shallow, and false theories which react on their practice, and that theoretical men construct theories which are very slightly connected with facts. A society in which the two classes should form distinct castes, the one being subordinated to the other, looks like nothing better than a pedantic dream.

The general result is that the distinction between spiritual and temporal power becomes unmeaning as soon as we explode the distinction between spirit and matter, time and eternity, the Church which has its sanctions in the one, and the State which has its sanctions in the other.

Why, then, it may be asked, do Positivists attach such importance to this distinction? If it arises out of a mere confusion of ideas, why has it such attractions for them? The passages referred to above* have led me to doubt

*See note, pp. 73–74.

whether Comte really meant much more than that his followers would do well under existing circumstances to stand aloof from practical politics, and to confine themselves to teaching the theory of their creed. Speculative men constantly throw very obvious remarks of this kind into the form of enormously wide general assertions, as our own experience shows: but however this may be, all religious reformers like to pour new wine into old bottles. Instances are to be found in abundance in the history of speculation, and especially in the history of religious speculation, in which people have tried to show that all previous writers and thinkers were merely their precursors, and that these precursors were groping blindly after great truths, certain aspects of which they dimly recognized, though the full knowledge of them was reserved for the reformers themselves. 'See how my theory reconciles and gives symmetry to all the great doctrines which you, my predecessors, who were all very well in your way, did not succeed in grasping,' is the remark more or less emphatically made by many a reformer when he looks on his work and, behold, it is very good. This taste was strongly developed in Comte, and as on the one hand he had a deep admiration for certain sides of Catholicism, and on the other a conviction that the doctrine of a future state and of the distinctions between spirit and matter as usually understood were unfounded, he was obliged either to invent some new meaning for the distinction between spirit and matter and spiritual and temporal power, or to admit that the Roman Catholic Church was based upon a delusion. He preferred the first branch of the alternative, and attempted to give a theory about spirit and matter, spiritual and temporal, which should replace and complete the old one.

Of this theory his disciples, so far as I know (for I write under correction), have never given any distinct account, and the want of such an account is closely connected with the objection to their system, which has been continually made, and, so far as I am aware, has never been answered. The objection is the familiar one that they expect the clock to go when the weights are cut off. They would like to have a priesthood and a spiritual rule after they have denied the existence of the conditions which make these things possible. The subject is so important that it will bear a little remark.

All religions whatever, the professors of which aspire to rule mankind, have the same problem to grapple with. Each has an ideal of human nature to which its professors wish mankind in general to conform, or which they wish them, at all events, to admit to be entitled to reverence, whether they conform to it or not. Each of these religions finds a number of earnest and disinterested supporters, who are so much struck with its moral beauty and its inherent essential attractions that they become converts to it, as a lawyer would say, 'upon the view.' Christ would have many disciples and worshippers if all notion of individual profit or loss hereafter from his worship were at an end. The earliest Buddhists looked, and the purest Buddhists still look, for nothing better for themselves than final absorption or annihilation. The loving, trusting, believing spirit wants neither reward nor punishment. He falls in love with his creed as a man might fall in love with a woman, without hope, but beyond the possibility of recovery. Persons like these are the core and heart of every great religion.

They form, however, a very small minority of the human race. The great mass of men is not capable of this kind of disinterested passion for anything whatever. On the other hand, they are open to offers. They can be threatened or bribed into a more or less nominal adherence to almost any creed which does not demand too much of them.* Indeed, they like it rather than not; but some degree of consideration is essential. The real leading motives of the mass of mankind are personal prudence and passion. Their centre is self; and every religion which means to govern men must recognize this fact and appeal to personal motives. It does not become a spiritual power in the true sense of the word power—it cannot, that is to say, impose itself *in invitos* until it has practically solved this problem. How Christianity, Mahommedanism, and Brahminism solved it we all know. Even Buddhism had, after a time, to set up its hell; but to the worldly, the selfish, the indifferent, Positivism has nothing whatever to say. Considered as an organized religion, it is superfluous to those who like it, and impotent as against those who like it not, and its attempts to attach new meanings to the word 'spiritual,' to arrogate to its professors spiritual power, to sit in the seats of the priests whom it helps to dethrone, are mere fictions meant to conceal its fundamental impotence. No Positivist has

*Mr. Harrison represents this passage as follows: 'The sensitive must be pained . . . to be told that "he" [the Creator] has simply made men to be threatened or bribed, for all the world as if the problem of life were a contested election and Mr. Stephen the agent of Omnipotence.' Where have I said that God is the author of all religions, or that He has made men 'simply to be threatened or bribed'? Where have I hinted that God attaches, or that men ought to attach, much moral significance to the nominal adherence of ordinary men to this creed or that?

ever yet been able to answer the question, How do you propose to deal with a person who either thinks in his heart or says boldly with his lips, 'Tried by your standard, I am a bad and selfish man. I mean to be bad and selfish, and as for your spiritual power, I set it and you at defiance, and I shall take my own course in despite of you.'* All that the Positivist can say to such a person is, 'For the present, take your own course. Our tastes differ. In time we shall be a majority, and then we shall persuade others to coerce you.' The answer to this is, 'I and people like me form the incalculable majority of mankind, and you will never persuade the mass of men or any mass of men till you can threaten them. Here and there a horse may be disposed to go by himself, but you cannot drive a coach without reins and a whip. Religious teachers who have no hold on the selfish must renounce the notion of being a power at all, either spiritual or temporal; for a power which can be defied with impunity is no power, and as for you, you will never be anything more than a Ritualistic Social Science Association.'

*This is not one of the passages of this book to which Mr. Harrison has found it convenient to refer. He has much to say on all sorts of subjects, but he never meets the plain question, How will you deal with the ordinary worldly man?

CHAPTER FOUR

THE DOCTRINE OF
LIBERTY IN ITS APPLICATION
TO MORALS

So far I have considered the theoretical grounds of Mr. Mill's principle and its practical application to liberty of thought and discussion. I now proceed to consider its application to morals. It may be well to restate it for fear that I may appear to be arguing with an imaginary opponent. 'The object of this Essay is to assert one very simple principle, as entitled to govern absolutely all the dealings of society with the individual in the way of compulsion and control, whether the means used be physical force or the moral coercion of public opinion. That principle is, that the sole end for which mankind are warranted, individually or collectively, in interfering with the liberty of action of any of their number, is self-protection.' [13/223 L] A little further on we are told that 'from this liberty of each individual, follows the liberty, within the same limits of combination among individuals; freedom to unite for any purpose not involving harm to others.' [15–16/226 L]

The following consequences would flow legitimately from this principle. A number of persons form themselves into an association for the purpose of countenancing each other in the practice of seducing women, and giving the widest possible extension to the theory that adultery is a good thing. They carry out these objects by organizing a system for the publication and circulation of lascivious novels and pamphlets calculated to inflame the passions of the young and inexperienced. The law of England would treat this as a crime.

It would call such books obscene libels, and a combination for such a purpose a conspiracy. Mr. Mill, apparently, would not only regard this as wrong, but he would regard it as an act of persecution if the newspapers were to excite public indignation against the parties concerned by language going one step beyond the calmest discussion of the expediency of such an 'experiment in living.' [81/281 L] Such an association would be impossible in this country, because if the law of the land did not deal with it, lynch law infallibly would. This Mr. Mill ought in consistency to regard as a lamentable proof of our bigotry and want of acquaintance with the true principles of liberty.*

The manner in which he discusses an illustration closely analogous to this, and in which he attempts to answer an objection which must suggest itself to everyone, throws the strongest possible light on the value of his own theory. His illustration is as follows: 'Fornication, for example, must be tolerated and so must gambling; but should a person be free to be a pimp, or to keep a gambling house?' [99/296 L] He puts the arguments on each side without drawing any conclusion, and the strongest of them are as follows:

> On the side of toleration it may be said . . . that if the principles which we
> have hitherto defended are true, society has no business *as* society to decide
> anything to be wrong which concerns only the individual; that it cannot

*Upon this Mr. Morley says: 'I venture to propound two questions to Mr. Stephen. 1. Is the practice of seducing women a self-regarding practice. [sic] 2. Is the *circulation* of pamphlets calculated to inflame the passions of the young an act which hurts nobody but the circulator?'

I reply that each of these questions must, on Mr. Mill's principles (though not on mine), be answered in the affirmative. As to the first, according to Mr. Mill, the seduction of a woman, force and fraud apart, is distinctly a self-regarding act. The man's act regards the man, and the woman's act regards the woman. In passages already quoted Mr. Mill distinctly justifies the toleration of fornication on the ground that society as society has no business to decide anything to be wrong which concerns only the individual. He doubts whether this extends to the case of a pimp; but surely seduction is an even more personal matter than fornication. To question 2 (whether the circulation of pamphlets calculated to inflame the passions of the young is an act which hurts nobody but the circulator), I answer Yes, on Mr. Mill's principles it is, though not on mine. The whole of his argument on the liberty of thought and discussion is directed to prove the proposition that the 'appropriate region of human liberty' includes 'absolute freedom of opinion and sentiment on all subjects, *practical* or speculative, scientific, *moral*, or theological'; [15/225 L] and he adds, 'The liberty of expressing and publishing opinions may seem to fall under a different principle, since it belongs to that part of the conduct of an individual which concerns other people, but being almost of as much importance as the liberty of thought itself, and resting in great part on the same reasons, is practically inseparable from it.' [15/225-26 L]

go beyond discussion, and that one person should be as free to persuade as another to dissuade. In opposition to this it may be contended that, although the public, or the State are not warranted in authoritatively deciding, for purposes of repression or punishment, that such or such conduct affecting only the interests of the individual is good or bad, they are fully justified in assuming, if they regard it as bad, that its being so or not is at least a disputable question: That, this being supposed, they cannot be acting wrongly in endeavouring to exclude the influence of solicitations which are not disinterested, of instigators who cannot possibly be impartial—who have a direct personal interest on one side, and that the side which the State believes to be wrong, and who confessedly promote it for personal objects only. [99–100/296–97 L]

There is a kind of ingenuity which carries its own refutation on its face. How can the State or the public be competent to determine any question whatever if it is not competent to decide that gross vice is a bad thing? I do not think the State ought to stand bandying compliments with pimps. 'Without offence to your better judgment, dear sir, and without presuming to set up my opinion against yours, I beg to observe that I am entitled for certain purposes to treat the question whether your views of life are right as one which admits of two opinions. I am far from expressing absolute condemnation of an

---

Having regard to these quotations, I continue the quotation from Mr. Morley:

'The answer to these questions shows the illustration to be utterly pointless.' That is, he would answer each in the negative.

Which of us has misrepresented Mr. Mill, Mr. Morley or I?

Mr. Morley goes on to state the case of Wilkes and the Franciscans of Medmenham Abbey. 'These debauchees,' he says, 'were as gross and scandalous a set of profligates as ever banded together. But they conformed to the conditions laid down in the doctrine of liberty, and no one thought of interfering with them.' He then refers to Wilkes's 'Essay on Women,' and asks: 'Does Mr. Stephen hold that Wilkes was justifiably punished for this improperly imputed crime? i.e. for composing an obscene libel which he published only to his private friends in his own house.' I reply that I see no objection whatever to the punishment either of the Franciscans of Medmenham or of Wilkes, except the practical objections pointed out on pp. 88–89 and 94–96. The only reason why such acts should go unpunished is that no police or other public authority can be trusted with the power to intrude into private society, and to pry into private papers. It is like the case of the rule of evidence which protects from disclosure communications made during marriage between husbands and wives. The evil is that justice is sometimes defeated, the good that the confidence of married life is to some extent protected, and the good is held (I think rightly) to overbalance the harm.

experiment in living from which I dissent (I am sure that mere dissent will not offend a person of your liberality of sentiment), but still I am compelled to observe that you are not altogether unbiassed by personal considerations in the choice of the course of life which you have adopted (no doubt for reasons which appear to you satisfactory, though they do not convince me). I venture, accordingly, though with the greatest deference, to call upon you not to exercise your profession; at least I am not indisposed to think that I may, upon full consideration, feel myself compelled to do so.' My feeling is that if society gets its grip on the collar of such a fellow it should say to him, 'You dirty rascal, it may be a question whether you should be suffered to remain in your native filth untouched, or whether my opinion about you should be printed by the lash on your bare back. That question will be determined without the smallest reference to your wishes or feelings; but as to the nature of my opinion about you, there can be no question at all.'

Most people, I think, would feel that the latter form of address is at all events the more natural. Which is the more proper I shall try to show further on, but by way of preface it will be as well to quote the other passage from Mr. Mill to which I have referred. After setting forth his theory as to personal vices being left to take their own course, he proceeds as follows:

> The distinction here pointed out between the part of a person's life which concerns only himself, and that which concerns others many persons will refuse to admit. How (it may be asked) can any part of the conduct of a member of society be a matter of indifference to the other members? No person is an entirely isolated being; it is impossible for a person to do anything seriously or permanently hurtful to himself, without mischief reaching at least to his near connections, and often far beyond them. [80/280 L]

He proceeds to enforce this by highly appropriate illustrations, which I need not quote. Further on he quotes a passage from an advocate of the suppression of intemperance, of which the following is a sample: 'If anything invades my social rights, certainly the traffic in strong drink does. It invades my primary right of security by constantly creating and stimulating social disorder.' [89/288 L] Upon this Mr. Mill observes:

> A theory of "social rights," the like of which probably never before found its way into distinct language: being nothing short of this—that it is the absolute social right of every individual, that every other individual should

act in every respect precisely as he ought; that whosoever fails thereof in the smallest violates my social right, and entitles me to demand from the legislature the removal of the grievance. So monstrous a principle is far more dangerous than any single interference with liberty. . . . The doctrine ascribes to all mankind a vested interest in each other's moral, intellectual, and even physical perfection, to be defined by each according to his own standard. [89–90/288 L]

At the risk of appearing paradoxical, I own that the theory which appears to Mr. Mill so monstrous appears to me defective only in its language about rights and legislation, upon which I shall have more to say hereafter. It is surely a simple matter of fact that every human creature is deeply interested not only in the conduct, but in the thoughts, feelings, and opinions of millions of persons who stand in no other assignable relation to him than that of being his fellow-creatures. A great writer who makes a mistake in his speculations may mislead multitudes whom he has never seen. The strong metaphor that we are all members one of another is little more than the expression of a fact. A man would no more be a man if he was alone in the world than a hand would be a hand without the rest of the body.

I will now turn to the manner in which Mr. Mill deals with the objection just stated, and I must observe by the way that nothing proves his candour and honesty so clearly as the force with which he states objections to which he has no, or very weak, answers to make. His answer is twofold. He first admits that where 'by conduct of this sort' (*i.e.*, self-regarding vices) 'a person is led to violate a distinct and assignable obligation to any other person or persons, the case is taken out of the self-regarding class, and becomes amenable to moral disapprobation in the proper sense of the term. If, for example, a man, through intemperance . . . becomes unable to pay his debts, . . . he is deservedly reprobated, and might be justly punished, but it is for the breach of duty . . . to his creditors, not for his extravagance.' [81/281 L] A party of people get drunk together at a public-house. Public opinion ought to stigmatize those only who could not afford it. The rest are 'trying an experiment in living' [81/281 L] which happens to suit their taste, and no one else has anything to say to it.

So far Mr. Mill's plea is a qualified admission. He admits that when one man's misconduct injures other definite persons in a definite way he may be punished. 'But with regard to the merely contingent, or, as it may be called, constructive injury which a person causes to society, by conduct which neither violates any specific duty to the public, nor occasions perceptible hurt to any assignable individual except himself; the inconvenience is one which society can afford to bear, for the sake of the greater good of human freedom.' [82/ 282 L] It is natural to ask why? especially as the question is whether 'human freedom,' understood as Mr. Mill understands it, is good or bad? The answer to the inquiry is twofold. First, 'Society has had absolute power over all the early portion of their existence: it has had the whole period of childhood and nonage in which to try whether it could make them capable of rational conduct in life.' The existing generation being itself imperfect cannot indeed make its pupils 'perfectly wise and good,' but it is well able to make the rising generation as a whole as good as and a little better than itself. 'If society lets any considerable number of its members grow up as mere children incapable of being acted upon by rational considerations of distant motives, society has itself to blame for the consequences.' [82/282 L] Secondly, by issuing commands to grown-up people it will make people rebel, and 'the strongest of all the arguments against the interference of the public with purely personal conduct, is that when it does interfere, the odds are that it interferes wrongly, and in the wrong place.' [83/283 L]

This is Mr. Mill's whole case, and it appears to me so weak that I fear that I may have misunderstood or understated it. If so, I have done so unconsciously. As it stands it seems to involve the following errors.

First, there is no principle on which the cases in which Mr. Mill admits the justice of legal punishment can be distinguished from those in which he denies it. The principle is that private vices which are injurious to others may justly be punished, if the injury be specific and the persons injured distinctly assignable, but not otherwise. If the question were as to the possibility in most cases of drawing an indictment against such persons I should agree with him. Criminal law is an extremely rough engine, and must be worked with great caution; but it is one thing to point out a practical difficulty which limits the application of a principle and quite another to refute the principle itself. Mr. Mill's proviso deserves attention in considering the question whether a given act should be punished by law, but he applies it to 'the moral coercion of public opinion,' [13/223 L] as well as to legal coercion, and to this the practical difficulty which he points out does not apply. A set of young noblemen of great fortune and hereditary influence, the representatives of ancient names, the natural leaders of the society of large districts, pass their whole time and employ all their means in gross debauchery. Such people are far more injurious to society than common pickpockets, but Mr. Mill says that if anyone having the opportunity of making them ashamed of themselves uses it in order to coerce them into decency, he sins against liberty, unless their example does assignable harm to specific people. It might be right to say, 'You, the Duke of A, by extravagantly keeping four mistresses—to wit, B and C in London, and D and E in Paris—set an example which induced your friend F to elope with Mrs. G. at——on——, and you are a great blackguard for your pains, and all the more because you are a duke.' It could never be right to say, 'You, the Duke of A, are scandalously immoral and ought to be made to smart for it, though the law cannot touch you.' The distinction is more likely to be overlooked than to be misunderstood.*

Secondly, the arguments against legal interference in the cases not admitted to be properly subject to it are all open to obvious answers.

Mr. Mill says that if grown-up people are grossly vicious it is the fault of society, which therefore ought not to punish them.

This argument proves too much, for the same may be said with even greater force of gross crimes, and it is admitted that they may be punished.

It is illogical, for it does not follow that because society caused a fault it is not to punish it. A man who breaks his arm when he is drunk may have to have it cut off when he is sober.

It admits the whole principle of interference, for it assumes that the power of society over people in their minority is and ought to be absolute, and

*Mr. Morley says: 'But these two forms of remonstrance by no means exhaust the number. An advocate of Mr. Mill's principle might say to the debauched duke one of three things' (which he goes on to specify). Once more Mr. Morley totally misunderstands me. The object of the illustration is to expose the futility of Mr. Mill's distinction between the cases in which you may and the cases in which you may not find fault with a man for vice, which is that you may do so when his vice inflicts specific injury on a definite person, and not otherwise. Thus the gist of the charge against the Duke of A would be that his example hurt F. To use the language of special pleading, the declaration would be demurrable unless it averred special damage. This, I say, is futile. It deserves notice that Mr. Morley has not a word to say on the argument of which this illustration is a very subordinate part.

minority and majority are questions of degree, and the line which separates them is arbitrary.

Lastly, it proceeds upon an exaggerated estimate of the power of education. Society cannot make silk purses out of sows' ears, and there are plenty of ears in the world which no tanning can turn even into serviceable pigskin.

Mr. Mill's other arguments are that compulsion in such cases will make people rebel, and, above all, that the moral persecutor himself may very probably be mistaken.

This is true and important, but it goes to show not that compulsion should not be used at all, but that its employment is a delicate operation.

The Brahmins, it is said, being impressed with the importance of cattle to agriculture, taught people to regard the bull as a holy beast. He must never be thwarted, even if he put his nose into a shop and ate the shopkeeper's grain. He must never be killed, even in mercy to himself. If he slips over a cliff and breaks his bones and the vultures are picking out his eyes and boring holes between his ribs, he must be left to die. In several Indian towns the British Government has sent half the holy bulls to Mahommedan butchers, and the other half to draw commissariat wagons. Many matters go better in consequence of this arrangement, and agriculture in particular goes no worse. Liberty is Mr. Mill's Brahminee bull.

I find it difficult to understand how Mr. Mill's doctrine about individual liberty is to be reconciled with another of his theories to which I shall have occasion to refer more fully farther on. This is the theory about justice which is put forward in his essay on Utilitarianism. After a long and interesting discussion of the different senses in which the word 'justice' is used, he at last works out a conclusion which is expressed as follows: 'We do not call anything wrong, unless we mean to imply that a person ought to be punished in some way or other for doing it; if not by law, by the opinion of his fellow-creatures; if not by opinion, by the reproaches of his own conscience. This seems the real turning point of the distinction between morality and simple expediency. It is part of the notion of Duty in every one of its forms, that a person may rightfully be compelled to fulfil it.' [246 U] In other passages he says, 'The sentiment of justice, in that one of its elements which consists of the desire to punish, is thus, I conceive, the natural feeling of retaliation or vengeance, rendered by intellect and sympathy applicable to those injuries, that is to those hurts, which wound us through, or in common with society at large. This sentiment, in itself, has nothing moral in it; what is moral is, the exclusive subordination of it to the social sympathies, so as to wait on and obey their call. For the natural feeling tends to make us resent indiscriminately whatever anyone does that is disagreeable to us; but when moralized by the social feeling, it only acts in the directions conformable to the general good.' [248–49 U]

The passages seem to me to affirm the very principles for which I have been contending, and to be totally inconsistent with the doctrine of the essay on Liberty. The first passage involves the following consequence: Persons who call debauchery wrong mean to imply that debauched persons ought to be punished either by public opinion or by their own consciences. The second passage involves the following consequence: The sentiment of justice when moralized by the social feeling is the feeling of vengeance against a debauched person acting in a direction conformable to the general good—that is to say, acting in the direction of restraining him from following his vicious habits, which set a bad example to people at large. I do not know how it is possible to express in a more emphatic way the doctrine that public opinion ought to put a restraint upon vice, not to such an extent merely as is necessary for definite self-protection, but generally on the ground that vice is a bad thing from which men ought by appropriate means to restrain each other.

It may perhaps be replied that this is small criticism, and that Mr. Mill might have answered it conclusively by striking out two or three lines of his essay on Liberty, and by admitting that its doctrine is somewhat too widely expressed. I do not think that is the case. If the expressions in question had been withdrawn from the essay on Liberty, the whole theory would have fallen to the ground. Mr. Mill's writings form chains of thought from which no link can be withdrawn without destroying the value of the chain. Erase the few lines in question from the essay on Liberty and what remains is a commonplace hardly worth recording. The doctrine of the book would in that case be as follows: Men are not justified in imposing *the restraint of criminal law* on each other's conduct except for the purpose of self-protection, but they are justified in restraining each other's conduct by the action of public opinion, not only for the purpose of self-protection, but for the common good, including the good of the persons so restrained. Now, this doctrine would be quite a different thing from the one for which Mr. Mill contends. I do not think it would be correct, but it would be hardly worth discussing. It would not affect in practice the questions of liberty of opinion and discussion. The restraints of criminal law in these days are few, and most of them may be justified on any one of several grounds. Moreover, there are many reasons against extending the sphere of criminal law which are altogether independent of general considerations about liberty, as I shall show hereafter. Criminal law, in short, has found its level in this country, and, though in many respects of great importance, can hardly be regarded as imposing any restraint on decent people which is ever felt as such. To the great mass of mankind a law forbidding robbery is no more felt as a restraint than the necessity of wearing clothes is felt as a restraint. The only restraints under which anyone will admit that he frets are the restraints of public opinion, the 'social intolerance' of which Mr. Mill gives such a striking account. This is the practically important matter, this it is which formerly retarded (it does not at present very much retard) the expression of unusual opinions on religion, the adoption by women of practices unusual among women, the modification of existing notions as to ranks of society and the like. This, in a word, is the great engine by which the whole mass of beliefs, habits, and customs, which collectively constitute positive morality, are protected and sanctioned. The very object of the whole doctrine of liberty as stated by Mr. Mill is to lay down a principle which condemns all such interference with any experiments in living which particular people may choose to make. It is that or it is nothing, for the wit of man cannot frame any distinction between the cases in which moral and physical coercion respectively are justifiable except distinctions which arise out of the nature of criminal law and the difficulty of putting it into operation, and this is a small and technical matter. The result is that Mr. Mill's doctrine that nothing but self-defence can justify the imposition of restraint by public opinion on a man's self-regarding vices is not merely essential to the coherence of his theory, but is by far the most important part of it in practice.

I now pass to what I have myself to offer on the subject of the relation of morals to legislation, and the extent to which people may and ought to be made virtuous by Act of Parliament, or by 'the moral coercion of public opinion.'

I have no simple principle to assert on this matter. I do not believe that the question admits of any solution so short and precise as that which Mr. Mill supplies. I think, however, that the points relevant to its solution may be classified, and its discussion simplified by the arrangement suggested in previous chapters—namely, by considering whether the object for which the compulsion is employed is good, whether the compulsion employed is likely to be effective, and whether it will be effective at a reasonable expense.

The object is to make people better than they would be without compulsion. This statement is so very general that it can scarcely be understood without some preliminary observations as to the general position of morality in human affairs, and the manner in which it is produced and acted upon.

Men are so closely connected together that it is quite impossible to say how far the influence of acts apparently of the most personal character may extend. The sentiments of the founder of a great religion, the reflections of a great philosopher, the calculations of a great general may affect the form of the mould in which the lives, thoughts, and feelings of hundreds of millions of men may be cast. The effect of Henry VIII's personal feelings on the English Reformation is only a single illustration which happens to have come to light of the operations of a principle which usually works in secret. There are events in every man's life which might easily have been otherwise, but which give their whole colour to it. A happy marriage, which might have been prevented by any one of numberless accidents, will lead a man to take a cheerful view of life. Some secret stab in the affections, of which two or three people only are aware, may convert a man who would otherwise have been satisfied and amiable into a stoic, a sour fanatic, or a rebel against society, as the case may be. If Dante had been personally happy, or Shakespeare personally wretched, if Byron had married Miss Chaworth, if Voltaire had met with no personal ill-usage, their literary influence would have been very different. The result is that we can assign no limits at all to the importance to each other of men's acts and thoughts. Still less can we assign limits to that indefinable influence which they exercise over each other by their very existence, by the very fact of their presence, by the spirit which shines through their looks and gestures, to say nothing of their words and thoughts. If the inhabitants of the earth were all perfectly healthy and robust in mind and body, if there were not too many of them, if they rose rapidly to maturity and died before they began to lose their faculties, each man's happiness would be increased not only by the difference between his present condition and the condition in which he individually would then be placed, but by the difference between the position of a strong and healthy man living in a strong and healthy world and the same man living in a sickly world. It is easy to ride to death the analogy between health and disease and virtue and vice. They differ in several essential respects, but they resemble each other in several leading points. Vice is as infectious as disease, and happily virtue is infectious, though health is not. Both vice and virtue are transmissible, and, to a considerable extent, hereditary. Virtue and vice resemble health and disease in being dependent upon broad general causes which, though always present, and capable of being greatly modified by human efforts, do not always force themselves on our attention. Good air, clean water, and good food are now coming to be recognized as the great conditions of health. The maintenance of a high moral standard, the admiration and honour of virtue and the condemnation of vice, what is called in a school or a regiment a good moral tone, is the great condition of virtue. When soldiers speak of an army which is thoroughly frightened as 'demoralized,' they use an expression which by its significance atones for its politeness.

Besides this, we must recollect that the words 'virtue' and 'vice,' and their equivalents, have different meanings in different parts of the world and in different ages. I shall have occasion to speak elsewhere of Mr. Mill's ethical opinions more fully, and to say how far I agree with him and how far I disagree on several points. For the present, it is enough to say that I agree with him in taking its tendency to produce happiness as the test of the moral quality of an action, but this is subject to several important qualifications, of which I may mention one by way of illustration. Different people form very different ideals of happiness. The ideals of different nations, ages, and classes differ as much as the ideals of different individuals. The Christian ideal is not the Roman ideal, the Roman Catholic ideal is not the Protestant ideal, nor is the ideal of a lay Roman Catholic the same as that of a devotee. Compare the morals of Corneille, for instance, with the morals of Port Royal, or the morals of Port Royal with those of the Jesuits. They differ like the oak, the elm, and the larch. Each has a trunk and leaves and branches and roots, and whatever belongs to a tree: but the roots, the bark, the grain of the wood, the shape of the leaves, and the branches differ in every particular.

Not only are the varieties of morality innumerable, but some of them are conflicting with each other. If a Mahommedan, for instance, is fully to realize his ideal, to carry out into actual fact his experiment of living, he must be one of a ruling race which has trodden the enemies of Islam under their feet, and has forced them to choose between the tribute and the sword. He must be able to put in force the law of the Koran both as to the faithful and as to unbelievers. In short, he must conquer. Englishmen come into a country where Mahommedans had more or less realized their ideal, and proceed to govern it with the most unfeigned belief in the order of ideas of which liberty is the motto. After a time they find that to govern without any principles at all is impossible, though they think it would be very pleasant, and they are thus practically forced to choose between governing as Englishmen and governing as Mahommedans. They govern as Englishmen accordingly. To suppose that this process does not in fact displace and tend to subvert Mahommedan ideas is absurd. It is a mere shrinking from unpleasant facts.

This is only one illustration of the general truth that the intimate sympathy and innumerable bonds of all kinds by which men are united, and the differences of character and opinions by which they are distinguished, produce and must forever produce continual struggles between them. They are like a pack of hounds all coupled together and all wanting to go different ways. Mr. Mill would like each to take his own way. The advice is most attractive, and so long as the differences are not very apparent it may appear to be taken, but all the voting in the world will not get the couples off, or prevent the stronger dogs from having their own way in the long run and making the others follow them. We are thus brought to the conclusion that in morals as well as in religion there is and must be war and conflict between men. The good man and the bad man, the men whose goodness and badness are of different patterns, are really opposed to each other. There is a real, essential, eternal conflict between them.

At first sight it may appear as if this was a cynical paradox, but attention to another doctrine closely connected with it will show that it is far less formidable than it appears to be at first sight. The influences which tend to unite men and which give them an interest in each other's welfare are both more numerous and more powerful than those which throw them into collision. The effect of this is not to prevent collisions, but to surround them with acts of friendship and goodwill which confine them within limits and prevent people from going to extremities. The degree to which a man feels these conflicting relations and practically reconciles them in his conduct is not at all a bad measure of the depth, the sensibility, and the vigour of his character. The play of contradictory sentiments gives most of its interest to tragedy, and the conflict itself is the tragedy of life. Take as one instance out of a million the Cid's soliloquy on the alternative in which he is placed between allowing the outrage offered to his own father to go unpunished, and punishing it by killing the father of his mistress:

> Cher et cruel espoir d'une âme généreuse
> Mais ensemble amoureux,
> Digne ennemi de mon plus grand bonheur;
> Fer, qui cause ma peine,
> M'es-tu donné pour venger mon honneur?
> M'es-tu donné pour perdre Chimène?[1]

This is a single illustration of the attitude of all mankind to each other. Complete moral tolerance is possible only when men have become completely indifferent to each other—that is to say, when society is at an end. If, on the other hand, every struggle is treated as a war of extermination, society will come to an end in a shorter and more exciting manner, but not more decisively.

A healthy state of things will be a compromise between the two. There are innumerable differences which obviously add to the interest of life, and without which it would be unendurably dull. Again, there are differences which can neither be left unsettled nor be settled without a struggle, and a real one, but in regard to which the struggle is rather between inconsistent forms of good than between good and evil. In cases of this sort no one need see an occasion for anything more than a good-tempered trial of strength and skill, except those narrow-minded fanatics whose minds are incapable of taking in more than one idea at a time, or of having a taste for more things than one, which one thing is generally a trifle. There is no surer mark of a poor, contemptible, cowardly character than the inability to conduct disputes of this sort with fairness, temper, humanity, goodwill to antagonists, and a determination to accept a fair defeat in good part and to make the best of it. The

---

1. Pierre Corneille (1606–84), *Le Cid,* act 1, sc. 6, lines 315–20. For an English language translation of the play see *The Golden Age,* ed. Norris Houghton (New York: Dell Publishing, 1963).

peculiar merit of English people, a virtue which atones for so many vices that we are apt to misapprehend its nature and forget its weak sides, is our general practical recognition of this great truth. Every event of our lives, from school-boy games up to the most important struggles of public life, even, as was shown in the seventeenth century, if they go the length of civil war, is a struggle in which it is considered a duty to do your best to win, to treat your opponents fairly, and to abide by the result in good faith when you lose, without resigning the hope of better luck next time. War there must be, life would be insupportable without it, but we can fight according to our national practice like men of honour and people who are friends at bottom, and without attaching an exaggerated value to the subject matter of our contention.

The real problem of liberty and tolerance is simply this: What is the object of contention worth? Is the case one—and no doubt such cases do occur—in which all must be done, dared, and endured that men can do, dare, or endure; or is it one in which we can honourably submit to defeat for the present subject to the chance of trying again? According to the answer given to this question the form of the struggle will range between internecine war and friendly argument.

These explanations enable me to restate without fear of misapprehension the object of morally intolerant legislation. It is to establish, to maintain, and to give power to that which the legislator regards as a good moral system or standard. For the reasons already assigned I think that this object is good if and in so far as the system so established and maintained is good. How far any particular system is good or not is a question which probably does not admit of any peremptory final decision; but I may observe that there are a considerable number of things which appear good and bad, though no doubt in different degrees, to all mankind. For the practical purpose of legislation refinements are of little importance. In any given age and nation virtue and vice have meanings which for that purpose are quite definite enough. In England at the present day many theories about morality are current, and speculative men differ about them widely, but they relate not so much to the question whether particular acts are right or wrong, as to the question of the precise meaning of the distinction, the manner in which the moral character of particular actions is to be decided, and the reasons for preferring right to wrong conduct. The result is that the object of promoting virtue and preventing vice must be admitted to be both a good one and one sufficiently intelligible for legislative purposes.

If this is so, the only remaining questions will be as to the efficiency of the means at the disposal of society for this purpose, and the cost of their application. Society has at its disposal two great instruments by which vice may be prevented and virtue promoted—namely, law and public opinion; and law is either criminal or civil. The use of each of these instruments is subject to certain limits and conditions, and the wisdom of attempting to make men good either by Act of Parliament or by the action of public opinion depends entirely upon the degree in which those limits and conditions are recognized and acted upon.

First, I will take the case of criminal law. What are the conditions under which and the limitations within which it can be applied with success to the object of making men better? In considering this question it must be borne in mind that criminal law is at once by far the most powerful and by far the roughest engine which society can use for any purpose. Its power is shown by the fact that it can and does render crime exceedingly difficult and dangerous. Indeed, in civilized society it absolutely prevents avowed open crime committed with the strong hand, except in cases where crime rises to the magnitude of civil war. Its roughness hardly needs illustration. It strikes so hard that it can be enforced only on the gravest occasions, and with every sort of precaution against abuse or mistake. Before an act can be treated as a crime, it ought to be capable of distinct definition and of specific proof, and it ought also to be of such a nature that it is worthwhile to prevent it at the risk of inflicting great damage, direct and indirect, upon those who commit it. These conditions are seldom, if ever, fulfilled by mere vices. It would obviously be impossible to indict a man for ingratitude or perfidy. Such charges are too vague for specific discussion and distinct proof on the one side, and disproof on the other. Moreover, the expense of the investigations necessary for the legal punishment of such conduct would be enormous. It would be necessary to go into an infinite number of delicate and subtle inquiries which would tear off all privacy from the lives of a large number of persons. These considerations are, I think, conclusive reasons against treating vice in general as a crime.

The excessive harshness of criminal law is also a circumstance which very greatly narrows the range of its application. It is the *ratio ultima* of the majority against persons whom its application assumes to have renounced the common bonds which connect men together. When a man is subjected to legal punishment, society appeals directly and exclusively to his fears. It renounces the attempt to work upon his affections or feelings. In other words, it puts itself into distinct, harsh, and undisguised opposition to his wishes; and the effect of this will be to make him rebel against the law. The violence of the rebellion will be measured partly by the violence of the passion the indulgence of which is forbidden, and partly by the degree to which the law can count upon an ally in the man's own conscience. A law which enters into a direct contest with a fierce imperious passion, which the person who feels it does not admit to be bad, and which is not directly injurious to others, will generally do more harm than good; and this is perhaps the principal reason why it is impossible to legislate directly against unchastity, unless it takes forms which everyone regards as monstrous and horrible. The subject is not one for detailed discussion, but anyone who will follow out the reflections which this hint suggests will find that they supply a striking illustration of the limits which the harshness of criminal law imposes upon its range.

If we now look at the different acts which satisfy the conditions specified, it will, I think, be found that criminal law in this country actually is applied to the suppression of vice and so to the promotion of virtue to a very considerable extent; and this I say is right.

The punishment of common crimes, the gross forms of force and fraud, is no doubt ambiguous. It may be justified on the principle of self-protection, and apart from any question as to their moral character. It is not, however, difficult to show that these acts have in fact been forbidden and subjected to punishment not only because they are dangerous to society, and so ought to be prevented, but also for the sake of gratifying the feeling of hatred—call it revenge, resentment, or what you will—which the contemplation of such conduct excites in healthily constituted minds. If this can be shown, it will follow that criminal law is in the nature of a persecution of the grosser forms of vice, and an emphatic assertion of the principle that the feeling of hatred and the desire of vengeance above-mentioned are important elements of human nature which ought in such cases to be satisfied in a regular public and legal manner.

The strongest of all proofs of this is to be found in the principles universally admitted and acted upon as regulating the amount of punishment. If vengeance affects, and ought to affect, the amount of punishment, every circumstance which aggravates or extenuates the wickedness of an act will operate in aggravation or diminution of punishment. If the object of legal punishment is simply the prevention of specific acts, this will not be the case. Circumstances which extenuate the wickedness of the crime will often operate in aggravation of punishment. If, as I maintain, both objects must be kept in view, such circumstances will operate in different ways according to the nature of the case.

A judge has before him two criminals, one of whom appears, from the circumstances of the case, to be ignorant and depraved, and to have given way to very strong temptation, under the influence of the other, who is a man of rank and education, and who committed the offence of which both are convicted under comparatively slight temptation. I will venture to say that if he made any difference between them at all every judge on the English bench would give the first man a lighter sentence than the second.

What should we think of such an address to the prisoners as this? 'You, A, are a most dangerous man. You are ignorant, you are depraved, and you are accordingly peculiarly liable to be led into crime by the solicitations or influence of people like your accomplice B. Such influences constitute to men like you a temptation practically all but irresistible. The class to which you belong is a large one, and is accessible only to the coarsest possible motives. For these reasons I must put into the opposite scale as heavy a weight as I can, and the sentence of the court upon you is that you be taken to the place from whence you came and from thence to a place of execution, and that there you be hanged by the neck till you are dead. As to you, B, you are undoubtedly an infamous wretch. Between you and your tool A there can, morally speaking, be no comparison at all. But I have nothing to do with that. You belong to a small and dangerous class. The temptation to which you gave way was slight, and the impression made upon me by your conduct is that you really did not care very much whether you committed this crime or not. From a moral point of view, this may perhaps increase your guilt; but it shows that the motive to be overcome is less powerful in your case than in A's. You belong, moreover, to a class, and occupy a position in society, in which exposure and loss of character are much dreaded. This you will have to undergo. Your case is a very odd one, and it is not likely that you will wish to commit such a crime again, or that others will follow your example. Upon the whole, I think that what has passed will deter others from such conduct as much as actual punishment. It is, however, necessary to keep a hold over you. You will therefore be discharged on your own recognizance to come up and receive judgment when called upon, and unless you conduct yourself better for the future, you will assuredly be so called upon, and if you do not appear, your recognizance will be inexorably forfeited.'

Caricature apart, the logic of such a view is surely unimpeachable. If all that you want of criminal law is the prevention of crime by the direct fear of punishment, the fact that a temptation is strong is a reason why punishment should be severe. In some instances this actually is the case. It shows the reason why political crimes and offences against military discipline are punished so severely. But in most cases the strength of the temptation operates in mitigation of punishment, and the reason of this is that criminal law operates not merely by producing fear, but also indirectly, but very powerfully, by giving distinct shape to the feeling of anger, and a distinct satisfaction to the desire of vengeance which crime excites in a healthy mind.

Other illustrations of the fact that English criminal law does recognize morality are to be found in the fact that a considerable number of acts which need not be specified are treated as crimes merely because they are regarded as grossly immoral.

I have already shown in what manner Mr. Mill deals with these topics. It is, I venture to think, utterly unsatisfactory. The impression it makes upon me is that he feels that such acts ought to be punished, and that he is able to reconcile this with his fundamental principles only by subtleties quite unworthy of him. Admit the relation for which I am contending between law and morals, and all becomes perfectly clear. All the acts referred to are unquestionably wicked. Those who do them are ashamed of them. They are all capable of being clearly defined and specifically proved or disproved, and there can be no question at all that legal punishment reduces them to small dimensions, and forces the criminals to carry on their practices with secrecy and precaution. In other words, the object of their suppression is good, and the means adequate. In practice this is subject to highly important qualifications, of which I will only say here that those who have due regard to the incurable weaknesses of human nature will be very careful how they inflict penalties upon mere vice, or even upon those who make a trade of promoting it, unless special circumstances call for their infliction. It is one thing however to tolerate vice so long as it is inoffensive, and quite another to give it a legal right not only to exist, but to assert itself in the face of the world as an 'experiment in living' as good as another, and entitled to the same protection from law.

I now pass to the manner in which civil law may and does, and as I say properly, promote virtue and prevent vice. This is a subject so wide that I prefer indicating its nature by a few illustrations to attempting to deal with it systematically. It would, however, be easy to show that nearly every branch of civil law assumes the existence of a standard of moral good and evil which the public at large have an interest in maintaining, and in many cases enforcing, a proceeding which is diametrically opposed to Mr. Mill's fundamental principles.*

The main subject with which law is conversant is that of rights and duties, and all the commoner and more important rights and duties presuppose some theory of morals. Contracts are one great source of rights and duties. Is there any country in the world the courts of which would enforce a contract which the Legislature regarded as immoral? and is there any country in which there would be much difficulty in specific cases in saying whether the object or the consideration of a contract was or was not immoral? Other rights are of a more general nature, and are liable to be violated by wrongs. Take the case of

---

*Mr. Morley says on this: 'A good deal of rather bustling ponderosity is devoted to proving that the actual laws do in many points assume the existence of a standard of moral good and evil, and that this proceeding is diametrically opposed to Mr. Mill's fundamental principles. To this one would say first that the actual existence of laws of any given kind is wholly irrelevant to Mr. Mill's contention, which is that it would be better if laws of such a kind did not exist. Secondly, Mr. Mill never says, nor is it at all essential to his doctrine to hold, that a government ought not to have a "standard of moral good and evil which the public at large have an interest in maintaining, and in many instances enforcing." He only set apart a certain class of cases to which the right or duty of enforcement of the criminal standard does not extend—self-regarding cases.'

As to the first point, surely it is not irrelevant to show that Mr. Mill is at issue with the practical conclusions to which most nations have been led by experience. Those to whom I address

a man's right to his reputation, which is violated by defamation. How, without the aid of some sort of theory of morals, can it be determined whether the publication of defamatory matter is justifiable or not?

Perhaps the most pointed of all illustrations of the moral character of civil law is to be found in the laws relating to marriage and inheritance. They all proceed upon an essentially moral theory as to the relation of the sexes. Take the case of illegitimate children. A bastard is *filius nullius*—he inherits nothing, he has no claim on his putative father. What is all this except the expression of the strongest possible determination on the part of the Legislature to recognize, maintain, and favour marriage in every possible manner as the foundation of civilized society? It has been plausibly maintained that these laws bear hardly upon bastards, punishing them for the sins of their parents. It is not necessary to my purpose to go into this, though it appears to me that the law is right. I make the remark merely for the sake of showing to what lengths the law does habitually go for the purpose of maintaining the most important of all moral principles, the principle upon which one great department of it is entirely founded. It is a case in which a good object is promoted by efficient and adequate means.

These illustrations are so strong that I will add nothing more to them from this branch of the law, but I may refer to a few miscellaneous topics which bear on the same subject. Let us take first the case of sumptuary laws. Mr. Mill's principles would no doubt condemn them, and, as they have gone out

---

myself may be disposed to doubt whether a principle which condemns so many of the institutions under which they live can be right.

As to the second point, Mr. Mill says in express words: 'Society, as society, has no right to decide anything to be wrong which concerns only the individual.' [This is a paraphrase of 99/296 L.] This I think is equivalent to denying that society ought to have a moral standard, for by a moral standard I understand a judgment that certain acts are wrong, whoever they concern. Whether they concern the agent only or others as well is and must be an accident. Mr. Morley, however, thinks that Mr. Mill's opinion was that society may and ought to have a moral standard, but ought not to enforce it in the case of self-regarding acts. I say, and attempt throughout the whole of this chapter to prove, that as regards the 'moral coercion of public opinion,' [13/223 L] this is neither possible nor desirable, and that as regards legal coercion, the question whether it is possible and desirable depends upon considerations drawn from the nature of law, civil and criminal. Whether I am right or wrong I cannot see that I have not understood Mr. Mill, or that I have not contradicted him.

of fashion, it may be said that unless my principle does so too, it is the worse for my principle. I certainly should not condemn sumptuary laws on the principle that the object in view is either bad or improper for legislation. I can hardly imagine a greater blessing to the whole community than a reduction in the lavish extravagance which makes life so difficult and laborious. It is difficult for me to look at a lace machine with patience. The ingenuity which went to devise it might have made human life materially happier in a thousand ways, and its actual effect has been to enable a great number of people to wear an imitation of an ornament which derives what little merit it has principally from its being made by hand. If anyone could practically solve the problem of securing the devotion of the higher forms of human ingenuity to objects worthy of them, he would be an immense benefactor to his species. Life, however, has become so complicated, vested interests are so powerful and so worthy of respect, it is so clear that the enforcement of any conceivable law upon such a subject would be impossible, that I do not think anyone in these days would be found to propose one. In a simpler age of the world and in a smaller community such laws may have been very useful. The same remarks apply to laws as to the distribution of property and to the regulation of trade.

Laws relating to education and to military service and the discipline of the army have a moral side of the utmost importance. Mr. Mill would be the first to admit this; indeed, in several passages of his book he insists on the fact that society has complete control over the rising generation as a reason why it should not coerce adults into morality. This surely is the very opposite of the true conclusion. How is it possible for society to accept the position of an educator unless it has moral principles on which to educate? How, having accepted that position and having educated people up to a certain point, can it draw a line at which education ends and perfect moral indifference begins? When a private man educates his family, his superiority over them is founded principally on his superior age and experience; and as this personal superiority ceases, the power which is founded upon it gradually ceases also. Between society at large and individuals the difference is of another kind. The fixed principles and institutions of society express not merely the present opinions of the ruling part of the community, but the accumulated results of centuries of experience, and these constitute a standard by which the conduct of individuals may be tried, and to which they are in a variety of ways, direct and indirect, compelled to conform. This, I think, is one of the meanings which may be attached to the assertion that education never ceases. As a child grows into a man, and as a young man grows into an old man, he is brought under the influence of successive sets of educators, each of whom sets its mark upon him. It is no uncommon thing to see aged parents taught by their grown-up children lessons learned by the children in their intercourse with their own generation. All of us are continually educating each other, and in every instance this is and must be a process at once moral and more or less coercive.*

As to Mr. Mill's doctrine that the coercive influence of public opinion ought to be exercised only for self-protective purposes, it seems to me a paradox so startling that it is almost impossible to argue against it. A single consideration on the subject is sufficient to prove this. The principle is one which it is impossible to carry out. It is like telling a rose that it ought to smell sweet only for the purpose of affording pleasure to the owner of the ground in which it grows. People form and express their opinions on each other, which, collectively, form public opinion, for a thousand reasons; to amuse themselves; for the sake of something to talk about; to gratify this or that momentary feeling; but the effect of such opinions, when formed, is quite independent of the grounds of their formation. A man is tried for murder, and just escapes conviction. People read the trial from curiosity; they discuss it for the sake of the discussion; but if, by whatever means, they are brought to think that the man was in all probability guilty, they shun his society as they would shun any other hateful thing. The opinion produces its effect in precisely the same way whatever was its origin.

The result of these observations is that both law and public opinion do in many cases exercise a powerful coercive influence on morals, for objects which are good in the sense explained above, and by means well calculated to attain

---

* Mr. Morley says in reference to this passage and the preceding passages from pp. 99–100: 'Mr. Stephen . . . proves the contradictory of assertions which his adversary never made, as when he cites judicial instances which imply the recognition of morality by the law.' I think Mr. Morley misunderstands my argument, which nevertheless appears to me very plain. It is simply this: I say laws can and do promote virtue and diminish vice by coercion in the cases and in the ways specified, and their interference does more good than harm. The contradictory of this proposition would be that in the cases specified legal interference does more harm than good. Surely if Mr. Mill's general principle is true, this must follow from it. Therefore in denying it I deny a necessary inference from the principle which I attack.

those objects, to a greater or less extent at a not inadequate expense. If this is so, I say law and public opinion do well, and I do not see how either the premisses or the conclusion are to be disproved.

Of course there are limits to the possibility of useful interference with morals, either by law or by public opinion; and it is of the highest practical importance that these limits should be carefully observed. The great leading principles on the subject are few and simple, though they cannot be stated with any great precision. It will be enough to mention the following:

1. Neither legislation nor public opinion ought to be meddlesome. A very large proportion of the matters upon which people wish to interfere with their neighbours are trumpery little things which are of no real importance at all. The busybody and world-betterer who will never let things alone, or trust people to take care of themselves, is a common and a contemptible character. The commonplaces directed against these small creatures are perfectly just, but to try to put them down by denying the connection between law and morals is like shutting all light and air out of a house in order to keep out gnats and blue-bottle flies.

2. Both legislation and public opinion, but especially the latter, are apt to be most mischievous and cruelly unjust if they proceed upon imperfect evidence. To form and express strong opinions about the wickedness of a man whom you do not know, the immorality or impiety of a book you have not read, the merits of a question on which you are uninformed, is to run a great risk of inflicting a great wrong. It is hanging first and trying afterwards, or more frequently not trying at all. This, however, is no argument against hanging after a fair trial.

3. Legislation ought in all cases to be graduated to the existing level of morals in the time and country in which it is employed. You cannot punish anything which public opinion, as expressed in the common practice of society, does not strenuously and unequivocally condemn. To try to do so is a sure way to produce gross hypocrisy and furious reaction. To be able to punish, a moral majority must be overwhelming. Law cannot be better than the nation in which it exists, though it may and can protect an acknowledged moral standard, and may gradually be increased in strictness as the standard rises. We punish, with the utmost severity, practices which in Greece and Rome went almost uncensured. It is possible that a time may come when it

may appear natural and right to punish adultery, seduction, or possibly even fornication, but the prospect is, at present, indefinitely remote, and it may be doubted whether we are moving in that direction.

4. Legislation and public opinion ought in all cases whatever scrupulously to respect privacy. To define the province of privacy distinctly is impossible, but it can be described in general terms. All the more intimate and delicate relations of life are of such a nature that to submit them to unsympathetic observation, or to observation which is sympathetic in the wrong way, inflicts great pain, and may inflict lasting moral injury. Privacy may be violated not only by the intrusion of a stranger, but by compelling or persuading a person to direct too much attention to his own feelings and to attach too much importance to their analysis. The common usage of language affords a practical test which is almost perfect upon this subject. Conduct which can be described as indecent is always in one way or another a violation of privacy.

There is one perfect illustration of this, of which I may say a few words. It is the case of the confessional and casuistry generally. So far as I have been able to look into the writings of casuists, their works appear to contain a spiritual penal code, in which all the sins of act and thought, of intention and imagination, which it is possible for men to commit, are described with legal minuteness and with specific illustrations, and are ranged under the two heads of mortal and venial, according as they subject the sinner to eternal damnation or only to purgatory. Nothing can exceed the interest and curiosity of some of the discussions conducted in these strange works, though some of them (by no means so large a proportion as popular rumour would suggest) are revolting. So far as my observation has gone, I should say that nothing can be more unjust than the popular notion that the casuists explained away moral obligations. Escobar in particular (Pascal's *bête noire*)[2] gives me rather the impression of a sort of half-humorous simplicity.*

2. In his *Provincial Letters*, Pascal criticizes Antonio Escobar y Mendoza (1589–1669), a Spanish casuist, for tending to inculcate a loose system of morals. See the edition of *Provincial Letters* translated by A. J. Krailsheimer for Penguin Books (London, 1967), pp. 97–98 (Letters V and VI).

*His habit of putting all his illustrations in the first person has a very strange effect. Here for instance is a catalogue of the mortal sins which an advocate may commit. 'Defendi litem injustam, seu minus probabilem, quando minimè poteram, et debebam de minori probabilitate consulentem admonere. Ob studii defectum falso de probabilitate causæ judicavi, quam improba-

The true objection to the whole system, and the true justification of the aversion with which it has been regarded, is that it is perhaps the greatest intrusion upon privacy, the most audacious and successful invasion by law of matters which lie altogether out of the reach of law, recorded in history. Of course if the postulate on which it is founded is true—if, in fact, there is a celestial penal code which classifies as felonies or misdemeanours punishable respectively with hell or purgatory all human sins—and if priests have the power of getting the felonies commuted into misdemeanours by confession and absolution—there is no more to be said; but this supposition need not be seriously considered. It is, I think, impossible to read the books in question without feeling convinced that a trial in a court which administers such laws upon evidence supplied exclusively by the criminal must be either a mere form, a delusion of a very mischievous kind, or a process which would destroy all the self-respect of the person submitted to it and utterly confuse all his notions of right and wrong, good and evil. That justice should be done without the fullest possible knowledge of every fact connected with every transgression is impossible. That every such fact should be recalled, analyzed, dwelt upon, weighed and measured, without in a great measure renewing the evil of the act itself, and blunting the conscience as to similar acts in future, seems equally impossible. That any one human creature should ever really strip his soul stark naked for the inspection of any other, and be able to hold up his head afterwards, is not, I suppose, impossible, because so many people profess to do it; but to lookers-on from the outside it is inconceivable.

The inference which I draw from this illustration is that there is a sphere, none the less real because it is impossible to define its limits, within which law and public opinion are intruders likely to do more harm than good. To try to

---

bilem omnino post studium rejicerem. Induxi partem ad pactum, cum nulla justitia inniti cognoscerem, et nihil ab altero posset exigi nisi parum aliquid quod fortasse daretur in vexationis redeptionem.' (I got my client too good terms in a compromise.) 'Plures causas quam discutere poteram suscepi' (I held briefs in too many committee-rooms at once.) 'Leges, statuta et ordinationes ignoravi' (I did not know all the local government acts), &c., &c.—Escobar, Theol. Mor. 286. The last appears to me to be a very hard law. It is difficult to imagine the state of mind of a man who really thought that he was authorised to declare as a part of the law of God that a lawyer who did not know all 'laws, statutes, and ordinances' would be eternally damned unless he repented.

regulate the internal affairs of a family, the relations of love or friendship, or many other things of the same sort, by law or by the coercion of public opinion, is like trying to pull an eyelash out of a man's eye with a pair of tongs. They may put out the eye, but they will never get hold of the eyelash.

These, I think, are the principal forms in which society can and actually does promote virtue and restrain vice. It is impossible to form any estimate of the degree in which it succeeds in doing so, but it may perhaps be said that the principal importance of what is done in this direction by criminal law is that in extreme cases it brands gross acts of vice with the deepest mark of infamy which can be impressed upon them, and that in this manner it protects the public and accepted standard of morals from being grossly and openly violated. In short, it affirms in a singularly emphatic manner a principle which is absolutely inconsistent with and contradictory to Mr. Mill's—the principle, namely, that there are acts of wickedness so gross and outrageous that, self-protection apart, they must be prevented as far as possible at any cost to the offender, and punished, if they occur, with exemplary severity.

As for the influence of public opinion upon virtue and vice, it is incalculably great, but it is difficult to say much as to its extent, because its influence is indefinite, and is shown in an infinite variety of ways. It must also be observed that, though far more powerful and minute than the influence of law, it is infinitely less well instructed. It is also exceedingly liable to abuse, for public opinion is multiform, and may mean the gossip of a village or the spite of a coterie, as well as the deliberate judgment of a section of the rational part of mankind. On the other hand, its power depends on its nature and on the nature of the person on whom it acts. A calm, strong, and rational man will know when to despise and when to respect it, though no rules can be laid down on the subject. It is, however, clear that this much may be said of it in general. If people neither formed nor expressed any opinions on their neighbours' conduct except in so far as that conduct affected them personally, one of the principal motives to do well and one of the principal restraints from doing ill would be withdrawn from the world.

I have now said what I had to say on the action of law and of public opinion in regard to the encouragement of virtue and the prevention of vice; and I hope I have shown that the object is one which they can and do promote in a variety of ways, the expense of which, if indeed it is to be regarded as an expense at all, is by no means disproportioned to the importance of the object in view.

Before taking leave of this part of the subject, I will make some observations upon a topic closely connected with it—I mean the compulsion which is continually exercised by men over each other in the sternest of all possible shapes—war and conquest. The effects of these processes upon all that interests men as such can hardly be overrated. War and conquest determine all the great questions of politics and exercise a nearly decisive influence in many cases upon religion and morals. We are what we are because Holland and England in the sixteenth century defeated Spain, and because Gustavus Adolphus and others successfully resisted the Empire in Northern Germany. Popular prejudice and true political insight agree in feeling and thinking that the moral and religious issues decided at Sadowa and Sedan were more important than the political issues. Here, then, we have compulsion on a giant scale producing vast and durable political, moral, and religious effects. Can its good and evil, its right and wrong, be measured by the single simple principle that it is good when required for purposes of self-protection, otherwise not?

I have more than once referred in passing to this great question. I have already pointed out in general terms the practical impossibility of applying Mr. Mill's principle to it. The preceding observations enable me to enter upon it more fully. First, then, I would observe that, as has already been shown, struggles in different shapes are inseparable from life itself as long as men are interested in each other's proceedings, and are actuated by conflicting motives and views. The great art of life lies not in avoiding these struggles, but in conducting them with as little injury as may be to the combatants, who are, after all, rather friends than enemies, and without attaching an exaggerated importance to the object of contention. In short, toleration is in its proper sphere so long as its object is to mitigate inevitable struggles. It becomes excessive and irrational if and in so far as it aims at the complete suppression of these struggles, and so tends to produce a state of indifference and isolation, which would be the greatest of all evils if it could be produced.

In a very large proportion of cases—it may perhaps be said in the great majority of cases—these conflicts can be carried on without resorting to physical force. In each society taken by itself the class of cases in which the use of physical force is necessary is determined by the range of criminal law, and the principle that criminal law ought to be employed only for the prevention of acts of force or fraud which injure others than the agent may be accepted as a rough practical rule, which may generally be acted upon, though, as I have shown, it is no more than a practical rule, and even in that character is subject to numerous exceptions.

When, however, we come to consider the relations of independent nations to each other, a totally different set of considerations present themselves. Nations have no common superior. Their relations do not admit of being defined with the accuracy which the application of criminal law requires, nor if they were so defined would it be possible to specify or to inflict the sanctions of criminal law. The result of this is that nations always do consider for themselves in every particular case as it arises how their interests are to be asserted and protected, and whether or not at the expense of war. Even in the case of such references to arbitration as we have lately seen this is true. The arbitrators derive their whole authority from the will of the parties, and their award derives its authority from the same source.

Such being the relations between nation and nation, all history, and especially all modern history, shows that what happens in one nation affects other nations powerfully and directly. Indeed, the question what a nation is to be— how much or how little territory, how many or how few persons it is to comprehend—depends largely on the state of other nations. A territory more or less compact, inhabited by a population more or less homogeneous, is what we mean by a nation; but how is it to be determined where the lines are to be drawn? Who is to say whether the Rhine or the Vosges is to divide France from Germany?—whether the English and the Welsh, the Scotch and the Irish, are or are not homogeneous enough to form one body politic? To these questions one answer only can be truly given, and that is, Force, in the widest sense of the word, must decide the question. By this I mean to include moral, intellectual, and physical force, and the power and attractiveness of the beliefs and ideas by which different nations are animated. All great wars are to a greater or less extent wars of principle and sentiment; all great conquests embrace more or less of a moral element. Given such ideas as those of Protestants and Catholics in the sixteenth century suddenly seizing upon the nations of Europe, religious wars were inevitable, and in estimating their character we must take into account not merely the question, Who was on the offensive? Who struck the first blow? but much more the question, Which of the conflicting theories of life, which of the opposing principles brought into collision, was the noblest, the truest, the best fitted for the development of the powers of human nature, most in harmony with the facts which surround and constitute human life?

The most pointed and instructive modern illustration of this that can possibly be given is supplied by the great American civil war. Who, looking at the matter dispassionately, can fail to perceive the vanity and folly of the attempt to decide the question between the North and the South by lawyers' metaphysics about the true nature of sovereignty or by conveyancing subtleties about the meaning of the Constitution and the principles on which written documents ought to be interpreted? You might as well try to infer the fortunes of a battle from the shape of the firearms. The true question is, What was the real gist and essence of the dispute? What were the two sides really fighting for? Various answers may be given to these questions which I need neither specify nor discuss, but the answer to them which happens to be preferred will, I think, settle conclusively the question which way the sympathies of the person who accepts that answer should go.

It seems, then, that compulsion in its most formidable shape and on the most extensive scale—the compulsion of war—is one of the principles which lie at the root of national existence. It determines whether nations are to be and what they are to be. It decides what men shall believe, how they shall live, in what mould their religion, law, morals, and the whole tone of their lives shall be cast. It is the *ratio ultima* not only of kings, but of human society in all its shapes. It determines precisely, for one thing, how much and how little individual liberty is to be left to exist at any specific time and place.

From this great truth flow many consequences, some of which I have already referred to. They may all be summed up in this one, that power precedes liberty—that liberty, from the very nature of things, is dependent upon power; and that it is only under the protection of a powerful, well-organized, and intelligent government that any liberty can exist at all.

I will not insist further upon this, but I would point out that the manner in which war is conducted is worthy of much greater attention than it has received, as illustrating the character and limits of the struggles of civil life. The points to be noticed are two. In the first place, in war defeat after fair fight inflicts no disgrace, and the cheerful acceptance of defeat is in many cases the part of honourable and high-spirited men. Not many years ago an account was published of a great review held by the Emperor of Russia. Schamyl, who had so long defied him in the Caucasus, was said to have come forward and declared that as the Emperor had had no more obstinate enemy, so he should now have no more faithful subject than himself, that he saw that it was God's will that Russia should rule, and that he knew how to submit himself to the will of God. If the story was true and the speech sincere, it was the speech of a wise, good, and brave man.

In the second place, though war is the very sternest form of coercion which can be devised, and though the progress of civilization makes wars more and more coercive as time goes on, there is at all times some recognition of the principle that they are not to be carried beyond certain bounds—a principle which continually tends to assert itself with increasing vigour and distinctness. The laws of war, as they are called, show that even in that extreme case of collision of interests there are ties of good feeling which lie deeper than the enmity, and are respected in spite of it. War is the ultimate limitation upon freedom. From war downwards to the most friendly discussion on a question which must ultimately be decided one way or another, there is an infinite series of degrees each of which differs from the rest, and each of which constitutes a distinct shade of coercion, a definite restraint upon liberty. In most of these instances anything which can be described as self-protection plays an inappreciably small part, if it plays any.

So far I have been considering the theory about liberty advanced by Mr. Mill, who is beyond all comparison the most influential and also the most reasonable of its advocates—I might say its worshippers. Mr. Mill, however, is far too rational to be taken as an exponent of the popular sentiment upon the subject, and upon this popular sentiment I should like to make some observations. It is always difficult to criticize sentiments, because they are so indeterminate and shifting that to argue against them is like firing a gun at a cloud. The words 'liberty' and 'freedom' are used by enthusiastic persons in all sorts of ways. Freedom sometimes means simply victory. It sometimes means a government which puts the restraints in the right place, and leaves men free to do well. This is obviously the Freedom of which Mr. Tennyson finely speaks as the

> Grave mother of majestic works
> From her isle altar gazing down,
> Who godlike grasps the triple forks
> And kinglike wears the crown.[3]

Freedom often means authority, as when Roman Catholic archbishops talk of the freedom or liberty of the Church, and when Lord Clarendon (I think) speaks of the kings of England as being 'as free and absolute as any kings in the world.'

No way of using the word, however, is so common as when it is used to signify popular government. People who talk of liberty mean, as a general rule, democracy or some kind of government which stands rather nearer to democracy than the one under which they are living. This, generally speaking, is the Continental sense of the word. Now democracy has, as such, no definite or assignable relation to liberty. The degree in which the governing power interferes with individuals depends upon the size of the country, the closeness with which people are packed, the degree in which they are made conscious by actual experience of their dependence upon each other, their national temper, and the like. The form of the government has very little to do with the matter.

It would, of course, be idle to suppose that you can measure the real importance of the meaning of a popular cry by weighing it in logical scales. To understand the popular enthusiasm about liberty, something more is wanted than the bare analysis of the word. In poetry and popular and pathetic language of every kind liberty means both more and less than the mere absence of restraint. It means the absence of those restraints which the person using the words regards as injurious, and it generally includes more or less distinctly a positive element as well—namely, the presence of some distinct original power acting unconstrainedly in a direction which the person using the word regards as good. When used quite generally, and with reference to the present

3. Alfred Lord Tennyson, "Of Old Sat Freedom on the Heights," in *The Works of Tennyson*, ed. Hallam, Lord Tennyson. The Ebersley Edition, 9 vols. (New York: AMS Press, 1970), 1:241.

state of the political and moral world, liberty means something of this sort: The forward impulses, the energies of human nature are good; they were regarded until lately as bad, and they are now in the course of shaking off trammels of an injurious kind which had in former ages been imposed upon them.* The cry for liberty, in short, is a general condemnation of the past and an act of homage to the present in so far as it differs from the past, and to the future in so far as its character can be inferred from the character of the present.

If it be asked, What is to be thought of liberty in this sense of the word, the answer would obviously involve a complete discussion of all the changes in the direction of the diminution of authority which have taken place in modern times, and which may be expected hereafter as their consequence. Such an inquiry, of course, would be idle, to say nothing of its being impossible. A few remarks may, however, be made on points of the controversy which are continually left out of sight.

The main point is that enthusiasm for liberty in this sense is hardly compatible with anything like a proper sense of the importance of the virtue of obedience, discipline in its widest sense. The attitude of mind engendered by continual glorification of the present time, and of successful resistance to an authority assumed to be usurped and foolish, is almost of necessity fatal to the recognition of the fact that to obey a real superior, to submit to a real necessity and make the best of it in good part, is one of the most important of all virtues—a virtue absolutely essential to the attainment of anything great and lasting. Everyone would admit this when stated in general terms, but the gift of recognizing the necessity for acting upon the principle when the case actually arises is one of the rarest in the world. To be able to recognize your superior, to know whom you ought to honour and obey, to see at what point resistance ceases to be honourable, and submission in good faith and without

---

*On this passage, extending to p. 116, Mr. Morley observes that you do not condemn the past by recognizing the fact that its institutions are unsuited for the present, and that I write as if 'the old forms had not been disorganised by internal decrepitude' previously to the growth of those commonplaces about liberty, which, as I say, have 'shattered to pieces' the old forms of discipline. He says Mr. Stephen 'is one of those absolute thinkers who bring to the problems of society the methods of geometry.'

This is rather an inversion of parts. The very thing of which I complain in this passage is the accent of triumph and passion with which the word 'liberty' is generally used, so as to suggest that every restraint is oppressive. A calm statement of the advantages and disadvantages of

mental reservation becomes the part of courage and wisdom, is supremely difficult. All that can be said about these topics on the speculative side goes a very little way. It is like the difficulty which everyone who has had any experience of the administration of justice will recognize as its crowning difficulty, the difficulty of knowing when to believe and when to disbelieve a direct assertion on a matter of importance made by a person who has the opportunity of telling a lie if he is so minded.

In nearly every department of life we are brought at last by long and laborious processes, which due care will usually enable us to perform correctly, face to face with some ultimate problem where logic, analogy, experiment, all the apparatus of thought, fail to help us, but on the value of our answer to which their value depends. The questions, Shall I or shall I not obey this man? accept this principle? submit to this pressure? and the like, are of the number. No rule can help towards their decision; but when they are decided, the answer determines the whole course and value of the life of the man who gave it. Practically, the effect of the popularity of the commonplaces about liberty has been to raise in the minds of ordinary people a strong presumption against obeying anybody, and by a natural rebound to induce minds of another class to obey the first person who claims their obedience with sufficient emphasis and self-confidence. It has shattered to pieces most of the old forms in which discipline was a recognized and admitted good, and certainly it has not produced many new ones.

The practical inference from this is that people who have the gift of using pathetic language ought not to glorify the word 'liberty' as they do, but ought, as far as possible, to ask themselves before going into ecstasies over any particular case of it, Who is left at liberty to do what, and what is the restraint from which he is liberated? By forcing themselves to answer this question dis-

particular institutions, and of the degree in which they are adapted to the present state of the world, is always good; but, as far as my experience goes, I should say that for one such utterance before the public in which the word 'liberty' is used, fifty or more are coloured by rhetorical exaggeration, condemnation of all restraints as restraints, and of the past as the past. The gist of this passage is to show that such language is hollow bombast, and that what Mr. Morley calls the historical method, that is, the unimpassioned discussion of the special effects and objects of each particular restraint, is the only true one.

tinctly, they will give their poetry upon the subject a much more definite and useful turn than it has at present.

Of course these remarks apply, as all such remarks must, in opposite directions. When liberty is exalted as such, we may be sure that there will always be those who are opposed to liberty as such, and who take pleasure in dwelling upon the weak side of everything which passes by the name. These persons should ask themselves the converse questions before they glorify acts of power: Who is empowered to do what, and by what means? or, if the words chosen for eulogy are 'order' and 'society,' it would be well for them to ask themselves, What order and what sort of society it is to which their praises refer?

In illustration of these remarks, I would refer to the works of two remarkable writers, Mr. Buckle and De Maistre. They form as complete a contrast as could be found in literary history. Each is a Manichee—a believer in Arimanes and Oromasdes, a good principle and a bad one; but Mr. Buckle's Arimanes, the past, the backward impulse, is De Maistre's Oromasdes; and De Maistre's Arimanes, the present, the forward impulse, is Mr. Buckle's Oromasdes. Mr. Buckle generalizes all history as consisting in a perpetual struggle between the spirit of scepticism, which is progress and civilization, and the spirit of protection, which is darkness and error.[4] De Maistre does not draw out his opposition so pointedly; but in his opinion the notion of progress, the belief that the history of mankind is the history of a series of continual changes for the better, from barbarism up to modern civilization, is the 'erreur mère' of these days. His own belief (very cloudily expressed) is that in ancient times men had a direct vision of truth of all sorts, and were able to take the *a priori* road to knowledge. It is impossible in a few lines to do, or attempt to do, justice to De Maistre's strange and versatile genius. For the purpose of my illustration, therefore, I will confine myself to Mr. Buckle, whose works are much better known in this country and whose theories are more definite. I mention De Maistre merely for the sake of the remark that if it were worthwhile to do so, the converse of the observations which I am about to make on Mr. Buckle might be made upon him.

4. Stephen is referring to Henry Thomas Buckle's (1821–1862) *History of Civilization in England* (1857–61), which he reviewed in *Edinburgh Review* vol. 107 (1858) and vol. 114 (1861).

It seems to me, then, that Mr. Buckle's ardent advocacy of scepticism and his utter condemnation of what he calls the spirit of protection is much as if a man should praise the centrifugal at the expense of the centripetal force, and revile the latter as a malignant power striving to drag the earth into the sun. It would be just as reasonable to reply, No, you, the centrifugal force, are the eternal enemy. You want to hurl the world madly through space into cold and darkness, and would do it, too, if our one friend the centripetal force did not persist in drawing it back towards the source of light and heat. The obvious truth is that the earth's orbit is a resultant, and that whatever credit it deserves must be rateably divided between its two constituent elements.

It surprises me that people should be enthusiastic either about the result or about either of the causes which have contributed to its production. As to the general result, what is it? Say, roughly, three hundred million Chinese, two hundred million natives of India, two hundred million Europeans and North Americans, and a miscellaneous hundred million or two—Central Asians, Malays, Borneans, Javanese, South Sea Islanders, and all sorts and conditions of blacks; and, over and above all the rest, the library at the British Museum. This is the net result of an indefinitely long struggle between the forces of men, and the weights of various kinds in the attempt to move which these forces display themselves. Enthusiasts for progress are to me strange enough. 'Glory, glory: the time is coming when there will be six hundred million Chinese, five hundred million Hindoos, four hundred million Europeans, and Heaven only knows how many hundred million blacks of various shades, and when there will be two British Museums, each with a library. "Ye unborn ages, crowd not on my soul."' This appears to me a very strange psalm, but it becomes infinitely stranger when a fiercer note is sounded: 'Yea, verily, and but for the accursed restraints imposed by tyrants on the powers of man, there would now have been eight hundred million Chinese, seven hundred million Hindoos, and so on in proportion, all alive and kicking, and making this world of ours like a Stilton cheese run away with by its own mites.' To the first enthusiast I feel inclined to say, There is no accounting for tastes. To the second, You are unjust. Your cheese-mites owe their existence not merely to impulse, but to that which resisted it. The cheese confined while it fed them. Disembody force, divorce it from matter and friction, in a word set it free, and it ceases to exist. It is a *chimæra bombinans in vacuo*.

If we apply these generalities to the more limited and yet, in comparison to our capacity, boundless field of political history, it surely needs little proof that, whatever our present condition may be worth, we are what we are (to use Mr. Buckle's terms) by virtue of protection as well as by virtue of scepticism. If a stream of water flows down a hill, the amount of fluid delivered at a given point depends upon the friction of the sides and bottom of the channel as well as upon the force of gravitation. It is quite true that since the seventeenth century—to go no farther back—the Puritan, the Whig, and the Radical have been more successful than the Cavalier, the Tory, and the Conservative; but the existing state of society is the result of each set of efforts, not of either set by itself, and certainly not the result of the forward effort by itself. Unless a man is prepared to say that all the existing evils of society are due to our having moved too slowly—that the clock is wrong solely because it has a pendulum, and that to take off the pendulum and allow the weights to pull the wheels round with no restriction at all will ensure universal happiness— he has no right to regard the forward impulse as an unmixed good. It appears to me that the *erreur mère,* so to speak, of most modern speculations on political subjects lies in the fact that nearly every writer is an advocate of one out of many forces, which, as they act in different directions, must and do come into collision and produce a resultant according to the direction of which life is prosperous or otherwise.

The same doctrine may be stated in less abstract terms as follows: There are a number of objects the attainment of which is desirable for men, and which collectively may be called good, happiness, or whatever else you please so long as some word is used which sufficiently marks the fact that there is a real standard towards which human conduct must be directed, if the wishes which prompt us to action, and which are the deepest part of our nature—which are, indeed, our very selves in the attitude of wishing—are to be satisfied. These objects are very numerous. They cannot be precisely defined, and they are far from being altogether consistent with each other. Health is one of them. Wealth, to the extent of such a command of material things as enables men to use their faculties vigorously, is another. Knowledge is a third. Fit opportunities for the use of the faculties is a fourth. Virtue, the state in which given sets of faculties are so related to each other as to produce good results (whatever good may mean), is the most important and the most multiform and intricate of all. Reasonable men pursue these objects or some of them openly and avowedly. They find that they can greatly help or impede each other in the pursuit by exciting each other's hopes or fears, by promising payment for this and threatening punishment for that, and by leaving other matters to individual taste. This last department of things is the department of liberty in the proper sense of the word. Binding promises and threats always imply restraint. Thus the question, How large ought the province of liberty to be? is really identical with this: In what respects must men influence each other if they want to attain the objects of life, and in what respects must they leave each other uninfluenced?

If the object is to criticize and appreciate historical events, the question between liberty and law, scepticism and protection, and the like, will have to be stated thus: What are the facts? Which of them were caused, and to what extent, by the influence of men on each other's hopes and fears? Which of them were caused by the unrestrained and unimpelled impulses of individuals towards particular objects? How far did each class of results contribute to the attainment of the objects of life? To ask these questions is to show that they cannot be answered. Discussions about liberty are in truth discussions about a negation. Attempts to solve the problems of government and society by such discussions are like attempts to discover the nature of light and heat by inquiries into darkness and cold. The phenomenon which requires and will repay study is the direction and nature of the various forces, individual and collective, which in their combination or collision with each other and with the outer world make up human life. If we want to know what ought to be the size and position of a hole in a water pipe, we must consider the nature of water, the nature of pipes, and the objects for which the water is wanted; but we shall learn very little by studying the nature of holes. Their shape is simply the shape of whatever bounds them. Their nature is merely to let the water pass, and it seems to me that enthusiasm about them is altogether thrown away.[5]

---

5. Lon L. Fuller (1902–78), the important philosopher of law, cites this passage as being of great significance in understanding the nature of liberty. See his "Means and Ends," in *The Principles of Social Order: Selected Essays of Lon L. Fuller*, ed. Kenneth I. Winston (Durham, NC: Duke University Press, 1981), p. 59.

The result is that discussions about liberty are either misleading or idle, unless we know who wants to do what, by what restraint he is prevented from doing it, and for what reasons it is proposed to remove that restraint.

Bearing these explanations in mind, I may now observe that the democratic motto involves a contradiction. If human experience proves anything at all, it proves that, if restraints are minimized, if the largest possible measure of liberty is accorded to all human beings, the result will not be equality but inequality reproducing itself in a geometrical ratio. Of all items of liberty, none is either so important or so universally recognized as the liberty of acquiring property. It is difficult to see what liberty you leave to a man at all if you restrict him in this matter. When Lord Byron called Sir Walter Scott 'Apollo's mercenary son,' Sir Walter replied, 'God help the bear who may not lick his own paws.' All private property springs from labour for the benefit of the labourer; and private property is the very essence of inequality.

Assume that every man has a right to be on an equality with every other man because all are so closely connected together that the results of their labour should be thrown into a common stock out of which they are all to be maintained, and you certainly give a very distinct sense to Equality and Fraternity, but you must absolutely exclude Liberty. Experience has proved that this is not merely a theoretical but also a practical difficulty. It is the standing and insuperable obstacle to all socialist schemes, and it explains their failure.

The only manner in which the famous Republican device can be rendered at once fully intelligible and quite consistent is by explaining Liberty to mean Democracy. The establishment of a Democratic government, which proposes to recognize the universal brotherhood of mankind by an equal distribution of property, is as definite a scheme as it is possible to imagine, and when the motto is used in real earnest and not as a piece of meretricious brag, this is what is does mean. When so used the words 'or death' should be added to the motto to give it perfect completeness. Put together and interpreted in the manner stated, these five words constitute a complete political system, describing with quite sufficient distinctness for all practical purposes the nature of the political constitution to be established, the objects to which it is to be directed, and the penalty under which its commands are to be obeyed. It is a system which embodies in its most intense form all the bitterness and resentment which can possibly be supposed to be stored up in the hearts of the most disappointed envious and ferociously revengeful members of the human race against those whom they regard as their oppressors. It is the poor saying to the rich, We are masters now by the establishment of liberty, which means democracy, and as all men are brothers, entitled to share and share alike in the common stock, we will make you disgorge or we will put you to death. It is needless to say more about this doctrine than that those who are attracted by the Republican motto would do well to ask themselves whether they understand by it anything short of this? and, if so, where and on what principle they draw the line. I think anyone who has mind enough to understand the extreme complexity of the problem will see that the motto contributes either far too much or else nothing whatever towards its solution.

I have now said what I had to say about liberty, and I may briefly sum up the result. It is that if the word 'liberty' has any definite sense attached to it, and if it is consistently used in that sense, it is almost impossible to make any true general assertion whatever about it, and quite impossible to regard it either as a good thing or a bad one. If, on the other hand, the word is used merely in a general popular way without attaching any distinct signification to it, it is easy to make almost any general assertion you please about it; but these assertions will be incapable of either proof or disproof as they will have no definite meaning. Thus the word is either a misleading appeal to passion, or else it embodies or rather hints at an exceedingly complicated assertion, the truth of which can be proved only by elaborate historical investigations. 'The cause of liberty, for which Hampden died on the field and Sydney on the scaffold,' means either that Hampden and Sydney *were right* in resisting Charles I and Charles II, respectively, or else merely that they *did as a fact* die in resisting those kings. The first assertion obviously requires, before it can be accepted, a full account of all the circumstances by way of proof. The second tells us nothing worth knowing except a bare matter of fact, and would be consistent with Hampden's having been shot when trying to rob on the highway and Sydney's having been hanged for highway robbery.

This may appear to be quibbling, but I believe that it will be found on examination to be no more than an illustration, and a very important one, of the first condition of accurate and careful thought—the precise definition of fundamental terms. Men have an all but incurable propensity to try to prejudge all the great questions which interest them by stamping their prejudices upon their language. Law, in many cases, means not only a command, but a beneficent command. Liberty means not the bare absence of restraint, but the absence of injurious restraint. Justice means not mere impartiality in applying general rules to particular cases, but impartiality in applying beneficent general rules to particular cases. Some people half consciously use the word 'true' as meaning useful as well as true. Of course language can never be made absolutely neutral and colourless; but unless its ambiguities are understood, accuracy of thought is impossible, and the injury done is proportionate to the logical force and general vigour of character of those who are misled. Not long ago Mr. Mill gave an important illustration of this. A political association forwarded to him some manifesto of their views, in which appeared the phrase 'the Revolution,' used in the sense in which French writers are accustomed to use it. Mr. Mill very properly replied that the expression thus used was bad English. 'The Revolution,' he said, always means in English some particular revolution, just as 'the man' always means some particular man. To talk of the English or the French Revolution is proper, but to talk of the Revolution generally is to darken counsel by words, which, in fact, are only the names of certain intellectual phantoms. He advised his correspondents to seek their political objects without introducing into English phraseology one of the worst characteristics of Continental phraseology, and without depriving it of one of the most valuable of its own characteristics. The advice was admirable, but ought not Mr. Mill to have remembered it himself in writing as he does about liberty?

It requires no great experience to see that, as a rule, people advance both in speculation and in politics principles of very great generality for the purpose of establishing some practical conclusion of a comparatively narrow kind, and this, I think, is the case in this discussion about liberty. What specific thing is there which anyone is prevented from doing, either by law or by public opinion, which any sensible person would wish to do? The true answer to this is that thirteen years ago a certain number of persons were, to a certain extent, deterred from expressing a disbelief in common religious opinions by the consciousness that their views were unpopular, and that the expression of them might injure their prospects in life. I have already said what I had to say on this, and need not return to it. As to legislation intended to discourage vice, I do not believe that anyone would succeed in getting himself listened to if he were to say plainly, 'I admit that this measure will greatly discourage and diminish drunkenness and licentiousness. I also admit that it will involve no cruelty, no interference with privacy—nothing that can in itself be described as an inadequate price for the promotion of sobriety or chastity. I oppose it on the broad, plain ground that if people like to get drunk and lead dissolute lives, no one else ought to interfere. I advocate liberty—to wit, the liberty of a set of lads and girls to get drunk of an evening at a particular house of entertainment specially provided for that and other purposes; and though I own that that evil can be prevented by fining the person who keeps the house 5l., the sacred principles of liberty forbid it, at least as regards people over twenty-one. Virtue up to twenty-one knows no compromise, but we must draw the line somewhere, and when the twenty-first birthday is passed liberty claims her prey, and I concede the demand. "Fiat libertas ruat justitia."' I think the public would say to such a speech, You and liberty may settle the matter as you please, but we see our way to a measure which will do no harm to anyone, and which will keep both young fools and old fools out of harm's way. If freedom does not like it, let her go and sit on the heights self-gathered in her prophet mind, and send the fragments of her mighty voice rolling down the wind. She will be better employed in spouting poetry on the rocks of the Matterhorn than in patronizing vice on the flags of the Haymarket.

CHAPTER FIVE

EQUALITY

The second great article of the modern creed which I have undertaken to examine is Equality. It is at once the most emphatic and the least distinct of the three doctrines of which that creed is composed. It may mean that all men should be equally subject to the laws which relate to all. It may mean that law should be impartially administered. It may mean that all the advantages of society, all that men have conquered from nature, should be thrown into one common stock, and equally divided amongst them. It may be, and I think it is in a vast number of cases, nothing more than a vague expression of envy on the part of those who have not against those who have, and a vague aspiration towards a state of society in which there should be fewer contrasts than there are at present between one man's lot and another's. All this is so vague and unsatisfactory that it is difficult to reduce it to a form definite enough for discussion. It is impossible to argue against a sentiment otherwise than by repeating commonplaces which are not likely to convince those to whom they are addressed if they require convincing, and which are not needed by those who are convinced already.

In order to give colour and distinctness to what is to be said on the one side, it is necessary to find distinct statements on the other. The clearest statement of the doctrine of equality with which I am acquainted is to be found in Bentham's 'Principles of Morals and Legislation.'* It consists principally of an

*Dumont's *Traités de Législation*, vol. i, pp. 180–191, ed. 1830.[1]

1. This work, which was edited by Etienne Dumont from a manuscript in English which he then translated into French, first appeared in English translation as: Jeremy Bentham, *Theory of Legislation*, trans. R. Hildreth (London: Trübner, 1864). Stephen reviewed this English language edition: see *Horae Sabbaticae*, vol. 3, pp. 210–29.

expansion of the principle that a given quantity of the material of happiness will produce the largest amount of actual happiness when it is so divided that each portion of it bears the largest possible ratio to the existing happiness of those to whom it is given. This, however, is subject to the remark that you may cut it up so small that the parts are worthless. To give a hundred pounds apiece to ten people, each of whom possesses a hundred pounds, doubles the wealth of ten people. To give a thousand pounds to a man who has already a thousand pounds doubles the wealth of only one person. To give a farthing to every one of 960,000 persons is to waste 1,000*l*. This argument no doubt shows that in so far as happiness depends on the possession of wealth by persons similarly situated in other respects, it is promoted rather by a general high level of comfort than by excessive accumulations of wealth in individual hands; but this is really a barren truth. It might be important if some benefactor of the human race were to wake one morning with his pockets stuffed full of money which he wished to distribute so as to produce a maximum of enjoyment, but it has very little relation to the state of the world as we know it. Moreover, Bentham's whole conception of happiness as something which could, as it were, be served out in rations, is open to great objection, though his way of using it gave extraordinary force and distinctness to his views on many important topics.

Upon this subject Mr. Mill has put forward a theory which, if not quite so simple or so perfectly distinct as his view about liberty, admirably serves the purposes of discussion. The parts of his writings to which I refer are part of the chapter in his essay on Utilitarianism (ch. v.) 'On the Connexion between Justice and Utility,' and the whole of his work on the Subjection of Women. Though these passages can hardly be said to give a definite theory of equality, which, indeed, was not the object with which they were written, they form a powerful and striking expression and, so to speak, condensation of a popular sentiment which in France and perhaps in some other countries is in these days more powerful than that which is inspired either by liberty or by fraternity.

Mr. Mill's views on this subject, then, seem to be as follows. Having considered other matters connected with Utilitarianism (to some of which I shall have to refer in connection with Fraternity), he proceeds to consider its connection with justice:

> In all ages of speculation, one of the strongest obstacles to the reception of
> the doctrine that Utility or Happiness is the criterion of right or wrong, has

been drawn from the idea of Justice. The powerful sentiment, and apparently clear perception, which that word recalls with a rapidity and certainty resembling an instinct, have seemed to the majority of thinkers to point to an inherent quality in things; to show that the Just must have an existence in Nature as something absolute—generically distinct from every variety of the Expedient, and, in idea, opposed to it, though (as is commonly acknowledged) never, in the long run, disjoined from it in fact. [240 U]

Commenting upon this, Mr. Mill proceeds to expound in a long and interesting chapter what I think is the true theory of justice. It may be thus stated: 'Justice,' like nearly every other word which men use in ethical discussions, is ambiguous, and is exceedingly likely to mislead those who use it unless its ambiguity is recognized and allowed for. It implies, first, the impartial application of a law to the particular cases which fall under it. It implies, secondly, that the law so to be administered shall either be for the general good, or at least shall have been enacted by the legislator with an honest intention to promote the good of those whom it is intended to benefit.

The same thing may be stated otherwise, as follows: The words 'just' and 'justice' may refer either to the judge who applies or to the legislator who makes a law, or to the law itself. The judge is just if he enforces the law impartially. The legislator is just if he enacts the law with an honest intention to promote the public good. When the law itself is called just or unjust, what is meant is that it does or does not in fact promote the interests of those whom it affects.

The corn laws, for instance, were unjust if and in so far as they were inexpedient. Those who passed them were unjust if and in so far as they knew, or ought to have known, that they were inexpedient. If on any occasion they were carried out partially, or if they were left unexecuted by those whose duty it was to carry them out, the persons guilty of such partiality or neglect were unjust, irrespectively of the question whether the laws themselves and whether the legislators who made them were just or unjust.

The principle as to morals is precisely similar. Justice in the common intercourse of society differs from legal justice only in the circumstance that morality is less definite in its form than law, and more extensive in its range. A man withdraws his confidence from his friend upon frivolous grounds. By calling this an injustice we imply that there is a known and well-understood though unwritten rule of conduct, to the effect that confidence once reposed by one person in another should not be withdrawn except upon reasonable grounds, and that this rule has not been impartially applied to the particular case. A rule of positive morality may be called unjust as well as a law. For instance, there are in most societies rules which impose social penalties on persons who have been guilty of unchastity, and these penalties are generally more severe upon women than upon men. Those who think it on the whole expedient to make the difference in question will regard these rules as just. Those who think it inexpedient will regard them as unjust, but it is impossible to discuss the question of their justice or injustice apart from that of their expediency or inexpediency.

I need not point out at length the manner in which Mr. Mill traces out the connection between justice and expediency. He shows, as it appears to me irresistibly, that justice means the impartial administration of rules (legal or moral) founded on expediency, and that it includes the idea of coercion and of a desire of revenge against wrongdoers. He also points out with great distinctness and force that many of the most popular commonplaces on the subject, which are often regarded as definitions or quasi-definitions of justice, are merely partial maxims, useful for practical purposes, but not going to the root of the matter.

> Most of the maxims of justice current in the world, and commonly appealed to in its transactions, are simply instrumental in carrying into effect the principles of justice which we have now spoken of. That a person is only responsible for what he has done voluntarily, or could voluntarily have avoided; that it is unjust to condemn any person unheard; that the punishment ought to be proportioned to the offence, and the like, are maxims intended to prevent the just principle of evil for evil from being perverted to the infliction of evil without the justification. The greater part of these common maxims have come into use from the practice of courts of justice, which have been naturally led to a more complete recognition and elaboration than was likely to suggest itself to others, of the rules necessary to enable them to fulfil their double function, of inflicting punishment when due, and of awarding to each person his right. [257 U]

Thus far I have nothing to add to Mr. Mill's statement. It may, I think, be put thus in other words: Justice involves the elements of power and benevolence.

Power acts by imposing general rules of conduct on men, which rules may or may not be benevolent and may or may not be impartially executed. In so far as they are benevolent and impartially applied to particular cases, justice is said to be done. Whether the law itself is just or unjust, impartiality in its application is absolutely essential to a just result. A general rule not applied impartially is for practical purposes no rule at all.

So far, I have only to assent, but Mr. Mill's doctrine that the words 'just' and 'unjust' always involve 'a desire that punishment may be suffered by those who infringe the rule' [250 U] calls, I think, for one important remark. The doctrine does not apply to the case in which the thing qualified as just or unjust is a law or rule. When a judge or a legislator is called unjust, no doubt the word implies personal censure, and this involves more or less distinctly a wish for the punishment of the unjust person. But to call a law unjust seems to me to be the same thing as to call it inexpedient. You cannot punish a law, nor would any rational person wish to punish a legislator who makes a bad law under an honest mistake. Still less would it be reasonable to punish the judge who applies a bad law impartially to a particular case. Nor can it be said that an unjust law is a law breaches of which ought not to be punished. To free from punishment every person who breaks a bad law would be to put an end to law altogether.

If the distinction between an unjust and an inexpedient law is to be maintained, it must be done by the help of some such theory as is involved in the expression 'rights of man.' It must be said that there are rights which are not the creatures of law, but which exist apart from and antecedently to it; that a law which violates any of these rights is unjust, and that a law which, without violating them, does more harm than good is simply inexpedient. I need not say how popular such theories have been or what influence they have exercised in the world, nor need I remind those who, like myself, have been trained in the school of Locke, Bentham, and Austin, that this theory is altogether irreconcilable with its fundamental doctrines. The analysis of laws (political or ethical), according to that school, is as follows. The first idea of all is force, the power to reward and punish. The next idea is command. Obey and you shall be rewarded. Disobey and you shall be punished. Commands impose duties and confer rights. Let A do what he will with this field, and let no one else interfere with him. A hereupon has a right of property in the field, and the rest of the world is under a duty to abstain from infringing that right. This theory is irreconcilable with any notion about natural rights which cannot be resolved into general expediency. It may of course be said that God is the ultimate legislator, and that God has imposed laws on men which they must obey under penalties. It may also be said, without using the name of God, The course of nature is thus and not otherwise, and if you do not adjust your institutions to the course of nature, they will fall to pieces. I for one do not quarrel with either of these assertions; but each resolves right into general utility—general as regards a larger or smaller class. If you regard God as the ultimate legislator, what other criterion of God's will can be discovered than the tendency of a rule or law to promote the welfare of men in general, or of such men as God is supposed to favour? If we take the course of nature as a guide in legislation, our object is simply to know how far and on what terms we (that is, I in the plural) can get what we want. On these grounds I think that the justice and the expediency of a law are simply two names for one and the same thing.*

I should certainly have expected that Mr. Mill would be of the same opinion, but on carefully reading his essay on Utilitarianism, and comparing it with his essay on the Subjection of Women, it appears to me that, though this is the opinion which all the rest of his speculations would make it natural for him to hold, he turns away from it in order to obtain support for his doctrine about women; 'an opinion,' as he tells us, which he has 'held from the very earliest period when' he 'had formed any opinions at all on social and political matters, and which, instead of being weakened and modified, has been constantly growing stronger by the progress of reflection and the experience of life' [119/261 SW]—in short, a pet opinion, which when once embraced by a logical mind is capable of turning all things unto itself. This opinion is, 'That the principle which regulates the existing social relations between the two sexes—the legal subordination of one sex to the other—is wrong in itself, and now one of the chief hindrances to human improvement; and that it ought to be replaced by a principle of perfect equality, admitting no power or privilege on the one side, nor disability on the other.' [119/261 SW] I shall have more to say upon this hereafter. At present I wish to point out how carefully the

*As to the question whose happiness a utilitarian would wish to consult, see post, Chap. VI, pp. 164–65.

foundation for it is laid in the essay on Justice. Although, as I have shown, the whole drift, not only of the particular argument, but of the doctrines of the school to which Mr. Mill belongs, and of which he is beyond all question the most distinguished living member, leads to the conclusion that equality is just only if and in so far as it is expedient, Mr. Mill gives to equality a character different from other ideas connected with justice.

The following extract will show this:

> Nearly allied to the idea of impartiality, is that of *equality;* which often enters as a component part both into the conception of justice and into the practice of it, and, in the eyes of many persons, constitutes its essence. But in this, more than in any other case, the notion of justice varies in different persons, and always conforms in its variations to their notion of utility. *Each person maintains that equality is the dictate of justice, except where he thinks that expediency requires inequality.* . . .[2] Those who think that utility requires distinctions of rank, do not consider it unjust that riches and social privileges should be unequally dispensed; but those who think this inequality inexpedient think it unjust also. [243–44 U]

If this means that the word 'just' as applied to a law or an institution is identical in meaning with the expression 'generally useful,' I fully agree with it, but I do not think this is the meaning. The words italicized appear to convey something further, and to imply that justice involves the notion that a presumption is in all cases to be made in favour of equality quite irrespectively of any definite experience of its utility; and if this is what Mr. Mill means, I disagree with him. It appears to me that the only shape in which equality is really connected with justice is this—justice presupposes general rules, legal or moral, which are to be applied to particular cases, by those who are in the position of judges with respect to them. If these general rules are to be maintained at all, it is obvious that they must be applied equally to every particular case which satisfies their terms. The rule, 'All thieves shall be imprisoned,' is not observed if A, being a thief, is not imprisoned. In other words, it is not observed if it is not applied equally to every person who falls within the definition of a thief, whatever else he may be. If the rule were, 'All thieves except those who have red hair shall be imprisoned, and they shall not,' the rule

2. Stephen's emphasis.

would be violated if a red-haired thief were imprisoned as much as if a black-haired thief were not imprisoned. The imprisonment of the red-haired thief would be an inequality in the application of the rule; for the equality consists not in the equal treatment of the persons who are the subjects of law, but in the equivalency between the general terms of the law and the description of the particular cases to which it is applied. 'All thieves not being red-haired shall be imprisoned' is equivalent to 'A being a thief with brown hair, B being a thief with black hair, C being a thief with white hair, &c., shall be imprisoned, and Z being a thief with red hair shall not be imprisoned.' In this sense equality is no doubt of the very essence of justice, but the question whether the colour of a man's hair shall or shall not affect the punishment of his crimes depends on a different set of considerations. It is imaginable that the colour of the hair might be an unfailing mark of peculiarity of disposition which might require peculiar treatment. Experience alone can inform us whether this is so or not.

The notion that apart from experience there is a presumption in favour of equality appears to me unfounded. A presumption is simply an avowedly imperfect generalization, and this must, of course, be founded on experience. If you have occasion to speak to a stranger in the streets of London, you address him in English, because you presume that he speaks that language; but this is founded on experience of the fact that London is inhabited by people who speak English. In precisely the same way the presumption (if any) to be made in favour of equality must be based upon experience, and as 'equality' is a word so wide and vague as to be by itself almost unmeaning, the experience on which the presumption is based must be experience of the effects of that particular kind of equality to which reference is made, or, at any rate, experience of facts from which inferences can be drawn as to what the effects of it would be like. In every view of the case, therefore, we are brought back to the result that the justice of equality means merely that equality is as a fact expedient.

I do not overlook another and far more important passage from the same chapter of Mr. Mill's writings which bears upon this subject. It is as follows:

This great moral duty {the adherence to maxims of equality and impartiality} rests upon a still deeper foundation, being a direct emanation from the first principle of morals, and not a mere logical corollary from secondary or derivative doctrines. It is involved in the very meaning of Utility, or the Greatest-Happiness Principle. That principle is a mere form of words without rational signification unless one person's happiness, supposed equal in degree (with the proper allowance made for kind), is counted for exactly as much as another's. Those conditions being supplied, Bentham's dictum 'everybody to count for one, nobody for more than one,' might be written under the principle of utility as an explanatory commentary. The equal claim of everybody to happiness in the estimation of the moralist and the legislator, involves an equal claim to all the means of happiness, except in so far as the inevitable conditions of human life, and the general interest in which that of every individual is included, sets limits to the maxim; and those limits ought to be strictly construed. As every other maxim of justice, so this is by no means to be held applicable universally; on the contrary, as I have already remarked, it bends to every person's ideas of social expediency. But in whatever case it is deemed applicable at all, it is held to be the dictate of justice. All persons are deemed to have a *right* to equality of treatment, except where some recognized social expediency requires the reverse, and hence all social inequalities which have ceased to be considered expedient, assume the character not of simple inexpediency, but of injustice, and appear so tyrannical that people are apt to wonder how they ever could have been tolerated. [257–58 U]

It is but very seldom that there is any difficulty in understanding Mr. Mill, but I cannot understand this passage. If justice, as applied to a law, is identical with expediency, how can a law be not simply inexpedient but unjust? If, in reference to a law, justice has some other meaning than general expediency, what is that meaning? So far as I know, Mr. Mill has nowhere explained in what it consists; but as I shall have occasion to show immediately, a considerable part of his argument about the subjection of women assumes that there is such a distinction, and the feeling that there is colours every page of it.

With regard to the remainder of the passage just quoted, I will content myself for the present with expressing my dissent from it. The reasons why I dissent will appear in discussing the subject of Fraternity. When stated I think they will show the real root of the differences—I do not say between Mr. Mill and myself, which is a matter of very small importance, but of the difference between two very large and influential classes of writers and thinkers who are continually confounded together.

Having tried to show in what sense justice and equality are connected, and in what sense they are independent of each other, I proceed to examine the question of the expediency of equality in some of its more important features.

The doctrine upon this subject which I deny and which I am disposed to think Mr. Mill affirmed—though, if he did, it was with somewhat less than his usual transparent vigour and decision—is that equality is in itself always expedient, or, to say the very least, presumably expedient, and that in every case of inequality the burden of proof lies on those who justify its maintenance.

I might cite in proof or illustration of this the whole of his essay on the Subjection of Women, a work from which I dissent from the first sentence to the last, but which I will consider on the present occasion only with reference to the particular topic of equality, and as the strongest distinct illustration known to me of what is perhaps one of the strongest, and what appears to me to be by far the most ignoble and mischievous of all the popular feelings of the age.

The object of Mr. Mill's essay is to explain the grounds of the opinion that 'the principle which regulates the existing social relations between the two sexes—the legal subordination of one sex to the other—is wrong in itself, and now one of the chief hindrances to human improvement; and that it ought to be replaced by a principle of perfect equality, admitting no power or privilege on the one side, or disability on the other.' [119/261 SW]

Mr. Mill is fully aware of the difficulty of his task. He admits that he is arguing against 'an almost universal opinion,' [120/261 SW] but he urges that it and the practice founded on it is a relic of a bygone state of things. 'We now live—that is to say, one or two of the most advanced nations of the world now live—in a state in which the law of the strongest seems to be entirely abandoned as the regulating principle of the world's affairs; nobody professes it, and as regards most of the relations between human beings, nobody is permitted to practise it. . . . This being the ostensible state of things, people flatter themselves that the rule of mere force is ended.' [124/264–65 SW] Still they do not know how hard it dies, and in particular they are unaware of the fact that it still regulates the relations between men and women. It is true that the actually existing generation of women do not dislike their position. The consciousness of this haunts Mr. Mill throughout the whole of his argument, and embarrasses him at every turn. He is driven to account for it by such assertions as that 'each individual of the subject class is in a chronic state of bribery and intimidation combined,' [129/268 *SW*] by reference to the affection which slaves in classical times felt for their masters in many cases, and by other suggestions of the same sort. His great argument against the present state of things is that it is opposed to what he calls 'the modern conviction, the fruit of a thousand years of experience' [135/273 *SW*]:

> That things in which the individual is the person directly interested, never go right but as they are left to his own discretion; and that any regulation of them by authority, except to protect the rights of others, is sure to be mischievous. . . . The peculiar character of the modern world . . . is that human beings are no longer born to their place in life, and chained down by an inexorable bond to the place they are born to, but are free to employ their faculties, and such favourable chances as offer, to achieve the lot which may appear to them most desirable. Human society of old was constituted on a very different principle. All were born to a fixed social position, and were mostly kept in it by law, or interdicted from any means by which they could emerge from it. . . . In consonance with this doctrine, it is felt to be an overstepping of the proper bounds of authority to fix beforehand, on some general presumption, that certain persons are not fit to do certain things. It is now thoroughly known and admitted that if some such presumptions exist, no such presumption is infallible. . . . {Hence we ought not} . . . to ordain that to be born a girl instead of a boy . . . shall decide the person's position all through life. [135, 134, 136/273, 272, 274 *SW*]

The result is that 'the social subordination of women thus stands out as an isolated fact in modern social institutions.' It is in 'radical opposition' to 'the progressive movement, which is the boast of the modern world.' This fact creates a '*prima facie* presumption' against it, 'far outweighing any which custom and usage could in such circumstances create' [137/275 *SW*] in its favour.

I will not follow Mr. Mill through the whole of his argument, much of which consists of matter not relevant to my present purpose, and not agreeable to discuss, though many of his assertions provoke reply. There is something—I hardly know what to call it; indecent is too strong a word, but I may say unpleasant in the direction of indecorum—in prolonged and minute discussions about the relations between men and women, and the characteristics of women as such. I will therefore pass over what Mr. Mill says on this subject with a mere general expression of dissent from nearly every word he says. The following extracts show the nature of that part of his theory which bears on the question of equality:

> The equality of married persons before the law . . . is the only means of rendering the daily life of mankind, in any high sense, a school of moral cultivation. Though the truth may not be felt or generally acknowledged for generations to come, the only school of genuine moral sentiment is society between equals. The moral education of mankind has hitherto emanated chiefly from the law of force, and is adapted almost solely to the relations which force creates. In the less advanced states of society, people hardly recognize any relation with their equals. To be an equal is to be an enemy. Society, from its highest place to its lowest, is one long chain, or rather ladder, where every individual is either above or below his nearest neighbour, and wherever he does not command he must obey. Existing moralities, accordingly, are mainly fitted to a relation of command and obedience. Yet command and obedience are but unfortunate necessities of human life: society in equality is its normal state. Already in modern life, and more and more as it progressively improves, command and obedience become exceptional facts in life, equal association its general rule. . . . We have had the morality of submission, and the morality of chivalry and generosity; the time is now come for the morality of justice. [159–60/293–94 SW]

In another part of the book this doctrine is stated more fully in a passage of which it will be enough for my purpose to quote a very few lines:

> There are many persons for whom it is not enough that the inequality {between the sexes} has no just or legitimate defence; they require to be told what express advantage would be obtained by abolishing it. To which let me first answer, the advantage of having all the most universal and pervading of all human relations regulated by justice instead of injustice. The vast amount of this gain to human nature, it is hardly possible, by any explanation or illustration, to place in a stronger light than it is placed in by the bare statement, to any one who attaches a moral meaning to words. [196/324 SW]

These passages show what Mr. Mill's doctrine of equality is, and how it forms the very root, the essence, so to speak, of his theory about the subjection of women. I consider it unsound in every respect. I think that it rests upon an unsound view of history, an unsound view of morals, and a grotesquely distorted view of facts, and I believe that its practical application would be as injurious as its theory is false.

The theory may be shortly restated in the following propositions, which I think are implied in or may be collected from the extracts given above.

1. Justice requires that all people should live in society as equals.

2. History shows that human progress has been a progress from a 'law of force' to a condition in which command and obedience become exceptional.

3. The 'law of the strongest' having in this and one or two other countries been 'entirely abandoned' in all other relations of life, it may be presumed not to apply to the relation between the sexes.

4. Notorious facts as to the nature of that relation show that in this particular case the presumption is in fact well founded.

I dissent from each of these propositions. First, as to the proposition that justice requires that all people should live in society as equals. I have already shown that this is equivalent to the proposition that it is expedient that all people should live in society as equals. Can this be proved? for it is certainly not a self-evident proposition.

I think that if the rights and duties which laws create are to be generally advantageous, they ought to be adapted to the situation of the persons who enjoy or are subject to them. They ought to recognize both substantial equality and substantial inequality, and they should from time to time be so moulded and altered as always to represent fairly well the existing state of society. Government, in a word, ought to fit society as a man's clothes fit him. To establish by law rights and duties which assume that people are equal when they are not is like trying to make clumsy feet look handsome by the help of tight boots. No doubt it may be necessary to legislate in such a manner as to correct the vices of society or to protect it against special dangers or diseases to which it is liable. Law in this case is analogous to surgery, and the rights and duties imposed by it might be compared to the irons which are sometimes contrived for the purpose of supporting a weak limb or keeping it in some particular position. As a rule, however, it is otherwise. Rights and duties should be so moulded as to clothe, protect, and sustain society in the position which it naturally assumes. The proposition, therefore, that justice demands that people should live in society as equals may be translated thus: 'It is inexpedient that any law should recognize any inequality between human beings.'

This appears to me to involve the assertion, 'There are no inequalities between human beings of sufficient importance to influence the rights and duties which it is expedient to confer upon them.' This proposition I altogether deny. I say that there are many such differences, some of which are more durable and more widely extended than others, and of which some are so marked and so important that unless human nature is radically changed, we cannot even imagine their removal; and of these the differences of age and sex are the most important.

The difference of age is so distinct a case of inequality that even Mr. Mill does not object to its recognition. He admits, as everyone must, that perhaps a third or more of the average term of human life—and that the portion of it in which the strongest, the most durable, and beyond all comparison the most important impressions are made on human beings, the period in which character is formed—must be passed by everyone in a state of submission, dependence, and obedience to orders the objects of which are usually most imperfectly understood by the persons who receive them. Indeed, as I have already pointed out, Mr. Mill is disposed rather to exaggerate than to underrate the influence of education and the powers of educators. Is not this a clear case of inequality of the strongest kind, and does it not at all events afford a most instructive precedent in favour of the recognition by law of a marked natural distinction? If children were regarded by law as the equals of adults, the result would be something infinitely worse than barbarism. It would involve a degree of cruelty to the young which can hardly be realized even in imagination. The proceeding, in short, would be so utterly monstrous and irrational that I suppose it never entered into the head of the wildest zealot for equality to propose it.

Upon the practical question all are agreed; but consider the consequences which it involves. It involves the consequence that, so far from being 'unfortunate necessities,' command and obedience stand at the very entrance to life, and preside over the most important part of it. It involves the consequence that the exertion of power and constraint is so important and so indispensable in the greatest of all matters that it is a less evil to invest with it every head of a family indiscriminately, however unfit he may be to exercise it, than to fail to provide for its exercise. It involves the consequence that by mere lapse of time and by following the promptings of passion men acquire over others a position of superiority and of inequality which all nations and ages, the most cultivated as well as the rudest, have done their best to surround with every association of awe and reverence. The title of Father is the one which the best part of the human race have given to God, as being the least inadequate and inappropriate means of indicating the union of love, reverence, and submission. Whoever first gave the command or uttered the maxim, 'Honour thy father and thy mother, that thy days may be long in the land,' had a far better conception of the essential conditions of permanent national existence and prosperity than the author of the motto Liberty, Equality, and Fraternity.

Now, if society and government ought to recognize the inequality of age as the foundation of an inequality of rights of this importance, it appears to me at least equally clear that they ought to recognize the inequality of sex for the same purpose, if it is a real inequality. Is it one? There are some propositions which it is difficult to prove, because they are so plain, and this is one of them. The physical differences between the two sexes affect every part of the human body, from the hair of the head to the soles of the feet, from the size and density of the bones to the texture of the brain and the character of the nervous system. Ingenious people may argue about anything, and Mr. Mill does say a great number of things about women which, as I have already observed, I will not discuss; but all the talk in the world will never shake the proposition that men are stronger than women in every shape. They have greater muscular and nervous force, greater intellectual force, greater vigour of character. This general truth, which has been observed under all sorts of circumstances and in every age and country, has also in every age and country led to a division of labour between men and women, the general outline of which is as familiar and as universal as the general outline of the differences between them. These are the facts, and the question is whether the law and public opinion ought to recognize this difference? How it ought to recognize it, what difference it ought to make between men and women as such, is quite another question.

The first point to consider is whether it ought to treat them as equals, although, as I have shown, they are not equals, because men are the stronger. I will take one or two illustrations. Men, no one denies, may, and in some cases ought to be liable to compulsory military service. No one, I suppose, would hesitate to admit that if we were engaged in a great war it might become necessáry, or that if necessary it would be right, to have a conscription both for the land and for the sea service. Ought men and women to be subject to it indiscriminately? If anyone says that they ought, I have no more to say, except that he has got into the region at which argument is useless. But if it is admitted that this ought not to be done, an inequality of treatment founded on a radical inequality between the two sexes is admitted, and if this admission is once made, where are you to draw the line? Turn from the case of liability to military service to that of education, which in Germany is rightly regarded as the other great branch of State activity, and the same question presents itself in another shape. Are boys and girls to be educated indiscriminately, and to be instructed in the same things? Are boys to learn to sew, to keep house, and to cook, and are girls to play at cricket, to row, and be drilled like boys? I cannot argue with a person who says Yes. A person who says No admits an inequality between the sexes on which education must be founded, and which it must therefore perpetuate and perhaps increase.

*Follow the matter a step further to the vital point of the whole question—marriage. Marriage is one of the subjects with which it is absolutely necessary for both law and morals to deal in some way or other. All that I need consider in reference to the present purpose is the question whether the laws and moral rules which relate to it should regard it as a contract between equals, or as a contract between a stronger and a weaker person involving subordination for certain purposes on the part of the weaker to the stronger. I say that a law which proceeded on the former and not on the latter of these views would be founded on a totally false assumption, and would involve cruel injustice in the sense of extreme general inexpediency, especially to women. If the parties to a contract of marriage are treated as equals, it is impossible to avoid the inference that marriage, like other partnerships, may be dissolved at pleasure. The advocates of women's rights are exceedingly shy of stating this plainly. Mr. Mill says nothing about it in his book on the Subjection of Women, though in one place he comes very near to saying so, [155–56/290–91 SW] but it is as clear an inference from his principles as anything can possibly be,

*With reference, I suppose, to this passage, which extends to p. 140, Mr. Harrison says of me: 'When he talks about marriage, it is in the tone of Petruchio taming the shrew.'

nor has he ever disavowed it.* If this were the law, it would make women the slaves of their husbands. A woman loses the qualities which make her attractive to men much earlier than men lose those which make them attractive to women. The tie between a woman and young children is generally far closer than the tie between them and their father. A woman who is no longer young, and who is the mother of children, would thus be absolutely in her husband's power, in nine cases out of ten, if he might put an end to the marriage when he pleased. This is one inequality in the position of the parties which must be recognized and provided for beforehand if the contract is to be for their common good. A second inequality is this. When a man marries, it is generally because he feels himself established in life. He incurs, no doubt, a good deal of expense, but he does not in any degree impair his means of earning a living. When a woman marries she practically renounces in all but the rarest cases the possibility of undertaking any profession but one, and the possibility of carrying on that one profession in the society of any man but one. Here is a second inequality. It would be easy to mention others of the deepest importance, but these are enough to show that to treat a contract of marriage as a contract between persons who are upon an equality in regard of strength, and power to protect their interests, is to treat it as being what it notoriously is not.

Again, the contract is one which involves subordination and obedience on the part of the weaker party to the stronger. The proof of this is, to my mind, as clear as that of a proposition in Euclid, and it is this:

1. Marriage is a contract, one of the principal objects of which is the government of a family.

2. This government must be vested either by law or by contract in the hands of one of the two married persons.

3. If the arrangement is made by contract, the remedy for breach of it must either be by law or by a dissolution of the partnership at the will of the contracting parties.

4. Law could give no remedy in such a case. Therefore the only remedy for breach of the contract would be a dissolution of the marriage.

*A passage near the end of the 'Essay on Liberty' strongly implies the opinion that divorce ought to be permitted at the discretion of the parties. [103/300 L] See p. 87, 1st ed.

5. Therefore, if marriage is to be permanent, the government of the family must be put by law and by morals in the hands of the husband, for no one proposes to give it to the wife.

Mr. Mill is totally unable to meet this argument, and apparently embraces the alternative that marriage ought to be dissoluble at the pleasure of the parties. After much argument as to contracts which appear to me visionary, his words are these: 'Things never come to an issue of downright power on one side, and obedience on the other, except where the connection has been altogether a mistake, and it would be a blessing to both parties to be relieved from it.' [157/292 SW]

This appears to me to show a complete misapprehension of the nature of family government and of the sort of cases in which the question of obedience and authority can arise between husband and wife. No one contends that a man ought to have power to order his wife about like a slave and beat her if she disobeys him. Such conduct in the eye of the law would be cruelty and ground for a separation. The question of obedience arises in quite another way. It may, and no doubt often does, arise between the very best and most affectionate married people, and it need no more interfere with their mutual affection than the absolute power of the captain of a ship need interfere with perfect friendship and confidence between himself and his first lieutenant. Take the following set of questions: 'Shall we live on this scale or that? Shall we associate with such and such persons? Shall I, the husband, embark in such an undertaking, and shall we change our place of residence in order that I may do so? Shall we send our son to college? Shall we send our daughters to school or have a governess? For what profession shall we train our sons?' On these and a thousand other such questions the wisest and the most affectionate people might arrive at opposite conclusions. What is to be done in such a case? for something must be done. I say the wife ought to give way. She ought to obey her husband, and carry out the view at which he deliberately arrives, just as, when the captain gives the word to cut away the masts, the lieutenant carries out his orders at once, though he may be a better seaman and may disapprove them. I also say that to regard this as a humiliation, as a wrong, as an evil in itself, is a mark not of spirit and courage, but of a base, unworthy, mutinous disposition—a disposition utterly subversive of all that is most worth having in life. The tacit assumption involved in it is that it is a degradation ever to give up one's own will to the will of another, and to me this appears the root of all evil, the negation of that which renders any combined efforts possible. No case can be specified in which people unite for a common object from making a pair of shoes up to governing an empire in which the power to decide does not rest somewhere; and what is this but command and obedience? Of course the person who for the time being is in command is of all fools the greatest if he deprives himself of the advantage of advice, if he is obstinate in his own opinion, if he does not hear as well as determine; but it is also practically certain that his inclination to hear will be proportioned to the degree of importance which he has been led to attach to the function of determining.

To sum the matter up, it appears to me that all the laws and moral rules by which the relation between the sexes is regulated should proceed upon the principle that their object is to provide for the common good of the two great divisions of mankind who are connected together by the closest and most durable of all bonds, and who can no more have really conflicting interests than the different members of the same body, but who are not and never can be equals in any of the different forms of strength.

This problem law and morals have solved by monogamy, indissoluble marriage on the footing of the obedience of the wife to the husband, and a division of labour with corresponding differences in the matters of conduct, manners, and dress. Substantially this solution appears to me to be right and true; but I freely admit that in many particulars the stronger party has in this, as in other cases, abused his strength, and made rules for his supposed advantage, which in fact are greatly to the injury of both parties. It is needless to say anything in detail of the stupid coarseness of the laws about the effects of marriage on property, laws which might easily be replaced by a general statutory marriage settlement analogous to those which every prudent person makes who has anything to settle. As to acts of violence against women, by all means make the law on this head as severe as it can be made without defeating itself. As to throwing open to women the one or two employments from which they are at present excluded, it is rather a matter of sentiment than of practical importance. I need not revive in this place a trite discussion. My object at present is simply to establish the general proposition that men and women are not equals, and that the laws which affect their relations ought to recognize that fact.

I pass to the examination of the opinion that laws which recognize any sort of inequality between human beings are mere vestiges of the past, against which as such there lies the strongest of all presumptions.

Mr. Mill's view as exhibited in the passages above quoted or referred to may, I think, be reduced to these two propositions: 1. History shows that human progress has been a progress from a 'law of force' to a condition in which command and obedience become exceptional. 2. The 'law of the strongest' having in this and one or two other countries been 'entirely abandoned' in all other relations of life, it may be presumed not to apply to the relations between the sexes.

I think these propositions completely unsound. They appear to me to rest on a mistaken view of history and on a misinterpretation of its facts.

In the first place they involve the assumption that the progress of society is from bad to good; for to say that it is from good to bad, and that we ought to promote it, would be absurd. No doubt, however, Mr. Mill's assumption is that the progress of society is from bad to good; that the changes of the last few centuries in our own and the other leading nations of Western Europe and in the United States have been changes for the better.

This is an enormously wide assumption, and it is one to which I certainly cannot assent, though I do not altogether deny it. I think that the progress has been mixed, partly good and partly bad. I suspect that in many ways it has been a progress from strength to weakness; that people are more sensitive, less enterprising and ambitious, less earnestly desirous to get what they want, and more afraid of pain, both for themselves and others, than they used to be. If this should be so, it appears to me that all other gains, whether in wealth, knowledge, or humanity, afford no equivalent. Strength, in all its forms, is life and manhood. To be less strong is to be less of a man, whatever else you may be. This suspicion prevents me, for one, from feeling any enthusiasm about progress, but I do not undertake to say it is well founded. It is not and it cannot be more than a suspicion, and the fallacies of the imagination in this matter are so obvious and so nearly irresistible that it is impossible for anyone to be too much on his guard against giving way to them. The doubt is enough, however, to stop enthusiasm. I do not myself see that our mechanical inventions have increased the general vigour of men's characters, though they have, no doubt, increased enormously our control over nature. The greater part of our humanity appears to me to be a mere increase of nervous sensibility in which I feel no satisfaction at all. It is useless to lament or even to blame the inevitable. It is rash to draw general conclusions as to the character of a process extending over centuries from the observations which one man can make in a few years, but it is at least equally rash to rejoice over the inevitable, and to assume that it is good. To observe and to take our part in the changes in which we live is rational; but for my part I will neither bless them at all nor curse them at all, and no one, I think, has a right to do otherwise without showing cause for what he does. The inference applicable to the present subject is that, even if the inequality between men and women is a vestige of the past, and is likely to be destroyed by the same process which has destroyed so many other things, that is no reason for helping the process on. The proper reflection upon its approaching removal may be, The more's the pity. Mr. Woodhouse liked his gruel thin, but not too thin. At a certain point of wateriness he would probably have turned off the tap. If Emma had been a disciple of Mr. Mill's, she might have remarked, 'Reflect, dear sir, that you are interrupting the stream of progress. Such remains of cohesiveness as are exhibited by the grits which form the substratum of your simple meal are relics of the past, and as such are probably defects in your gruel instead of merits.'

Be that as it may, let us consider the question whether the 'law of force'—the 'law of the strongest'—really has been abandoned? whether if it were abandoned it would tend to produce equality? and whether the general course of events in recent times has tended or does now tend to set it aside? First, and by way of introduction to the other questions, let us consider what it is.

Force is an absolutely essential element of all law whatever. Indeed law is nothing but regulated force subjected to particular conditions and directed towards particular objects. The abolition of the law of force cannot therefore mean the withdrawal of the element of force from law, for that would be the destruction of law altogether.

The general tenor of Mr. Mill's argument rather indicates that by the 'law of force' and the 'law of the strongest' he means force unregulated by any law at all. If this was what he meant, he should have said it; but he could not have said it without being at once involved in an obvious contradiction to facts, for the marriage institutions of modern Europe are anything but a case of force unregulated by law. They are cases of laws which regulate in the sternest way the most impetuous of human passions. Can anyone doubt that the principles of monogamy and the indissolubility of marriage effectually controlled the most ardent passions of the strongest-willed races in the world during the dark and the middle ages, or that the control so exercised was in its results eminently beneficial to the human race at large and to women in particular? De Maistre claims, and in this case I think justly, great credit for the mediæval clergy for having upheld these principles, which are the central principles of our version of morals, against the repeated attacks which were made upon them by the passions of kings and nobles in the most violent periods of history.

Assuming, then, that the 'law of force' is a somewhat indefinite expression for the general importance of force, and that Mr. Mill means to assert that force tends to lose its importance, I proceed to his whole conception of the theory of equality and its history.

It is no doubt perfectly true that in all the institutions of the nations which principally interest us, and in particular in such of their institutions as have to do with law and government, there is a constant tendency to the rejection of distinctions and to the simplification of laws. This is due to a variety of causes. In the first place the societies in question have a tendency to increase. The different kingdoms into which our own and the other great European nations were subdivided in the early stages of our history gradually ran into each other. The growth of wealth, and changes in the habits of life proceeding from an infinite number of causes not only rendered old institutions unsuitable for later times, but in many cases made them unintelligible. Thus, for instance, the word 'murder,' which for centuries has been the name of a crime, was, it seems, originally the name of a fine laid upon a township in which a person unknown was found slain, unless the legal presumption that the unknown man was a Dane could be disproved by positive testimony that he was an Englishman, by a proceeding called a 'presentment of Englishry.' The strange distinction introduced in favour of the Danes, and maintained in favour of the French, was not finally removed till the fourteenth year of Edward III. By that time the presentment of Englishry had become unmeaning and was abolished, and the name of the fine had passed into the name of the crime in respect of which the fine was imposed.

This was one case out of a multitude of the growth of equality, by the rejection of a distinction between the murders of men of different races which had become senseless. Probably every part of the institutions of every nation in the world would afford illustrations of the same principle. The history of the Roman law from the days of the Twelve Tables to the time of Justinian is little else than one continued illustration of it. Another, and one of the utmost importance, is afforded by a process which Mr. Mill refers to in a passage quoted above about the distinction which exists between the present and the former arrangements of society for the purpose of assigning to men their position in life. In former times, Mr. Mill tells us, 'All were born to a fixed social position, and were mostly kept in it by law, or interdicted from any means by which they could emerge from it.' [134/273 SW] Sir Henry Maine refers to, and to a certain extent gives the theory of, this matter in a passage which he sums up by saying, 'The movement of the progressive societies has hitherto been a movement from status to contract'[3]—a movement, that is, from a condition of things in which the relations between man and man are determined by membership of a family or of a tribe, or of a conquering or conquered race, towards a condition of things in which they depend upon contract. This is no doubt quite true, and to Sir Henry Maine's account of the matter, which is as interesting as it is ingenious, I have no objection to make. I will only observe upon it that in this, as in other cases, he confines himself to the investigation of or to speculations about matters of fact; and neither says nor, as it seems to me, assumes, as Mr. Mill always does, that to show that the course of events has in fact led from A to B, and appears to be in the direction of C, proves that B is better than A, and that C is better than B.

The question with which I have to deal is whether these facts authorize Mr. Mill's two doctrines: namely, first, the doctrine that the law of the strongest, or the law of force, has been abandoned in these days—an assertion which, I think, must, for the reasons already assigned, be taken to mean that force tends to be less and less important in human affairs; and, secondly, the doctrine that this abandonment of the law of force is equivalent to the growth of

3. Henry Sumner Maine (1822–88), *Ancient Law,* 10th ed. (London: John Murray, 1882), p. 165 (final line of chapter five in all editions).

equality. Both of these doctrines I deny, and I deny that the facts which I have admitted tend even to prove them.

As to the first, I say that all that is proved by the fact that status, to use Sir H. Maine's expression, tends to be replaced by contract, is that force changes its form. Society rests ultimately upon force in these days, just as much as it did in the wildest and most stormy periods of history. Compare Scotland in the fourteenth century with Scotland in the nineteenth century. In the fourteenth century the whole country was a scene of wild confusion, of which one of the most learned of Scott's novels (though it was written after his genius had received its fatal blow), 'The Fair Maid of Perth,' gives a striking picture. 'My name,' says one of the characters, 'is the Devil's Dick of Hellgarth, well known in Annandale for a gentle Johnstone. I follow the stout Laird of Wamphray, who rides with his kinsman, the redoubted Lord of Johnstone, who is banded with the doughty Earl of Douglas; and the Earl, and the Lord, and the laird, and I, the esquire, fly our hawks where we find our game, and ask no man whose ground we ride over.' [Chapter VIII] Every page of the book is full of the feuds of Highland and Lowland, Douglas and March, burghers and nobles, Clan Chattan and Clan Quhele. The first impression on comparing this spirited picture with the Scotland which we all know—the Scotland of quiet industry, farming, commerce, and amusement, is that the fourteenth century was entirely subject to the law of force, and that Scotland in the nineteenth century has ceased to be the theatre of force at all. Look a little deeper and this impression is as false, not to say as childish, as the supposition that a clumsy rowboat, manned by a quarrelsome crew, who can neither keep time with their oars, nor resist the temptation to fight among themselves, displays force, and that an ocean steamer which will carry a townful of people to the end of the earth at the rate of three hundred miles a day so smoothly that during the greater part of the time they are unconscious of any motion or effort whatever, displays none. The force which goes to govern the Scotland of these days is to the force employed for the same purpose in the fourteenth century what the force of a line-of-battle ship is to the force of an individual prize-fighter. The reason why it works so quietly is that no one doubts either its existence, or its direction, or its crushing superiority to any individual resistance which could be offered to it. The force of the chain of champions of whom the Devil's Dick was the last link is now stored up in the vast mass of peaceable and rational men, who, in case of need, would support the law, and from them it is drawn off as required. It can be defied only on the smallest possible scale, and by taking it at a disadvantage. A criminal may overpower an isolated policeman just as a pigmy might with his whole weight hold down the last joint of the little finger of a giant's left hand, if the hand were in a suitable position; but deliberate individual resistance to the law of the land for mere private advantage is in these days an impossibility which no one ever thinks of attempting. Force not only reigns, but in most matters it reigns without dispute, but it does not follow that it has ceased to exist.

This proposition is true, not merely in its general and abstract shape, but also of every relation of life in detail. Nowhere is it more strikingly illustrated than in the relation of marriage. Mr. Mill says: 'I readily admit that numbers of married people, even under the present law (in the higher classes of England probably a great majority), live in the spirit of a just law of equality. Laws never would be improved, if there were not numerous persons whose moral sentiments were better than the existing laws.' [161/295 SW] This is an admission that most marriages under the existing laws are happy. The reason, says Mr. Mill, is because the moral tone of particular classes is superior to the law. I say that it is because the law is good, and the people in question obey it. I go beyond Mr. Mill in his opinion about marriages, I should say that in all classes of life they are much more often happy than otherwise; but I say that is because as a general rule both husbands and wives keep the solemn promises which they made at their marriage, including the wife's promise to obey her husband. Surely the natural inference to draw from the fact that an institution works well is that it is founded on true principles, and answers its purpose. The administration of justice in this country is singularly pure. The inference is not that the judges are superior to the law, but that the law in which they are trained is favourable to the pure administration of justice.

Mr. Mill is not quite consistent upon this head, for he tells us distinctly that if the family in its best forms is a school of sympathy and tenderness, 'it is still oftener, as respects its chief, a school of wilfulness, overbearingness, unbounded self-indulgence, and a double-dyed and idealized selfishness, of which sacrifice itself is only a particular form'; the individual happiness of the wife and children 'being immolated in every shape to his {the head of the family's} smallest preferences.' 'What better,' he asks, 'is to be looked for under the existing form of the institution?' [153/289 SW] If this is at all like the truth, I cannot understand how marriage can be or ever can have been anything but an odious tyranny and school of every kind of vice; nor can I reconcile such statements with the one just quoted as to the general happiness of marriage. Certainly the higher classes of society in this country are not less strict in their views as to the duties of married life than their inferiors. Few ladies would like to be told that they were disobedient wives. Few gentlemen would feel it otherwise than a reproach to learn that they were not masters in their own homes; but how can this be, if authority on the one side and obedience on the other are fundamentally immoral? Mr. Mill's theory involves the absurd consequence that good fruit grows on a bad tree. Mine involves the natural consequence that a good institution produces good results. The real reason why the marriages of sensible and well-educated people in all ranks of life are happy is that people know their respective places, and act accordingly. The power exists and is exercised, but as the right to exercise it is undisputed, and as its exercise is unresisted, it acts smoothly, and the parties concerned are seldom unpleasantly reminded of its existence.

An exact parallel to the case of married life is to be found in the common case of hospitality. You go into a handsome, well-appointed house, full of well-behaved people. You observe that one of the company exerts himself in every possible way to promote the enjoyment and to provide for the amusement or occupation of the rest, and that he in all cases studiously though unostentatiously takes, in a certain sense, the lowest place. You are told that this man has an undoubted legal right to order all the rest out of his house at a moment's notice—say in a storm in the middle of the night—to forbid them to touch an article of furniture, to open a book, or to eat a crumb of bread:* and this appears harsh; yet if he were deprived of that right, if the presence of his guests rendered its existence doubtful for a moment in any particular, not one

---

*Mrs. Fawcett (who wrote a pamphlet on this chapter) considered that she had answered this by showing that a man who exercised this right would not only act in a very brutal manner, but expose himself to social penalties by so acting. This is as true as it is irrelevant. It is the only remark of Mrs. Fawcett's which I think it necessary to notice, and I notice it only as an illustration of what she understands by argument.

of them would cross his doors; matters go well, not because the master of the house has no powers, but because no one questions them, and he wishes to use them for the general comfort of the society.

To say that the law of force is abandoned because force is regular, unopposed, and beneficially exercised is to say that day and night are now such well-established institutions that the sun and moon are mere superfluities.

It should be observed that though marriage is the most important of all contracts, it is far from being the only one which confers upon one of the parties authority over the other. Nearly every contract does so. A man passes his life in a Government office. He contracts to serve the public on certain terms. Is there here no authority on the part of the employer over the employed? Dismissal from such a post would be as severe a punishment, in most cases, as could be inflicted on a man, a far more severe punishment than a short term of imprisonment or a heavy fine unaccompanied by dismissal. The power of a French Minister of the Interior over an immense multitude of subordinates is as real and quite as formidable as the power of a feudal lord over his vassals ever was. It is true that it is founded on contract and not on status. In the one case the man was born to a certain position, and in the other he entered into it by agreement, but that makes very little real difference between the two cases. In each case there is a stronger and a weaker person, and in each the weaker is subject to the authority of the stronger.

The truth is that the change above referred to, from status to contract, is very far indeed from being universally favourable to equality. I will not speculate on the nature of the change itself. It may be the best and most glorious of all conceivable states of society that all the relations between man and man should be resolved into the single relation of the earning and paying of wages in various forms; but whether this is so or not, it is perfectly certain that the result of the arrangement is to produce not equality but inequality in its harshest and least sympathetic form. The process is this. Society is converted into one immense machine, the powers of which are all concentrated into one body, which is called the public force. It consists of a legislative and an executive body backed up in case of need by soldiers and policemen. The direction in which this force is to act is ascertained by laws which apply with continually increasing precision and inflexibility to all sorts of cases. Each person is left to make use of these laws for his own purposes in his own way. They may be reduced to these four:

1. Thou shalt not commit crimes. 2. Thou shalt not inflict wrong. 3. Thou shalt perform thy contracts. 4. Thou and thine may keep whatever you can get. To say that such a state of society is favourable to equality, that it tends to supersede obedience and command, that it has superseded force, and the like, sounds more like a poor kind of irony than anything else. What equality is there between the rich and the poor, between the strong and the weak, between the good and the bad? In particular, what equality is there between the well-born and well-bred man, the son of a good, careful, prudent, prosperous parent, who has transmitted to him a healthy mind and body, and given him a careful education; and the ill-born, ill-bred man whose parents had nothing to teach which was not better unlearned, and nothing to transmit which would not have been better uninherited. It is quite true that in these days we have not much titular inequality. It is quite true that we have succeeded in cutting political power into very little bits, which with our usual hymns of triumph we are continually mincing, till it seems not unlikely that many people may come to think that a single man's share of it is not worth having at all. But with all this, real substantial inequalities in every respect, inequalities of wealth, inequalities of talent, of education, of sentiment, and of religious belief, and therefore inequalities in the most binding of all obligations, never were so great as they are at this moment. I doubt much whether the power of particular persons over their neighbours has ever in any age of the world been so well defined and so easily and safely exerted as it is at present. If in old times a slave was inattentive, his master might no doubt have him maimed or put to death or flogged; but he had to consider that in doing so he was damaging his own property, that when the slave had been flogged he would still continue to be his slave; and that the flogging might make him mischievous or revengeful, and so forth. If a modern servant misconducts himself, he can be turned out of the house on the spot, and another can be hired as easily as you would call a cab. To refuse the dismissed person a character may very likely be equivalent to sentencing him to months of suffering and to a permanent fall in the social scale. Such punishments are inflicted without appeal, without reflection, without the smallest disturbance of the smooth surface of ordinary life.

The older mode of organizing society has, like other things, been made the subject of much romantic exaggeration, but it is clear that it had a side which was favourable to poverty and weakness, though it produced its inequalities, as our own social maxims do. To try to make men equal by altering social arrangement is like trying to make the cards of equal value by shuffling the pack. Men are fundamentally unequal, and this inequality will show itself arrange society as you like. If the object were to secure the greatest amount of equality, the way to do it would be by establishing a system of distinctions, a social hierarchy corresponding as nearly as possible to the real distinctions between men, and by making the members of each class equal among themselves. Something by no means unlike this has actually been done by the caste system in India, and the result is that Hindoo society, though in some ways elastic and possessed of a considerable power of assimilating new ideas, is stable and conservative to a degree utterly unknown and hardly even imaginable in Europe. If we were possessed of any test by which men could be marshalled according to their intrinsic differences with unfailing accuracy, we should really obtain the repose, the absence of conscious and painful restraint, the calm play of unresisted and admitted force which people appear to expect from the establishment of what they call equality. The establishment of even this ideal state of things would leave some of the most important of social problems unsolved, but it is almost an identical proposition that it would afford not merely the best but the only full solution of the great problem of harmonising self-interest with the interests of the public at large. A nation in which everyone held the position for which he was best fitted, and in which everyone was aware of that fact, would be a nation in which every man's life would be passed in doing that which would be at once most agreeable to himself and most beneficial to his neighbours, and such a nation would have solved at all events several of the great problems of life.

It is needless to insist on the plain fact that such an ideal is unattainable; but the maintenance of broad and well-marked distinctions which really exist at a given time and place is a step towards it. The distinctions of age and sex are universal. Distinctions of race are at given times and places most important, and the fact that they have been exaggerated and abused is no reason for denying their existence. Distinctions of wealth and of the education and other qualities which are associated with the acquisition and retention of wealth are no less real. Such distinctions will continue to exist and to produce inequalities of every description, whether or not they are recognized by law, and whether or not they are permitted to affect the distribution of political authority. Leave them to find their own level by unrestricted competition, and they will display themselves in their most naked and their harshest form.

Let us suppose, to take a single illustration, that men and women are made as equal as law can make them, and that public opinion followed the law. Let us suppose that marriage became a mere partnership dissoluble like another; that women were expected to earn their living just like men; that the notion of anything like protection due from the one sex to the other was thoroughly rooted out; that men's manners to women became identical with their manners to men; that the cheerful concessions to acknowledged weakness, the obligation to do for women a thousand things which it would be insulting to offer to do for a man, which we inherit from a different order of ideas, were totally exploded; and what would be the result? The result would be that women would become men's slaves and drudges, that they would be made to feel their weakness and to accept its consequences to the very utmost. Submission and protection are correlative. Withdraw the one and the other is lost, and force will assert itself a hundred times more harshly through the law of contract than ever it did through the law of status. Disguise it how you will, it is force in one shape or another which determines the relations between human beings. It is far less harsh when it is subjected to the provisions of a general law made with reference to broad general principles than when it acts through a contract, the terms of which are settled by individuals according to their own judgment. The terms of the marriage relation as settled by the law and religion of Europe are an illustration, of course on an infinitely wider and more important scale, of the very principle which in our own days has led to the prohibition of the employment of little children in certain classes of factories and of women in coalpits.

To recapitulate, I think that equality has no special connection with justice, except in the narrow sense of judicial impartiality; that it cannot be affirmed to be expedient in the most important relations of social life; and that history does not warrant the assertion that for a great length of time there has been a continual progress in the direction of the removal of all distinctions between man and man, though it does warrant the assertion that the form in which men's natural inequalities display themselves and produce their results changes from one generation to another, and tends to operate rather through contracts made by individuals than through laws made by public authority for the purpose of fixing the relations between human beings.

I now proceed to the most important of the remaining senses of the word 'equality'—the equal distribution of political power. This is perhaps the most definite sense which can be attached to the vague general word 'equality.' It is undoubtedly true that for several generations a process has been going on all over our own part of the world which may be described, not inaccurately, as the subdivision of political power. The accepted theory of government appears to be that everybody should have a vote, that the Legislature should be elected by these votes, and that it should conduct all the public business of the country through a committee which succeeds for the time in obtaining its confidence. This theory, beyond all question, has gone forth, and is going forth conquering and to conquer. The fact of its triumph is as clear as the sun at noonday, and the probability that its triumphs will continue for a longer time than we need care to think about is as strong as any such probability can well be. The question is, what will a reasonable man think of it? I think he will criticize it like any other existing fact, and with as little partiality on either side as possible; but I am altogether at a loss to understand how it can rouse enthusiastic admiration in anyone whatever. It certainly has done so for some reason or other. Nearly every newspaper, and a very large proportion of modern books of political speculation, regard the progress of democracy, the approaching advent of universal suffrage, with something approaching to religious enthusiasm. To this I for one object.

In the first place, it will be well to point out a distinction which, though perfectly clear and of the utmost importance, is continually overlooked. Legislate how you will, establish universal suffrage, if you think proper, as a law which can never be broken. You are still as far as ever from equality. Political power has changed its shape but not its nature. The result of cutting it up into little bits is simply that the man who can sweep the greatest number of them into one heap will govern the rest. The strongest man in some form or other will always rule. If the government is a military one, the qualities which make a man a great soldier will make him a ruler. If the government is a monarchy, the qualities which kings value in counsellors, in generals, in administrators, will give power. In a pure democracy the ruling men will be the wirepullers and their friends; but they will no more be on an equality with the voters than soldiers or Ministers of State are on an equality with the subjects of a monarchy. Changes in the form of a government alter the conditions of superiority much more than its nature. In some ages a powerful character, in others cunning, in others powers of despatching business, in others eloquence, in others a good hold upon current commonplaces and facility in applying them to practical purposes will enable a man to climb on to his neighbours' shoulders and direct them this way or that; but in all ages and under all circumstances the rank and file are directed by leaders of one kind or another who get the command of their collective force. The leading men in a trade union are as much the superiors and rulers of the members of the body at large, and the general body of the members are as much the superiors and rulers of each individual member, as the master of a family or the head of a factory is the ruler and superior of his servants or workpeople.

In short, the subdivision of political power has no more to do with equality than with liberty.[4] The question whether it is a good thing or a bad one stands on its own ground, and must be decided by direct reference to its effects. They are infinitely numerous and complicated, and it would be idle to try to describe them fully or even to give full illustrations of their character. The point to which I wish to direct attention is one which is continually overlooked because it is unpleasant—namely, that whatever may be the strong side of popular institutions as we know them, they have also a weak and dangerous side, and by no means deserve that blind admiration and universal chorus of applause with which their progress is usually received.

If I am asked, What do you propose to substitute for universal suffrage? Practically, What have you to recommend? I answer at once, Nothing. The whole current of thought and feeling, the whole stream of human affairs, is setting with irresistible force in that direction. The old ways of living, many of which were just as bad in their time as any of our devices can be in ours, are breaking down all over Europe, and are floating this way and that like hay-

4. For an illuminating remark on this, see Stephen's "Hobbes on Government," in *Horae Sabbaticae*, vol. 2, p. 12.

cocks in a flood. Nor do I see why any wise man should expend much thought or trouble on trying to save their wrecks. The waters are out and no human force can turn them back, but I do not see why as we go with the stream we need sing Hallelujah to the river god. I am not so vain as to suppose that anything that I can say will do either good or harm to any perceptible degree, but an attempt to make a few neutral observations on a process which is all but universally spoken of with passion on one side or the other may interest a few readers.

The substance of what I have to say to the disadvantage of the theory and practice of universal suffrage is that it tends to invert what I should have regarded as the true and natural relation between wisdom and folly. I think that wise and good men ought to rule those who are foolish and bad. To say that the sole function of the wise and good is to preach to their neighbours, and that everyone indiscriminately should be left to do what he likes, and should be provided with a rateable share of the sovereign power in the shape of a vote, and that the result of this will be the direction of power by wisdom, seems to me to be the wildest romance that ever got possession of any considerable number of minds.

As to the character of our present rulers, let us hear Mr. Mill. He is speaking of the year 1859, but I do not think matters have altered much since then. Mr. Mill says ('Essay on Liberty,' chap. iii) of the governing class of England—meaning 'chiefly the middle class' [66/268 L]—'Their thinking is done for them by men much like themselves, addressing them or speaking in their name, on the spur of the moment, through the newspapers.' [66/269 L] 'I am not,' he adds, 'complaining of this. I do not assert that anything better is compatible, as a general rule, with the present low state of the human mind. But that does not hinder the government of mediocrity from being mediocre government. No government by a democracy or a numerous aristocracy, either in its political acts or in the opinions, qualities, and tone of mind which it fosters, ever did or ever could rise above mediocrity, except in so far as the sovereign many have let themselves be guided (which in their best times they always have done) by the counsels and influence of a more highly gifted and instructed One or Few.' [66/269 L] The parenthesis, I think, would apply chiefly to a few years in the history of Athens; but be this as it may, I need not repeat the quotations which I have already made from the same chapter about the way in which 'society has now fairly got the better of the individual.' [61/264 L] The substance of it is that we all live under a leaden rule of petty contemptible opinions which crushes all individuality. The moral is this: 'The greatness of England is now all collective; individually small, we only appear capable of anything great by our habit of combining; and with this our moral and religious philanthropists are perfectly contented. But it was men of another stamp than this that made England what it has been; and men of another stamp will be needed to prevent its decline.' [70/272 L] 'The mind itself is bowed to the yoke: even in what people do for pleasure, conformity is the first thing thought of; they like in crowds; they exercise choice only among things commonly done.' [61–62/265 L] There is much more to the same purpose which I need not quote. It would be easy to show from other parts of Mr. Mill's later works what a low opinion he has of mankind at large.* His whole essay on the Subjection of Women goes to prove that of the two sexes which between them constitute the human race, one has all the vices of a tyrant, and the other all the vices of a slave. Families are generally schools of selfishness 'double-dyed and idealized.' All women are either bribed or intimidated, and men have reduced them to that position. What the children must be who have such homes and such educators it is needless to say. All this, and much else of the same kind, appears to me to be harsh, unjust, and exaggerated; but I am entitled to ask how a man who thinks thus of his fellow-creatures can, with any degree of consistency, be the advocate of liberty in the sense of the negation of all government, and of equality in any sense at all? Given a herd of stupid fools who are never to be coerced, and who are to keep everyone from rising above their [sic] own level, and what will you ever get to the end of time except a herd of stupid fools? Mankind upon this system would be like a set of what Strauss calls the Ur-affen, or primeval apes of Mr. Darwin's theory, with just sense enough to defeat the operation of natural selection. Their one maxim would be to single out every ape who had got a few rudiments of

---

*Mr. Morley refers to this in connection with my assertion on p. 31, that 'the great defect of Mr. Mill's later writings seems to me to be that he has formed too favourable an estimate of human nature.' He asks, 'which of these contradictory assertions' I 'wish to stand by.' The statements are consistent. Mr. Mill may have 'formed too favourable an estimate of human nature' (i.e., in the abstract and in the future), 'and yet have had a low opinion of mankind at large,' i.e., of the actual concrete world before him. See pp. 180–81 as to the habits of mind which might lead him to do so.

human qualities in him, and, instead of making him their king, stone him to death. 'Non meus hic sermo.' I merely point out the tendency of a celebrated theory, but after it has been fully discounted, I think that some truth unquestionably remains in it.

I should certainly not agree with Mr. Mill's opinion that English people in general are dull, deficient in originality, and as like each other as herrings in a barrel appear to us. Many and many a fisherman, common sailor, workman, labourer, gamekeeper, policeman, non-commissioned officer, servant, and small clerk have I known who were just as distinct from each other, just as original in their own way, just as full of character, as men in a higher rank of life.

For my part I should limit myself to this, that the number of people who are able to carry on anything like a systematic train of thought, or to grasp the bearings of any subject consisting of several parts, is exceedingly small. I should add to this that the work of governing a great nation, if it is to be done really well, requires an immense amount of special knowledge and the steady, restrained, and calm exertion of a great variety of the very best talents which are to be found in it.

I never yet met with anyone who denied that if the institutions by which this country is governed were constructed solely with a view to the efficient transaction of public business, they would have to assume a very different shape from their present one. No one can justify, though he may explain, upon historical grounds, an arrangement by which the whole government of the country is vested in a popular assembly like the House of Commons, ruling as king through a committee which may be dismissed at a moment's notice. This committee, while it is in power, has to work through a set of public offices, hardly one of which has even any pretence to have been specially adapted for its work, while all the more important of them were established with reference to a state of things which has long since passed away. Some degree of permanence, some amount of discretionary authority, some scope for the formation and execution of considerable schemes, are the very first essentials of good government. Under the system which universal suffrage has given and is giving to us they are all but entirely wanting. Endless discussion, continual explanation, the constant statement and re-statement to Parliament of every matter on which Government is to act hamper to the last degree the process of governing. Nothing can be done at all till the importance of doing it has been made obvious to the very lowest capacity; and whatever can be made obvious to such capacities is sure in course of time to be done, although it may be obvious to people capable of taking a wider view that it ought not to be done. When once done, it is the hardest thing in the world to get it undone.

The net result of these evils, all of which are the direct consequence of the system of having the government of the country directly subordinated to the rule of the majority of the voters for the time being, of making it, in other words, as nearly as may be a faithful representative of the fluctuations of public feeling and opinion, has never been fully stated, nor do I think it can be so stated. A few observations on the subject will, however, be worth making, as they will afford a general indication of the enormous price which we pay for the advantages of obtaining the general consent to whatever is done and of interesting a great many people in the transaction of public affairs.

Assume that arrangements had been made by which a body of able men were able to devote their time continuously, steadily, and systematically to the task of employing the public force for the general welfare of the community, and assume that they could follow out their views without being obliged to be continually stopping to obtain the popular consent at every step. Would there be no work for them to do? I say there would in every department of the State be more work than any one generation of such men could hope to accomplish, and I further say that the greater part of it is going and will go undone, and that much of it is ill done simply because there is so little continuity, so little permanent authority vested under our system in anyone whatever. In proof of this, I will refer shortly to the business of the principal departments of government. I pass over the Prime Minister with the remark that in the present state of things his parliamentary qualities are nearly everything and his administrative functions comparatively small. After him the first great officer of State is the Lord Chancellor. What with proper assistance he might do in the way of law reform I need not say. The reduction of the law and of the judicial institutions of the country to a rational shape is a question of time, labour, and special knowledge. The real difficulty, I do not say an insuperable one, but the real difficulty lies in the constitution of Parliament, and in the system of party government which makes every man who is out of office pick holes in the work of every man who is in office, and every man who is in office considers, not what is the best thing to be done, but what he is most likely to be able to carry in spite of opposition. No one acquainted with the subject can doubt that a systematic reform of the law would facilitate every business transaction in the country, add enormously to the value of every acre of land in it, and convert law into an embodiment of justice, a real standard of conduct in every department of life, and so produce a great effect on both the intellect and the morals of the country.

Next to the Lord Chancellor comes the Lord President of the Council. One of the first things which would occur to such a government as I have supposed to exist (if indeed it would not be pre-supposed in the establishment of such a government) would be the reflection that the present constitution of the Cabinet and the public offices is about as ill-conceived an arrangement for the real despatch of business as could be contrived, however well it may be adapted to the exigencies of party government. The original idea of the Privy Council, as appears from their proceedings, was far better suited to that purpose, though I do not say it is fit for these times. This is not the place for technicalities which scarcely anyone understands, but in general terms I may observe that a council for the real transaction of business ought to exercise a direct superintendence over every department of the government, and ought, either by means of committees or otherwise, to be kept aware of all the great executive questions which arise in different parts of the government and to give orders upon them. As matters now stand, each department is a little State with its own little king for the time being, and the control of the whole over the different parts is loose and vague to the highest possible degree. Each Minister may act as he likes in his own dominions up to the point at which any question before him seems likely to attract the attention of Parliament and threaten the stability of the Ministry. This is not the way to get important questions well settled. If the Cabinet were a real steady governing council whose duty it was to pass orders on all the most important matters which might arise in the different departments, Cabinet Ministers would have to work a great deal harder than they do at present at other matters than making speeches and preparing to answer parliamentary questions.

After the President of the Council come the five Secretaries of State. Of their offices, the Colonial Office, the War Office, the Admiralty, and the India Office have, and can have, very little to gain and they have everything to lose by uncertainty of tenure and continual accountability to every voter in England through his representatives. The relations between England and the colonies, and England and India, are relations which it is hardly possible to conduct in a satisfactory way through Parliament. The best thing that Parliament can do with these subjects, generally speaking, is to let them alone, and to a great extent it does so. A smaller and better instructed body, however, dealing with these matters steadily and quietly, might render great services to every part of the British Empire, or rather to every part of the two empires, colonial and Indian. With regard to the organization of the army and navy, it hardly admits of a question that they are special matters dependent upon special knowledge which has hardly any connection at all with party politics.

The Home Office, perhaps, affords the strongest of all possible illustrations of the extent of the field which lies open for government. If anyone were to attempt to say what the internal government of England is, how it is carried on, or how it is superintended, he would be smothered in the attempt under a chaos of acts, charters, commissioners, boards, benches, courts, and vestries of all sorts and conditions, which have no unity, are subject to no central control in most instances, and are supposed to atone for all their other defects by what Frenchmen praise as 'le self-government,' which not unfrequently means the right to misgovern your immediate neighbours without being accountable for it to anyone wiser than yourself. Can anyone doubt that if this jungle of institutions were carefully examined by anyone who had at once the will and the power to set things to rights, the subjects of education, crime, pauperism, health, and others too numerous to mention or hint at, might be set in quite a new light? Even as things are, a great deal of late years has been done in all these matters, and probably more will be done; but it might be done infinitely quicker and better if the consent of fewer people was required to what, if not absolutely necessary, is plainly desirable.

Foreign policy perhaps affords as strong an illustration as can be given of the importance of special knowledge. There is no department of public affairs (if we except Indian and colonial affairs) in which the general level of knowledge is so low. There is none in which popular passions are so violent, so ill-instructed, or so likely to produce incalculable mischief. The intensity of the ignorance of the great mass of English people about France and Germany could only be equalled by the fierce excitement and unruly and irrational state of sympathy into which they were thrown by the progress of the war. In reference, however, to foreign affairs, what is required is rather the acquisition of knowledge than either administrative or legislative activity. The organization of a diplomatic service, which might be, so to speak, the eyes of the nation as regarded foreign affairs, might often make the difference between peace and war, and might even enable us to avert invasion.

As to financial affairs, of course popular consent, given in some distinct and substantial form, is essential to taxation, and this is the historical explanation of the gradual assumption of sovereignty by the House of Commons. This consideration, no doubt, must always limit the extent to which government by a well-instructed few could be carried, and it is perhaps the most obvious and conclusive of the many obvious and conclusive reasons why no great change in the principles of the machinery of government can be expected by any reasonable man. I do not for a moment suggest that we can be governed otherwise than we are. I fully admit that for practical purposes the best course is to get out of our tools such work as is to be got out of them. I merely wish to refer to the fact that there are two sides to the account, and to excuse myself for not sharing in the general enthusiasm on the subject of our institutions. I do not say that any other institutions are or have been much better. The folly, the weakness, the ignorance of men leave deep marks on all human institutions, and they are quite as legible here and now as in any other time or place.

Equality, like Liberty, appears to me to be a big name for a small thing. The enthusiasm about it in recent times seems to me to have been due principally to two circumstances: the invidious position of the French privileged classes before the Revolution, and the enormous development of wealth in the United States. The first of these was, no doubt, a case in which distinctions had been maintained long after they had ceased to have any meaning whatever or to be of any sort of use. Such cases are very common. Men have a passion for pluming themselves upon anything which distinguishes them from their neighbours, and exaggeration on one side is met by passion on the other. The case of the French privileged classes certainly was as gross a case of a distinction without a difference as has ever occurred in the world, and the French were just in the mood to become rhetorical about it, and to make it the subject not of rational quiet alteration, but of outbursts of pathetic and other nonsense, the effects of which will long be felt in the world. Few things in history seem to me so beggarly as the degree to which the French allowed themselves to be excited about such things. It was shameful to permit them to grow, and more shameful not to be able to put them down in a quiet way without fireworks and theatrical illusions.

The success of equality in America is due, I think, mainly to the circumstance that a large number of people, who were substantially equal in all the more important matters, recognized that fact and did not set up unfounded distinctions. How far they actually are equal now, and how long they will continue to be equal when the population becomes dense, is quite another question. It is also a question which I cannot do more than glance at in two words in this place, whether the enormous development of equality in America, the rapid production of an immense multitude of commonplace, self-satisfied, and essentially slight people is an exploit which the whole world need fall down and worship.

Upon the whole, I think that what little can be truly said of equality is that as a fact human beings are not equal; that in their dealings with each other they ought to recognize real inequalities where they exist as much as substantial equality where it exists. That they are equally prone to exaggerate real distinctions, which is vanity, and to deny their existence, which is envy. Each of these exaggerations is a fault, the latter being a peculiarly mean and cowardly one, the fault of the weak and discontented. The recognition of substantial equality where it exists is merely the avoidance of an error. It does not in itself affect the value of the things recognized as equals, and that recognition is usually a step towards the development of inherent inequalities. If all equally are forbidden to commit crime, and are bound to keep their contracts, the sober, the far-seeing, and the judicious win, and the flighty, the self-indulgent, and the foolish lose. Equality, therefore, if not like liberty, a word of negation, is a word of relation. It tells us nothing definite unless we know what two or more things are affirmed to be equal and what they are in themselves, and when we are informed upon these points we get only statements about matters of fact, true or false, important or not, as it may be.

CHAPTER SIX

FRATERNITY

I now come to examine the last of the three doctrines of the Democratic creed—Fraternity. That upon some terms and to some extent it is desirable that men should wish well to and should help each other is common ground to everyone. At the same time I cannot but think that many persons must share the feeling of disgust with which I for one have often read and listened to expressions of general philanthropy. Such love is frequently an insulting intrusion. Lord Macaulay congratulated England on having been hated by Barère. To hate England was, he observed, the one small service which Barère could do to the country.[1] I know hardly anything in literature so nauseous as Rousseau's expressions of love for mankind when read in the light of his confessions. 'Keep your love to yourself, and do not daub me or mine with it,' is the criticism which his books always suggest to me. So far from joining in Mr. Swinburne's odd address to France, 'Therefore thy sins which are many are forgiven thee because thou has loved much,' it appears to me that the French way of loving the human race is the one of their many sins which it is most difficult to forgive. It is not love that one wants from the great mass of mankind, but respect and justice. It would be pedantic to attempt anything like a definition of love, but it may be said to include two elements at least—first, pleasure in the kind of friendly intercourse, whatever it may be, which is appropriate to the position of the persons who love each other; and next, a mutual wish for each other's happiness. If two people are so constituted that such intercourse between them as is possible is not agreeable to either party, or if

1. See "Barère," in *The Works of Lord Macaulay*. The Twentieth Century Edition, 20 vols in 10, 6:182–302.

their views of what constitutes happiness are conflicting, I do not see how they can love each other. Take, on the one side, a Roman Catholic priest passionately eager for the conversion of heretics, and deeply convinced that the greatest happiness of a heretic is that of being converted to the Roman Catholic religion. Take, on the other hand, a person who has long since made up his mind against the Roman Catholic religion and wishes for no further discussion upon the subject. The priest's love to the heretic if he happened to love him would be a positive nuisance to the heretic. The priest's society would be no pleasure to the heretic, and that which the priest would regard as the heretic's happiness, the heretic would regard as misery.

Love between the sexes is an evil if it is not mutual. No honourable man or woman would desire to be loved by a woman or man unless they [sic] intended to return that love. Of course no one doubts that the greater part of the happiness of mankind arises from the various forms of friendly feeling which they entertain towards each other, and the various services which in consequence of it they do each other; but it is one thing to feel this, and quite another to believe that a general love for all the human race is destined to become a universal religion which will supply the place of all the old ones.

This worship and service of humanity in the abstract are taught in many shapes. The one which I propose to examine is to be found in Mr. Mill's essay on Utilitarianism. It shares the merit which is characteristic of all his writings of being the gravest, the clearest, and the most measured statement with which I, at all events, am acquainted of the dogmatic form of the popular sentiment. The following are the passages in which Mr. Mill states his theory. They occur in the second, the third, and the fifth chapters of his essay on Utilitarianism:

> The utilitarian standard . . . is not the agent's own happiness, but the greatest amount of happiness altogether; and if it may possibly be doubted whether a noble character is always the happier for its nobleness, there can be no doubt that it makes other people happier, and that the world in general is immensely a gainer by it. . . . As between his own happiness and that of others, utilitarianism requires him {the agent} to be as strictly impartial as a disinterested and benevolent spectator. In the golden rule of Jesus of Nazareth, we read the complete spirit of the ethics of utility. To do as one would be done by, and to love one's neighbour as oneself, consti-

tute the ideal perfection of utilitarian morality. . . . The Greatest-Happiness principle . . . is a mere form of words without rational signification, unless one person's happiness, supposed equal in degree (with the proper allowance for kind), is counted for exactly as much as another's. Those conditions being supplied, Bentham's dictum, "Everybody to count for one, nobody for more than one," might be written under the principle of utility as an explanatory commentary. The equal claim of everybody to happiness in the estimation of the moralist and the legislator, involves an equal claim to all the means of happiness, except in so far as the inevitable conditions of human life, and the general interest in which that of every individual is included, set limits to the maxim; and those limits ought to be strictly construed. [213, 218, 257–58 U]

Such is Mr. Mill's answer to the question, What is the object of morals? What do you mean by right and wrong? Let us see how he answers the question, Why should we do right? In the chapter which he devotes to this subject he points out with truth that the external sanctions of morals apply as well to the utilitarian as to any other system, and that the same may be said of the conscientious sanction, but he finds the final sanction in an allied though somewhat different order of ideas, which he describes as 'a natural basis of sentiment for utilitarian morality.' [231 U]

This it is which, when once the general happiness is recognized as the ethical standard, will constitute the strength of the utilitarian morality. This firm foundation is that of the social feelings of mankind; the desire to be in unity with our fellow creatures, which is already a powerful principle in human nature, and happily one of those which tend to become stronger, without express inculcation, from the influences of advancing civilization. The social state is at once so natural, so necessary, and so habitual to man, that, except in some unusual circumstances or by an effort of voluntary abstraction, he never conceives himself otherwise than as a member of a body; and this association is riveted more and more as mankind are further removed from the state of savage independence. Any condition, therefore, which is essential to a state of society, becomes more and more an inseparable part of every person's conception of the state of things which he is born into, and which is the destiny of a human being. Now, society between human beings, except in the relation of master and slave, is manifestly impossible on any other footing than the interests of all are to be consulted. Society between equals can only exist on the understanding that the interests of all are to be regarded equally. And since in all states of civilization every person except an absolute monarch, has equals, every one is obliged to live on these terms with somebody; and in every age some advance is made towards a state in which it will be impossible to live permanently on other terms with anybody. In this way people grow up unable to conceive as possible to them a total disregard of other people's interests. They are under a necessity of conceiving themselves as at least abstaining from all the grosser injuries, and (if only for their own protection) living in a state of constant protest against them. . . . Not only does all strengthening of social ties, and all healthy growth of society, give to each individual a stronger personal interest in practically consulting the welfare of others; it also leads him to identify his *feelings* more and more with their good, or at least with an ever greater degree of practical consideration for it. He comes, as though instinctively, to be conscious of himself as a being who *of course* pays a regard to others. The good of others becomes to him a thing naturally and necessarily to be attended to, like any of the physical conditions of our existence. [231–32 U]

Everyone is interested in promoting this feeling in others even if he has it not himself. 'This mode of conceiving ourselves and human life, as civilization goes on, is felt to be more and more natural.' [232 U] Ultimately it may assume the character of a religion. 'If we now suppose this feeling of unity to be taught as a religion, and the whole force of education, of institutions, and of opinion, directed, as it once was in the case of religion, to make every person grow up from infancy surrounded on all sides both by the profession and by the practice of it, I think that no one, who can realize this conception, will feel any misgiving about the sufficiency of the ultimate sanction for the Happiness morality.' [232 U] Referring to Comte's 'Système de Politique Positive,' Mr. Mill adds:

I entertain the strongest objections to the system of politics and morals set forth in that treatise; but I think it has superabundantly shown the possibility of giving to the service of humanity, even without the aid of belief in

Providence, both the psychical power and the social efficacy of a religion; making it take hold of human life and colour all thought, feeling, and action, in a manner of which the greatest ascendency ever exercised by any religion may be but a type and foretaste; and of which the danger is, not that it should be insufficient, but that it should be so excessive as to interfere unduly with human freedom and individuality.

Neither is it necessary to the feeling which constitutes the binding force of the utilitarian morality on those who recognize it, to wait for the social influences which would make its obligation felt by mankind at large. In the comparatively early stage of human advancement in which we now live, a person cannot indeed feel that entireness of sympathy with all others, which would make any real discordance in the general direction of their conduct in life impossible; but already a person in whom the social feeling is at all developed, cannot bring himself to think of the rest of his fellow creatures as struggling rivals with him for the means of happiness, whom he must desire to see defeated in their object in order that he may succeed in his. The deeply-rooted conception which every individual even now has of himself as a social being, tends to make him feel it one of his natural wants that there should be harmony between his feelings and aims and those of his fellow creatures. If differences of opinion and of mental culture make it impossible for him to share many of their actual feelings—perhaps make him denounce and defy those feelings—he still needs to be conscious that his real aim and theirs do not conflict; that he is not opposing himself to what they really wish for, namely, their own good, but is, on the contrary, promoting it. This feeling in most individuals is much inferior in strength to their selfish feelings, and is often wanting altogether. But to those who have it, it possesses all the characters of a natural feeling. It does not present itself to their minds as a superstition of education, or a law despotically imposed by the power of society, but as an attribute which it would not be well for them to be without. This conviction is the ultimate sanction of the greatest-happiness morality. This it is which makes any mind of well-developed feelings, work with, and not against, the outward motives to care for others, afforded by what I have called the external sanctions; and when those sanctions are wanting, or act in an opposite direction, constitutes in itself a powerful internal binding force, in proportion to the sensitiveness and thoughtfulness of the character; since few but those whose mind is a moral blank could bear to lay out their course of life on the plan of paying no regard to others except so far as their own private interest compels. [232–33 U]

I have quoted these passages at a length which would have been tedious but for their great intrinsic merits. To one who for many years has studied Mr. Mill's writings, and who has observed his public career, it must be obvious that they express his deepest and most abiding convictions. Those who have done me the honour of following my speculations thus far will not, I hope, accuse me of egotism for observing that they also mark the point at which I differ from Mr. Mill most deeply. The difference, indeed, is one which lies altogether beyond the reach of argument, and which no doubt colours the whole of my opposition to his later teaching. He thinks otherwise than I of men and of human life in general. He appears to believe that if men are all freed from restraints and put, as far as possible, on an equal footing, they will naturally treat each other as brothers, and work together harmoniously for their common good. I believe that many men are bad, a vast majority of men indifferent, and many good, and that the great mass of indifferent people sway this way or that according to circumstances, one of the most important of which circumstances is the predominance for the time being of the bad or good. I further believe that between all classes of men there are and always will be real occasions of enmity and strife, and that even good men may be and often are compelled to treat each other as enemies either by the existence of conflicting interests which bring them into collision, or by their different ways of conceiving goodness.

Mr. Mill's theory of life, which seems to be acquiring a sort of secondary orthodoxy, appears to me, when reduced to its simplest elements, to be something of this sort. On the one hand, we have the external world, which in its relation to men may be regarded as a mass of the materials of happiness. On the other, an enormous number of human creatures substantially equal, substantially alike, substantially animated by the same desires and impulses. Divide the materials of happiness equally between them, and let them do as they like. They will live at peace, and collectively increase each other's happiness to an indefinite or indefinitely increasing extent; inasmuch as each human creature possesses faculties which, if fully developed to their utmost extent, as they will be upon this supposition, will be an equal blessing to his neighbours and to himself. Men are, or rather men if let alone will after a time be found to be, disposed to work together for their common good. Let them alone. The great instrument for bringing about this result is a social sentiment already powerful in some minds, and which will hereafter become a dominant religion. I shall conclude this work by an attempt to give the outline of what I myself think upon this subject, but before doing so I will say why this view appears to me untenable.

In the first place I do not agree with Mr. Mill's statement of the standard of utilitarianism as being 'not the agent's own happiness, but the greatest amount of happiness altogether,' or with Bentham's doctrine, 'everybody to count for one, nobody for more than one,' even when Mr. Mill's qualifications are added to it. In a certain sense I am myself a utilitarian.* That is to say, I think that from the nature of the case some external standard must always be supplied by which moral rules may be tested; and happiness is the most significant and least misleading word that can be employed for that purpose. It is, too, the only object to which it is possible to appeal in order to obtain support. A moral system which avowedly had no relation to happiness in any sense of the word would be a mere exercise of ingenuity for which no one would care. I know not on what other footing than that of expediency, generally in a wider or narrower sense, it would be possible to discuss the value of a moral rule or the provisions of a law.

It is also perfectly true that it is impossible, either in legislation or in ethical speculation, which has much in common with legislation, to recognize individual distinctions. 'Thou shalt do no murder' must of necessity mean, No one shall do any act which the law defines to be murder, and everyone, without exception, who does any such act shall be punished. In the same way, 'It is wrong to lie' means that certain kinds of untruths defined as lying by the person who utters the maxim are morally wrong, whoever makes use of them. Every law and every moral rule must thus, of necessity, be a general proposition, and as such must affect indiscriminately rather than equally the interests of as many persons as are subject to its influence. To say, however, that moral speculation or legislation presupposes on the part of the moralist or legislator

*See Note at the end of the volume [pp. 215–27].

a desire to promote equally the happiness of every person affected by his system or his law is, I think, incorrect. Laws and moral systems are conditions of life imposed upon men either by political power or by the force of argument. The legislator says to his subjects, You shall—the moralist says to his hearers or readers, I advise you to—live thus or thus; but each addresses himself to a body of men whom he regards as a whole, upon whom he is to impose, or to whom he is to suggest, the way of life which he wishes them to adopt, not the way which he supposes them to wish to adopt. The character of a code of laws or of morals is determined by the ideal of human life which it assumes, and this is the ideal of its author, not the ideal of those to whose conduct it applies.

In a word, the happiness which the lawgiver regards as the test of his laws is that which he, after attaching to their wishes whatever weight he thinks proper, wishes his subjects to have, not that which his subjects wish to have; and this is still more true of the moralist. The legislator is always obliged to pay the utmost attention to the wishes of his subjects, though in particular cases he may be able to oppose, counteract, and sometimes even to change them. As the moralist has to rely entirely on persuasion, he is under no such restriction. If he has sufficient confidence in his own views, or if he is indifferent about their adoption by others, he can rest his system upon a conception of happiness as different from the common one of his own time and country as he pleases, and such moral systems are often by no means the least influential. As individual weakness is one of the conditions which make law possible, so conscious ignorance is one great source of the authority of moral systems. Men feel conscious of their own weakness and ignorance, and, at the same time, they feel that to live without any sort of principle or rule of conduct, to be guided as we suppose animals to be, merely by the impulse of the moment, is morally impossible, and this feeling predisposes them to accept what is prescribed to them by persons who claim authority. If everyone knew his own mind with perfect distinctness, there would be little or no room for moral teaching.

For these reasons I should amend Mr. Mill's doctrine thus: The utilitarian standard is not the greatest amount of happiness altogether (as might be the case if happiness was as distinct an idea as bodily health), but the widest possible extension of the ideal of life formed by the person who sets up the standard. I am not quite sure whether or to what extent Mr. Mill would dissent from this view. He insists on the difference between kinds of happiness in several passages, in one of which he remarks: 'Of two pleasures, if there be one to which all or almost all who have experience of both give a decided preference, irrespective of any feeling of moral obligation to prefer it, that is the more desirable pleasure.' [211 U] This looks as if his opinion was that the legislator and the moralist respectively are to decide what constitutes the happiness which they are to promote. If so, we are agreed, but in that case I think Mr. Mill's way of expressing himself unfortunate. A legislator may regard a meat diet as an element of the happiness which he seeks to promote, but sheep, oxen, and pigs can hardly look on the butcher as a friend. The legislator may think it right that criminals should be punished for their crimes. The criminal classes would probably think otherwise. The legislator may include energy of character in his ideal of happiness, and may seek to develope it by establishing freedom of contract and compelling men to keep their contracts. The weak, the languid, and in some instances the enthusiastic and the affectionate may feel that they would prefer a system of law leaving less to individual taste and interfering to a greater extent with the relations of life. In all these and in numberless other cases there is a conflict between man and man, both as to the nature of happiness and as to the terms on which it is to be enjoyed. To base a universal moral system on the assumption that there is any one definite thing, or any one definite set of things, which can be denoted by the word 'happiness' is to build on the sand.

It is quite true that in every time and country all existing communities have views upon the subject sufficiently distinct for ordinary practical purposes, and this circumstance gives to such speculations as Bentham's the immense practical importance which belongs to them. Assume England, France, the United States, and other nations to be established living communities in each of which a certain view as to the nature and general objects of human existence has come to prevail, and Bentham's rules are of the utmost value. Go a step farther and convert those rules into a theory which is to explain and account for the power of these societies and the nature and comparative values of their views of human life, and the rules not only break down, but become contradictory; for they begin by telling us that everyone's happiness is to count for one, and then proceed to lay down rules based on a conception of general happiness which makes and must make all those who do not accept it unhappy. To try to get out of this by telling those who disagree with you that their notion of happiness is wrong and yours right is a mere evasion. It is the shoemaker telling the wearer of the shoe that it does not pinch. It may be quite right that it should pinch, but on the question whether it pinches or not the feelings of the wearer are the only possible test. A friend of mine was once remonstrating with an Afghan chief on the vicious habits which he shared with many of his countrymen, and was pointing out to him their enormity according to European notions. 'My friend,' said the Afghan, 'why will you talk about what you do not understand? Give our way of life a fair trial, and then you will know something about it.' To say to a man who is grossly sensual, false all through, coldly cruel and ungrateful, and absolutely incapable of caring for anyone but himself, We, for reasons which satisfy us, will in various ways discourage and stigmatize your way of life, and in some cases punish you for living according to your nature, is to speak in an intelligible, straightforward way. To say to him, We act thus because we love you, and with a view to your own happiness, appears to me to be a double untruth. In the first place, I for one do not love such people, but hate them. In the second place, if I wanted to make them happy, which I do not, I should do so by pampering their vices, which I will not.

It is perhaps a minor point that the application of Mr. Mill's test about the different kinds of happiness is impossible. Where are we to find people who are qualified by experience to say which is the happier, a man like Lord Eldon or a man like Shelley; a man like Dr. Arnold or a man like the late Marquis of Hertford; a very stupid prosperous farmer who dies of old age after a life of perfect health, or an accomplished delicate woman of passionate sensibility and brilliant genius, who dies worn out before her youth is passed, after an alternation of rapturous happiness with agonies of distress. Who can call up Mdme. de la Vallière and ask her whether she was happier as the mistress of Louis XIV or as a penitent in her own convent? and how are we to discover what difference a conviction of the truth of atheism would have made in her views on the subject? To ask these questions is to show that they can never be answered. They are like asking the distance from one o'clock to London Bridge. The legislator and the moralist no doubt may and must form their own opinions on the subject of the life which is suitable for that section of mankind with which they are concerned, and must do what they can to compel or persuade them to adopt it; but they ought to know what they are about. Their object is to get people to accept their view of happiness, not to make people happy in their own way. Love is far from being the only motive which leads them to undertake this task. Their motives are innumerable and are like the motives which prompt men to other undertakings—love of power, love of the exercise of power, the gratification of curiosity, zeal for the doctrines in which they believe, and a thousand other things. No doubt interest in the human race and its welfare, or in the welfare of certain parts of it on certain terms, has its place among the rest, but it does not stand alone.

This last remark introduces the second great qualification to Mr. Mill's view which occurs to my mind. It applies to his doctrine that, according to the utilitarian system of morals, each person's happiness ought to count for exactly as much as another's, a 'proper allowance' being made for kind. What allowance would be proper or how it could be calculated I do not stop to enquire, but the principle asserted appears to me to be purely gratuitous; and, indeed, Mr. Mill makes, so far as I know, no attempt to prove it, and yet the objections to it are strong and obvious. I repeat that laws and moral rules must from the nature of the case be indiscriminate, and must in that sense treat those who are subject to them as equals, but in no other sense than this is it the case that everyone's happiness either is or ought to be regarded either by moralists or legislators or by anyone else as of equal importance. As I have already shown, both the legislator and the moralist desire to promote, not the happiness of men simply, but their own conception of happiness, upon certain conditions. They wish, for instance, men who will be truthful and energetic to have those satisfactions which truthfulness and energy procure so long as they continue to be truthful and energetic.

Apart, however, from this, both legislators and moralists, as well as all other human creatures, care for their own happiness and the happiness of their friends and connections very much more than for the happiness of others. Mr. Mill asserts as if it was an obvious first truth that 'as between his own happiness and that of others, justice requires' (everyone) 'to be as strictly impartial as a disinterested and benevolent spectator.' [218 U] If this be so, I can only say that nearly the whole life of nearly every human creature is one continued course of injustice, for nearly everyone passes his life in providing the means of happiness for himself and those who are closely connected with him, leaving others all but entirely out of account. Nay, men are so constituted that personal and social motives cannot be distinguished and do not exist apart. When and in so far as we seek to please others, it is because it pleases us to give them pleasure. A man who takes pleasure in pleasing others is benevolent; a man who takes no pleasure in pleasing others is unkind or devoid of benevolence. A man who takes pleasure in hurting others is malignant; but whenever it is necessary to determine a person's character in regard to benevolence, it is necessary to determine the manner in which the pleasures or the sufferings of others affect him. So completely is every man his own centre that the nature of his relations to those who stand closest to him have to be expressed in terms of his own personal pleasure or pain. 'She was the very joy of his heart,' 'He did not care a straw for her,' would be natural ways of describing a most affectionate and a most indifferent husband's feelings towards their respective wives.

That this is in fact the case, that self-love is the fountain from which the wider forms of human affection flow and on which philanthropy itself is ultimately based, is, I think, admitted by the whole turn of the passage on the ultimate sanction of utilitarian morality which I quoted above. The point at which Mr. Mill and I should part company is his belief that this natural feeling for oneself and one's friends, gradually changing its character, is sublimated into a general love for the human race; and in that shape is capable of forming a new religion, of which we need only fear that it may be too strong for human liberty and individuality.

Probably the best way of showing how and why I differ from his view will be by stating my own view positively, and noticing incidentally the view to which I am opposed.

In general terms I think that morality depends upon religion—that is to say, upon the opinions which men entertain as to matters of fact, and particularly as to God and a future state of existence—and that it is incapable of being in itself a religion binding on mankind at large. I think that if we entirely dismiss from our minds not only the belief that there are, but a doubt whether there may not be, a God and a future state, the morality of people in general, and in particular the view which people in general will take of their relation to others, will have to be changed. I admit that in the case of a few peculiarly constituted persons it may be otherwise, but I think that minds so constituted as to be capable of converting morality pure and simple into a religion by no means deserve unqualified admiration. I think that the disposition and power to do so is in many instances a case not of strength but of weakness, and that it almost always involves a considerable amount of self-deception.

*Up to a certain point, I agree that the question whether the fundamental doctrines of religion are true is indifferent to morality. If we assume that this life is all, and that there is no God about whom we need think or care, the moral system, which I may call common, as opposed to Mr. Mill's transcendental, utilitarianism will stand on its own foundations. To give a specific illustration, Hume's doctrine, 'that personal merit consists entirely in the usefulness or agreeableness of qualities to the person himself possessed of them, or to others who have any intercourse with him,' and that 'every man who has any regard to his own happiness and welfare will best find his account in the practice of every moral duty,'[2] is quite independent of religion in my sense of the word. That up to a certain point 'true self-love and social are the same'[3] does not admit of serious dispute. So far, therefore, I am on common ground with Mr. Mill and with others who are even more enthusiastic in what he calls the service of humanity. The point at which the common utilitarian doctrine, as I understand it, stops is that which is marked by the word 'self-sacrifice'; and this is a word with which so many false associations are connected that I must shortly examine it before I proceed.

It is to me, and I should think from the general tone of his speculations it would be to Mr. Mill, impossible to use the word 'self-sacrifice' as it sometimes is used, as if it were the name of some mysterious virtue. By self-sacrifice I understand simply an instance in which, though the contrary is usually the

---

*With this passage before him (it extends to p. 177), Mr. Harrison says of my book: 'The key-note of the book would appear to be that there can be no general morality apart from hell.'

2. David Hume, *Enquiry concerning the Principles of Morals,* in *Enquiries concerning the Human Understanding and concerning the Principles of Morals,* 3rd ed., ed. L. A. Selby-Bigge, and revised by P. H. Nidditch (Oxford: Clarendon Press, 1975), p. 278.

3. Alexander Pope, *Essay on Man,* in *Poetical Works,* ed. Herbert Davis (Oxford: Oxford University Press, 1978), Fourth Epistle, p. 279.

case, the motives which have reference to others immediately and to self only mediately happen to be stronger than the motives which have immediate relation to self and only a mediate relation to others. The pleasure of pleasing others by common acts of courtesy is in most cases stronger than the trifling pain of self-denial which it implies. I should not therefore say that it was an act of self-sacrifice to be polite. On the other hand, the pleasure of providing for destitute and disagreeable relations who are dependent on you is usually a weaker motive than the pain of foregoing a marriage into which a man wishes to enter. Therefore if a man abstained from such a marriage for such a purpose I should call his act one of self-sacrifice. This, however, seems to me to mark the limit of self-sacrifice. I do not believe that anyone ever did or ever will, as long as men are men, intentionally perform an act of absolute self-sacrifice—that is to say, hurt himself without any reason whatever for doing so.

That any human creature ever, under any conceivable circumstances, acted otherwise than in obedience to that which for the time being was his strongest wish, is to me an assertion as incredible and as unmeaning as the assertion that on a particular occasion two straight lines enclosed a space. If a mother were cruelly to murder a child whom she idolised and whom she had a thousand special reasons for cherishing with peculiar tenderness and no motive whatever for injuring, if she firmly believed all the while that in doing so she was acting most wickedly and in a manner which would assuredly be punished by her own eternal damnation, and which would ensure the eternal damnation of the child as well, and lastly if she had absolutely no reason whatever for so acting, she would perform an act of absolute self-sacrifice. I say that the occurrence of such an act is an impossibility. If circumstances occurred to which the description appeared to apply, the inference would be either that the murderess had had some unknown motive of immense power, such as vengeance, sudden anger, jealousy, or the like, or that the act was an act of madness, which, properly speaking, is not an act at all, but a mere event. If this is admitted, the general proposition that absolute self-sacrifice is impossible is proved, and it follows that when we speak of self-sacrifice we mean only that the person who is said to have sacrificed himself was affected to an unusual degree by some common wish or motive, or was affected by some unusual wish or motive.

To return, then, to the assertion that common utilitarianism stops short at self-sacrifice. The meaning of it will be that that system affords no reason why, if the system were generally adopted, the common proportion between wishes and motives which immediately regard oneself, and wishes and motives which immediately regard others, should be disturbed either in particular cases or in the race at large. Common utilitarianism is simply a description in general terms of the ordinary current morality which prevails amongst men of the world. It is a morality which I do not in the least degree disparage. I cordially approve it, and think it good as far as it goes. The question is whether it ought to go farther than it does. To this I say Yes, if there is a God and a future state; No, if there is no God and no future state. The positive half of this assertion and its limitations I shall develope hereafter. For the present I confine myself to the negative half, and upon this I am at issue with Mr. Mill and many other persons, who think that, irrespectively of what I understand by religion, the common current utilitarianism may, and probably will, be rendered very much stricter than it is at present, and that the existing balance between social and personal wishes and motives may and probably will be considerably altered, so as to increase the relative power of the former.

In examining the subject, it will be necessary in the first place to take a short general view of the extent to which common utilitarianism would go. It seems to me that it fully accounts for and justifies all the common instances of benevolence with which we are familiar in every-day life; for, like every other moral system, it must, if rationally worked, take account of the two great factors of human conduct, habit and passion. I do not think that in the common relations of life it makes much difference whether one moral system or another is adopted. The feelings towards each other of husbands and wives, parents and children, relations, friends, neighbours, members of the same profession, business connections, members of the same nation, and so forth, grow up by themselves. Moral systems have to account for and more or less to regulate them, but human life forms the starting point of all systems worth having. Now universal experience shows that some of the wishes and motives which regard others more obviously than self are in almost all men stronger than some of the wishes and motives which regard self more obviously than others, and that if we were to take an average indicating the comparative power of the two classes of wishes and motives in ordinary men, a very large number of individual exceptions would always have to be made. In every army, for instance, there is an average amount of courage on which you may reckon with confidence in nearly every soldier. But there are also in every army a certain number of soldiers with whom the wishes and motives which go to make up the habit of courage rise to what we should call the pitch of heroism, and there are also a certain number in which they sink to the pitch of cowardice. Whether you choose to say that a soldier who mounts a breach at the imminent risk of his life does or does not perform an act of self-sacrifice is a question of taste and of propriety in the use of language. If that expression is used, it will be consistent to say that common utilitarianism will provide for an average amount of self-sacrifice. If that expression is not used, we may say that common utilitarianism stops short of self-sacrifice; but whichever phrase be employed, the same general meaning is conveyed. It is that though the ordinary motives of human society as we know it carry social benevolence—or fraternity, if the word is preferred—up to a point, they also stop at a point.

The point cannot be specifically fixed, and it varies considerably according to the dispositions of particular persons, but it may be negatively described thus. Common utilitarianism does not in ordinary cases give people any reason for loving their neighbours as themselves, or for loving large numbers of people at all, especially those whose interests are in any way opposed to their own. Common utilitarianism, in a word, comes to this: 'Thou shalt love thy neighbour and hate thine enemy.' Love your neighbour in proportion to the degree in which he approaches yourself and appeals to your passions and sympathies. In hating your enemy, bear in mind the fact that under immediate excitement you are very likely to hate him more than you would wish to do upon a deliberate consideration of all his relations to yourself and your friends, and of your permanent and remote as compared with your immediate interest. How religion affects this I shall consider hereafter. At present I limit myself to the point that, however this may be, Mr. Mill's theory supplies no ground for thinking that common utilitarianism will in fact be screwed up into transcendental utilitarianism, except in a few particular cases, which deserve no special admiration or sympathy.

Mr. Mill's theory is, shortly, that the progress of civilization will lead people to feel a general love for mankind so strong that it will in process of time assume the character of a religion, and have an influence greater than that of all existing religions. Mr. Mill admits that the feeling is at present an exceptional one. He says, 'this feeling in most individuals is much inferior in strength to their selfish feelings, and is often wanting altogether.' He adds, 'to those who have it, it possesses all the characters of a natural feeling,' [233 U] which implies that he knows what he feels like. I admit that there is a real feeling which more or less answers the description given by Mr. Mill, but I think that those who feel it deceive themselves as to its nature, as to its importance, and as to the probability of its increase.

First, as to its nature and importance. Mr. Mill appears to assume that an earnest desire for the good of other men is likely to produce their good. How far this is consistent with his doctrine about liberty I will not stop to enquire. He has misgivings on the point, as he says that the danger is lest the influence arising out of it should 'interfere unduly with human freedom and individuality.' [231 U] Be this as it may, it is surely clear that you cannot promote a man's happiness unless you know, to begin with, wherein it consists. But apart from some few commonplace matters, upon which men substantially agree, and which society no doubt settles as it goes on, men's notions of happiness differ widely. As to all that part of our happiness which depends upon the general organization of society, upon the sentiments with which we are to regard each other, upon political institutions of different kinds and the like, there are many and conflicting theories. Self in respect to all things, but above all in respect to these things, is each man's centre from which he can no more displace himself than he can leap off his own shadow. Milton's line about Presbyter and Priest thus applies precisely to Humanity and Self.[4] Humanity is only I writ large, and love for Humanity generally means zeal for MY notions as to what men should be and how they should live. It frequently means distaste for the present. He that loveth not his brother whom he hath seen is peculiarly apt to suppose that he loves his distant cousin whom he hath not seen and never will see. Mr. Mill, for instance, never loses an opportunity of speaking with contempt of our present 'wretched social arrangements,' the low state of society, [214 U] and the general pettiness of his contemporaries, but he looks forward to an age in which an all-embracing love of Humanity will regenerate the human race.

On one who does not think thus the anticipations of those who do produce a singular effect. They look like so many ideal versions of what the world

4. The final line of John Milton's poem, "On the New Forcers of Conscience under the Long Parliament," in *John Milton: Complete Poems and Major Prose*, ed. M. Y. Hughes (New York: The Odyssey Press, 1957), p. 145.

would be if it adopted universally the theorist's views of human life. Love for Humanity, devotion to the All or Universum, and the like, are thus little, if anything, more than a fanatical attachment to some favourite theory about the means by which an indefinite number of unknown persons (whose existence it pleases the theorist's fancy to assume) may be brought into a state which the theorist calls happiness. A man to whom this ideal becomes so far a reality as to colour his thoughts, his feelings, his estimate of the present and his action towards it, is usually, as repeated experience has shown, perfectly ready to sacrifice that which living people do actually regard as constituting their happiness to his own notions of what will constitute the happiness of other generations. It is, no doubt, true that in a certain sense he does thus rise, or, at any rate, get out of himself. Sympathy for others, interest in the affairs of others, impatience of what he regards as the wrongs of others, do become far stronger motives to him than they are to most men, and do affect his conduct more powerfully, but this in itself is no merit. It certainly gives no man a right to any other man's confidence. Nothing, as I have already pointed out, is a greater nuisance, or in many cases a greater injury, than the love of a person by whom you do not want to be loved. Every man's greatest happiness is that which makes him individually most happy, and of that he and only he can judge. If A places his greatest happiness in promoting that which he regards as B's greatest happiness, B never having asked him to do so, and A having no other interest in the matter than general feelings of sympathy, it is a hundred to one that B will tell A to mind his own business. If A represents a small class of men of quick feelings and lively talents, and B a much larger class of ignorant people, who, if they were let alone, would never have thought of the topics which their advisers din into their ears, the probability is that the few will by degrees work up the many into a state of violence, excitement, discontent, and clamorous desire for they know not what—which is neither a pleasant state in itself nor one fruitful of much real good to anyone whatever.

The man who works from himself outwards, whose conduct is governed by ordinary motives, and who acts with a view to his own advantage and the advantage of those who are connected with himself in definite, assignable ways, produces in the ordinary course of things much more happiness to others (if that is the great object of life) than a moral Don Quixote who is always liable to sacrifice himself and his neighbours. When you have to deal with a man who expects pay and allowances, and is willing to give a fair day's work for it as long as the arrangement suits him, you know where you are. Deal with such a man fairly, and in particular cases, if he is a man of spirit and courage, he will deal with you not only fairly but generously. Earn his gratitude by kindness and justice, and he will in many cases give you what no money could buy or pay for. On the other hand, a man who has a disinterested love for the human race—that is to say, who has got a fixed idea about some way of providing for the management of the concerns of mankind—is an unaccountable person with whom it is difficult to deal upon any well-known and recognized principles, and who is capable of making his love for men in general the ground of all sorts of violence against men in particular.

Besides this, the great mass of mankind are and always will be to a greater or less extent the avowed enemies of considerable sections of their fellow creatures; at all events, for certain purposes and up to a certain point. Those who love the human race as a whole must take sides in these enmities, probably against both parties, and this will increase the original trouble. This introduces one vitally important question, at which I can only glance, but which believers in the service of humanity and in the religion of fraternity ought to solve before they can find standing-room for their religion. The question is this: Are the interests of all mankind identical? are we all brothers? are we even fiftieth cousins? and, in any event, have we not a considerable number of family quarrels which require to be settled before the fact of our relationship (if any) can be regarded in any other light than as a bone of contention?

These questions do not trouble a man who starts from himself and his definite relations to other people. Such a person can be content to let sleeping dogs lie. He can say, 'I wish for my own good; I wish for the good of my family and friends; I am interested in my nation; I will do acts of good nature to miscellaneous people who come in my way; but if in the course of my life I come across any man or body of men who treats me or mine or the people I care about as an enemy, I shall treat him as an enemy with the most absolute indifference to the question whether we can or cannot trace out a relationship either through Adam or through some primeval ape. Show me a definite person doing a definite thing and I will tell you whether he is my friend or my enemy; but as to calling all human creatures indiscriminately my brothers and sisters, I will do no such thing. I have far too much respect for real relations to give these endearing names to all sorts of people of whom I know and for whom, practically speaking, I care nothing at all.'*

The believer in the religion of fraternity cannot speak thus. He is bound to love all mankind. If he wants me to do so too, he must show me a reason why. Not only does he show me none, as a rule, but he generally denies either the truth or the relevancy of that which, if true, is a reason—the doctrine that God made all men and ordered them to love each other. Whether this is true is one question; how it is proposed to get people to love each other without such a belief I do not understand. It would want the clearest of all imaginable revelations to make me try to love a considerable number of people whom it is unnecessary to mention, or affect to care about masses of men with whom I have nothing to do.

These are the grounds on which it appears to me that there is a great deal of self-deception as to the nature of fraternity, and that the mere feeling of eager indefinite sympathy with mankind in those cases in which it happens to exist is not deserving of the admiration which is so often claimed for it.

I will say in concluding this topic a very few words on the opinion that the progress of civilization, the growth of wealth and of physical science, and the general diffusion of comfort will tend to excite or deepen such sympathy. I think it more probable that it will have exactly the opposite effect. The whole tendency of modern civilization is to enable each man to stand alone and take care of his own interests, and the growth of liberty and equality will, as I have already shown, intensify these feelings. They will minimize all restraints and reduce everyone to a dead level, offering no attractions to the imagination or to the affections. In this state of society you will have plenty of public meetings, Exeter Halls, and philanthropic associations, but there will be no occasion for patriotism or public spirit. France in 1870, with its ambulances and its representatives of the Geneva Convention, did not show to advantage in

*Somewhere or other in this chapter Mr. Harrison finds ground for the remark—'Surely a man might unmask fraternity without vociferating that he is an egotist and a misanthrope.' No doubt he is good enough to add: 'All England knows' (I fear that an infinitesimally small portion of England knows or cares anything whatever about it) 'that it is only his way of expressing a kindly nature and a strong sense of duty.' The passage in the text is the only one to which these strange remarks can by any possibility apply. Are they just?

comparison with Holland three centuries before. There are many common-places about the connection between the decay of patriotism and the growth of luxury. No doubt they have their weak side, but to me they appear far more like the truth than the commonplaces which are now so common about the connection between civilization and the love of mankind. Civilization no doubt makes people hate the very thought of pain or discomfort either in their own persons or in the case of others. It also disposes them to talk and to potter about each other's affairs in the way of mutual sympathy and compliment, and now and then to get into states of fierce excitement about them; but all this is not love nor anything like it. The real truth is that the human race is so big, so various, so little known, that no one can really love it. You can at most fancy that you love some imaginary representation of bits of it which when examined are only your own fancies personified. A progress which leads people to attach increased importance to phantoms is not a glorious thing, in my eyes at all events. It is a progress towards a huge Social Science Association embracing in itself all the Exeter Halls that ever were born or thought of.

The general result of all this is that fraternity, mere love for the human race, is not fitted in itself to be a religion. That is to say, it is not fitted to take command of the human faculties, to give them their direction, and to assign to one faculty a rank in comparison with others which but for such interference it would not have.

I might have arrived at this result by a shorter road, for I might have pointed out that the most elementary notions of religion imply that no one human faculty or passion can ever in itself be a religion. It can but be one among many competitors. If human beings are left to themselves, their faculties, their wishes, and their passions will find a level of some sort or other. They will produce some common course of life and some social arrangement. Alter the relative strength of particular passions, and you will alter the social result; but religion means a great deal more than this. It means the establishment and general recognition of some theory about human life in general, about the relation of men to each other and to the world, by which their conduct may be determined. Every religion must contain an element of fact, real or supposed, as well as an element of feeling, and the element of fact is the one which in the long run will determine the nature and importance of the element of feeling. The following are specimens of religions, stated as generally as possible, but still with sufficient exactness to show my meaning.

1. The statements made in the Apostles' Creed are true. Believe them, and govern yourselves accordingly.

2. There is one God, and Mahomet is the prophet of God. Do as Mahomet tells you.

3. All existence is an evil, from which, if you knew your own mind, you would wish to be delivered. Such and such a course of life will deliver you most speedily from the misery of existence.

4. An infinitely powerful supreme God arranged all of you whom I address in castes, each with its own rule of life. You will be fearfully punished in all sorts of ways if you do not live according to your caste rules. Also all nature is full of invisible powers more or less connected with natural objects, which must be worshipped and propitiated.

All these are religions in the proper sense of the word. Each of the four theories expressed in these few words is complete in itself. It states propositions which are either true or false, but which, if true, furnish a complete practical guide for life. No such statement of what Mr. Mill calls the ultimate sanction of the morals of utility is possible. You cannot get more than this out of it: 'Love all mankind.' 'Influences are at work which at some remote time will make men love each other.' These are respectively a piece of advice and a prophecy, but they are not religions. If a man does not take the advice or believe in the prophecy, they pass by him idly. They have no power at all *in invitos,* and the great mass of men have always been *inviti,* or at the very least indifferent, with respect to all religions whatever. In order to make such maxims as these into religions, they must be coupled with some statement of fact about mankind and human life, which those who accept them as religions must be prepared to affirm to be true.

What statement of the sort is it possible to make? 'The human race is an enormous agglomeration of bubbles which are continually bursting and ceasing to be. No one made it or knows anything worth knowing about it. Love it dearly, O ye bubbles.' This is a sort of religion, no doubt, but it seems to me a very silly one. 'Eat and drink, for to-morrow ye die;' 'Be not righteous overmuch, why shouldest thou destroy thyself?'

Huc vina et unguenta et nimium brevis
Flores amœnos ferre jube rosæ,
dum res et ætas et Sororum
Fila trium patiuntur atra.

.   .   .   .

Omnes eodem cogimur.

These are also religions, and, if true, they are, I think, infinitely more rational
than the bubble theory. As a fact they always have been, and in all probability
they always will be, believed and acted upon by a very large proportion of the
human race. I have never seen any serious answer whatever to them, except the
answer that the theory which they presuppose is false in fact, that the two
great fundamental doctrines of the existence of God and a future state are
either true or at all events reasonably probable. To see these doctrines denied
can surprise no rational man. Everyone must be aware of the difficulties connected with them. What does surprise me is to see able men put them aside
with a smile as being unimportant, as mere metaphysical puzzles of an insoluble kind which we may cease to think about without producing any particular effect upon morality. I have referred so often to Mr. Mill that I must do
him the justice to say that I do not here refer to him. Though he does find the
ultimate sanction of morals in considerations which are independent of religion, he nowhere, so far as I am aware, underrates the importance of religious
belief. To do so is the characteristic of minds of a different order from his.

It is not very easy to insist upon the connection between morals and religion without running the risk of falling into very obvious commonplace; but
the extent to which the habit prevails of maintaining that morals are independent of religion makes it necessary to point out that it is impossible to
solve any one of the great questions which the word 'fraternity' suggests without distinct reference to the fundamental questions of religion.

First, fraternity implies love for someone—a desire to promote someone's
happiness. But what is happiness? In particular, is anything which can properly be called virtue essential to it?—if so, what is virtue—the way of life
which becomes a man? Every answer which can be given to these questions depends upon the further question, What are men? Is this life all, or is it only a
stage in something wider and larger? The great disproportion which exists between the stronger and more abiding human feelings and the objects to which

they relate has often been used as an argument in favour of immortality. Whether it is entitled to weight in that capacity I need not enquire, but the fact on which the inference is based is, I think, certain. We do care far more about all sorts of things and people than is at all rational if this life is all; and I think that if we dismiss from our minds every thought of life after death, if we determine to regard the grave as the end of all things, it will be not merely natural and proper to contract our sympathies and interests, and to revise the popular estimate of the comparative value of many things—health, for instance, and honesty—but not to do so will be simply impossible.

Our present conception of a virtuous man is founded entirely on the opinion that virtue is higher in kind than other objects which come into competition with it. Every phrase which we use upon such subjects, and, above all, the word 'I,' implies permanence and continuity in individuals. Conscience and self-respect imply that I am the same person as I was twenty years ago and as I shall be twenty years hence, if I am then in existence at all. The immense importance which men attach to their character, to their honour, to the consciousness of having led an honourable, upright life, is based upon the belief that questions of right and wrong, good and evil, go down to the very man himself and concern him in all that is most intimately, most essentially himself; whereas other things, however distressing—bodily disease, for instance, or poverty—are, in a sense, external to him. The most memorable and striking passage ever written by Mr. Mill refers to this matter. It is as follows:

> The theory, therefore, which resolves Mind into a series of feelings, with a background of possibilities of feeling, can effectually withstand the most invidious of the arguments directed against it. But, groundless as are the extrinsic objections, the theory has intrinsic difficulties which we have not yet set forth, and which it seems to me beyond the power of metaphysical analysis to remove. The thread of consciousness which composes the mind's phenomenal life consists not only of present sensations, but likewise in part {rather, all but entirely} of memories and expectations. Now what are these? . . . Nor can the phenomena involved in these two states of consciousness be adequately expressed without saying that the belief they include is that I myself formerly had, or that I myself and no other shall hereafter have, the sensations remembered or expected. The fact believed is that the sensations did actually form, or will hereafter form, part of the

self-same series of states or thread of consciousness of which the remembrance or expectations of those sensations is the part now present. If, therefore, we speak of the Mind as a series of feelings, we are obliged to complete the statement by calling it a series of feelings which is aware of itself as past and future, and we are reduced to the alternative of believing that the Mind or Ego is something different from any series of feelings or possibilities of them, or of accepting the paradox {I should have said of making the unmeaning and even contradictory assertion} that something which *ex hypothesi* is but a series of feelings can be aware of itself as a series. The truth is, that we are here face to face with that final inexplicability at which, as Sir W. Hamilton observes, we inevitably arrive when we reach ultimate facts, and in general one mode of stating it only appears more incomprehensible than another because the whole of human language is accommodated to the one and is so incongruous with the other that it cannot be expressed in any terms which do not deny its truth. The real stumbling-block is, perhaps, not in any theory of the fact, but in the fact itself. The true incomprehensibility, perhaps, is that something which has ceased, or is not yet in existence, can still be, in a manner present; that a series of feelings, the infinitely greater part of which is past or future, can be gathered up as it were into a single present conception, accompanied by a belief of reality. I think by far the wisest thing we can do is to accept the inexplicable fact without any theory of how it takes place, and when we are obliged to speak of it in terms which assume a theory, to use them with a reservation as to their meaning.[5]

With the greater part of this I cordially agree, but it appears to me that Mr. Mill avoids, with needless caution, the inference which his language suggests. His theory is this. All human language, all human observation implies that the mind, the I, is a thing in itself, a fixed point in the midst of a world of change, of which world of change its own organs form a part. It is the same yesterday, today, and tomorrow. It was what it is when its organs were of a different shape and consisted of different matter from their present shape and matter. It will be what it is when they have gone through other changes. I do not say that this proves, but surely it suggests, it renders probable, the belief

5. John Stuart Mill, *Collected Works of John Stuart Mill*, ed. J. M. Robson, 33 vols (Toronto: University of Toronto Press, 1963–1991), vol. 9, *An Examination of Sir William Hamilton's Philsophy* (1979), pp. 193–94.

that this ultimate fact, this starting-point of all knowledge, thought, feeling, and language, this 'final inexplicability' (an emphatic though a clumsy phrase), is independent of its organs, that it may have existed before they were collected out of the elements, and may continue to exist after they are dissolved into the elements.

The belief thus suggested by the most intimate, the most abiding, the most widespread of all experiences, not to say by universal experience, as recorded by nearly every word of every language in the world, is what I mean by a belief in a future state, if indeed it should not rather be called a past, present, and future state all in one—a state which rises above and transcends time and change. I do not say that this is proved, but I do say that it is strongly suggested by the one item of knowledge which rises above logic, argument, language, sensation, and even distinct thought—that one clear instance of direct consciousness in virtue of which we say 'I am.' This belief is that there is in man, or rather that man is, that which rises above words and above thoughts, which are but unuttered words; that to each one of us 'I' is the ultimate central fact which renders thought and language possible. Some, indeed, have even gone so far as to say—and their saying, though very dark, is not, I think, unmeaning—that the 'I' is even in a certain sense the cause of the external world itself. Be this how it may, it is surely clear that our words, the sounds which we make with our lips, are but very imperfect symbols, that they all presuppose matter and sensation, and are thus unequal to the task of expressing that which, to use poor but necessary metaphors, lies behind and above matter and sensation. Most words are metaphors from sensible objects. 'Spirit' means breathing, but I think no one will ever use words to much purpose unless he can feel and see that eloquence is eloquence and logic logic only if and in so far as the skin of language covers firm bone and hard muscle. It seems to me that we are spirits in prison, able only to make signals to each other, but with a world of things to think and to say which our signals cannot describe at all.

It is this necessity for working with tools which break in your hand when any really powerful strain is put upon them which so often gives an advantage in argument to the inferior over the superior, to the man who can answer to the purpose easy things to understand over the man whose thoughts split the seams of the dress in which he has to clothe them. It also supplies the key to the saying 'Silence is golden.' The things which cannot be adequately represented by words are more important than those which can. Nay, the attempt, even the successful attempt, to put into words thoughts not too deep for them has its inconveniences. It is like selling out stock which might have risen in value if it had been left alone. This also is the reason why our language on the deepest of all deep things is so poor and unsatisfactory, and why poetry sometimes seems to say more than logic. The essence of poetry is that it is an appeal to the hearer's or reader's good faith and power of perception. Logic drives its thoughts into your head with a hammer. Poetry is like light. You can shut your eyes to it if you will, but if, having eyes to open, you open them, it will show you a world of wonders. I have quoted the passage which forms, so to speak, the last word on this subject of the great logician of our age. I will quote, in order to give form to what I have been trying to say, a passage which is perhaps the most memorable utterance of its greatest poet. The poetry seems to me to go far deeper into the heart of the matter than the logic:

> It is mysterious, it is awful to consider that we not only carry each a future ghost within him, but are in very deed ghosts. These limbs, whence had we them? this stormy force, this life-blood with its burning passion? They are dust and shadow; a shadow-system gathered around our ME wherein through some moments or years the Divine Essence is to be revealed in the flesh. That warrior on his strong war-horse, fire flashes through his eyes, force dwells in his arms and heart; but warrior and war-horse are a vision, a revealed force, nothing more. Stately they tread the earth, as if it were a firm substance. Fools! the earth is but a film; it cracks in twain, and warrior and war-horse sink beyond plummet's sounding. Plummet's? Fantasy herself will not follow them. A little while ago they were not; a little while and they are not, their very ashes are not.
>
> So has it been from the beginning, so will it be to the end. Generation after generation takes to itself the form of a body, and forth-issuing from Cimmerian night on heaven's mission APPEARS. What force and fire is in each he expends. One grinding in the mill of industry, one hunter-like climbing the giddy Alpine heights of science, one madly dashed in pieces on the rocks of strife in war with his fellow, and then the heaven-sent is recalled, his earthly vesture falls away and soon even to sense becomes a vanished shadow. Thus, like some wild-flaming, wild-thundering train of Heaven's artillery does this mysterious MANKIND thunder and flame in

long-drawn, quick succeeding grandeur through the unknown deep. Thus, like a God-created, fire-breathing-spirit host, we emerge from the inane, haste stormfully across the astonished earth, then plunge again into the inane. Earth's mountains are levelled, and her seas filled up in our passage. Can the earth, which is but dead and a vision, resist spirits which have reality and are alive? On the hardest adamant some footprint of us is stamped in. The last rear of the host will read traces of the earliest van. But whence? Oh, Heaven? whither? Sense knows not, faith knows not, only that it is through mystery to mystery, from God and to God.

> We are *such stuff*
> As dreams are made of, and our little life
> Is rounded with a sleep.[6]

I quote this, of course, as poetry ought to be quoted—that is to say, for the sake not of definite propositions, but of vivid impressions. To canvass its precise logical value would be to misunderstand it, but I know of no statement which puts in so intense and impressive a form the belief which appears to me to lie at the very root of all morals whatever—the belief, that is, that I am one; that my organs are not I; that my happiness and their well-being are different and may be inconsistent with each other; that pains and pleasures differ in kind as well as in degree; that the class of pleasures and pains which arise from virtue and vice respectively cannot be measured against those say of health and disease, inasmuch as they affect different subjects or affect the same subjects in a totally different manner.

The solution of all moral and social problems lies in the answer we give to the questions, What am I? How am I related to others? If my body and I are one and the same thing—if, to use a phrase in which an eminent man of letters once summed up the opinions which he believed to be held by an eminent scientific man—we are all 'sarcoïdous peripatetic funguses,' and nothing more, good health and moderate wealth are blessings infinitely and out of all comparison greater than any others. I think that a reasonable fungus would systematically repress many other so-called virtues which often interfere with health and the acquisition of a reasonable amount of wealth. If, however, I

6. Thomas Carlyle, *Sartor Resartus,* in *The Works of Thomas Carlyle,* Centenary edition, 30 vols (New York: Charles Scribner's and Sons, n.d.), 1:211–12.

am something more than a fungus*—if, properly speaking, the fungus is not I at all, but only my instrument, and if I am a mysteriously permanent being who may be entering on all sorts of unknown destinies—a scale is at once established among my faculties and desires, and it become natural to subordinate, and if necessary to sacrifice, some of them to others.

To take a single instance. By means which may easily be suggested, every man can accustom himself to practise a variety of what are commonly called vices, and, still more, to neglect a variety of what are generally regarded as duties, without compunction. Would a wise man do this or not? If he regards himself as a spiritual creature, certainly not, because conscience is that which lies deepest in a man. It is the most important, or one of the most important, constituent elements of his permanence. Indeed, if there is any permanent element in him, his conscience in all probability cannot be destroyed, although it can be covered up and disregarded. To tamper with it, therefore, to try to destroy it, is of all conceivable courses of conduct the most dangerous, and may prepare the way to a wakening, a self-assertion, of conscience fearful to think of. But suppose that the fungus theory is the true one. Suppose that man is a mere passing shadow, and nothing else. What is he to say of his conscience? Surely a rational man holding such a theory of his own nature will be bound in consistency to try and to determine the question whether he ought not to prune his conscience just as he cuts his hair and nails. A man who regarded a cold heart and a good digestion as the best possible provision for life would have a great deal to say for his view. Each of these blessings is capable of being acquired, and those who do not regard them as the *summum bonum* can only on the fungus theory say to those who do, 'Our tastes differ.'

From all this I conclude that the question, How would fraternity induce us to act? depends upon the view which may be taken of the doctrine of a future state as I have explained and stated it.

The question, Who is my brother? depends perhaps more obviously and directly upon the question, Is there a God who cares for human society—a Providence? If not, morality is simply a matter of fact. Certain rules of conduct do as a fact tend to promote human happiness. The ultimate sanction of these rules is individual taste. Those who have a taste (which is admitted to be rare)

*Mr. Harrison sees in this an allusion to Comte. I had in my mind an entirely different person, as unlike Comte in every respect as one man can be to another.

for the good of the race as a whole can say to those who have it not, 'In our opinion you are brutes.' Those who care only for themselves and their friends, and for others in relation to them, may reply to this, 'In our opinion you are fools,' and neither party can get any farther.

If, on the other hand, there is a Providence, then morality ceases to be a mere fact and becomes a law. The very meaning of a belief in a Providence is that the physical and the moral world alike are the sphere of conscious arrangement and design; that men, the members of the moral world, transcend the material world in which they are placed, and that the law imposed on them is this—Virtue, that is to say, the habit of acting upon principles fitted to promote the happiness of men in general, and especially those forms of happiness which have reference to the permanent element in men, is connected with, and will, in the long run, contribute to the individual happiness of those who practise it, and especially to that part of their happiness which is connected with the permanent elements of their nature. The converse is true of vice.*

This law is unwritten and unspoken, and its sanctions (except for those who believe in a definite literal heaven and hell) are indefinite. These circumstances constitute the moral trial of life, and no doubt immensely diminish the force of the law in question, and enable anyone who is disposed to do so to deny its very existence. If, however, a man is led to accept this interpretation of life, it affords a real sanction for morals. I cannot understand how a person who believed that a Being capable of arranging the physical and moral world as we know it, had by so arranging it tacitly commanded him thus to act, could hesitate about the wisdom of obeying that command.

Utilitarianism appears to me to rest on its own foundations. It is a consequence from the ultimate fact that men have powers and wishes. Add a future state, and you give to happiness a special meaning, and establish a scale among different kinds of happiness. Add a belief in God, and virtue ceases to be a mere fact, and becomes the law of a society, the members of which may by a strong metaphor be called brothers if and in so far as they obey that law.

---

*With this passage before him Mr. Harrison says of my book, 'Virtue consists in practising it' (utilitarianism) 'under pain of eternal damnation.' 'Mr. Stephen is reticent about the form of future torment. But we see him shake his head, and he leaves us to infer that it will not be pleasant.' Is this fair or true?

Virtue as a law implies social relations, and the law 'Be virtuous' can hardly be obeyed except by a person who wishes good men to be happy, and who also wishes to some extent to make men good. Take away the belief in a future state, and belief in God ceases to be of any practical importance. Happiness means whatever each man likes. Morality becomes a mere statement as to facts—this is what you can get if you want it, and this is the way to get it. Love for mankind becomes a matter of taste, sanctioned by the fear of being called a fool or a brute, as the case may be, by people who do not agree with you.

These two ways of looking at the world and at morals are both complete, consistent, intelligible, and based upon facts. The practical distinction between them is that the first does and the second does not give a rational account of the feeling that it is a duty to be virtuous. If virtue is God's law, to be virtuous is man's duty. Where there is no lawgiver there can be no law; where there is no law there can be no duty, though of course there may be a taste for doing what, if there were a law, would be a duty. This taste may, for what I know, be inherited. I think it a mere question of curiosity whether it is or not, for when a man learns that his sense of duty is a mere fact which, however convenient to others, is apt to be very inconvenient to him, and rests upon nothing, he will easily get rid of it. The fact that our ancestors wore sword-belts may be a very good explanation of the fact that tailors usually put buttons in the small of the back of the coats of their descendants. So long as they look well and are not inconvenient there let them stay, but if they were found inconvenient they would be snipped off without mercy. Duty is so very often inconvenient that it requires a present justification as well as an historical explanation, and no such justification can be given to a man who wants one except that God is a legislator and virtue a law in the proper sense of the word.

It would be a matter of equal difficulty and interest to trace out systematically the relation of religious belief to a sense of duty. The relation, of course, depends upon the nature of the religion. Some forms of religion are distinctly unfavourable to a sense of social duty. Others have simply no relation to it whatever, and of those which favour it (as is the case in various degrees with every form of Christianity) some promote it far more powerfully than others. I should say that those of which the central figure is an infinitely wise and powerful Legislator whose own nature is confessedly inscrutable to man, but

who has made the world as it is for a prudent, steady, hardy, enduring race of
people who are neither fools nor cowards, who have no particular love for
those who are, who distinctly know what they want, and are determined to
use all lawful means to get it. Some such religion as this is the unspoken
deeply rooted conviction of the solid, established part of the English nation.
They form an anvil which has worn out a good many hammers, and will wear
out a good many more, enthusiasts and humanitarians notwithstanding.*

Though the sense of duty which is justified by this form of religion has become instinctive with many of those who feel it, I think that if the belief
should ever fail, the sense of duty which grows out of it would die by degrees.
I do not believe that any instinct will long retain its hold upon the conduct of
a rational and enterprising man when he has discovered that it is a mere instinct which he need not yield to unless he chooses. People who think otherwise would do well to remember that, though custom makes some duties so
easy to some people that they are discharged as a matter of course, there are
others which it is extremely difficult to discharge at all; and that obvious immediate self-interest, in its narrowest shape, is constantly eating away the

*Upon this passage Mr. Harrison observes: 'It is quite true that this is a type of character
which is very useful, may command success, and sometimes respect. But it is not a very amiable
type. It certainly is not a religious type. Its tendency, if anything, is towards harshness and
selfishness. It is true that there are such people, and that such people get on, and that the world
needs such people. In one sense the world—this world at least' (Mr. Harrison's main quarrel
with me is that I think the question whether there is any other world an important one)—'may
be said to be theirs.' But the aim of all religions, certainly of all forms of Christian religion, has
been to show how little this corresponded to eternal realities. They have striven to make these
irrepressible individualities bow before the religious ideal, to warn these hardy giants that their
triumph was not for ever, that humanity was at bottom a softer and kinder thing. After much
more in the same vein Mr. Harrison sums up thus: 'If you end in making religion consist in doing
the best for yourself on utilitarian principles your system of life will stand or fall by this, and the
legislator and future life which you throw in as sanctions will not make your system of life a
whit purer or loftier or kinder, they will only add sanction to its selfishness and vulgarity, if
selfish and vulgar it be in its essence.' I entirely agree that the sanctions of a law do not affect the
character of the provisions sanctioned, but the question is, what are the tempers or habits of
minds, what is the type of character sanctioned and approved of by the Author of this world, if
it has an intelligent Author, or favoured by its constitution if it has no such Author? I say that
this is a question of fact which must be determined by an appeal to experience, and Mr. Harrison's view and my own as to the teaching of experience do not seem to differ very widely. The
difference is that he appears from this passage to think that the facts are wrong, that religion
ought, somehow or other, to load the dice in favour of the type of character which he prefers,

edges of morality, and would destroy it if it had not something deeper for its support than an historical or physiological explanation. We cannot judge of the effects of Atheism from the conduct of persons who have been educated as believers in God and in the midst of a nation which believes in God. If we should ever see a generation of men, especially a generation of Englishmen, to whom the word 'God' had no meaning at all, we should get a light upon the subject which might be lurid enough. Great force of character, restrained and directed by a deep sense of duty, is the noblest of noble things. Take off the restraint which a sense of duty imposes, and the strong man is apt to become a mere tyrant and oppressor. Bishop Berkeley remarked on his countrymen in the early part of the last century, 'Whatever may be the effect of pure theory upon certain select spirits of a peculiar make or in other parts of the world, I do verily think that in this country of ours reason, religion, law are all together little enough to subdue the outward to the inner man; and that it must argue a wrong head and weak understanding to suppose that without them men will be enamoured of the golden mean, to which my countrymen are

---

and to set right the world and its Maker. I think that we must look to the facts for our morals as well as for other things. I think it would be a very good world if it would only last, and the hope that that part of it which upon the supposition of permanence is the best part will really last is just what a belief in a future state gives.

In another part of his article Mr. Harrison refers to the murderer of Lord Mayo, and observes, 'that wretched Punjabee curiously fulfilled' my 'conditions as to religion. The world could hardly produce a creature to whom a God of some kind and a future state of some kind were more intense realities. When he drove in his deadly knife he saw heaven opening to receive him with a force of illusion which Europeans cannot reach.' Surely the important question in estimating this man's conduct is whether his conviction was true or false. Suppose that Mahommedanism is true, that it did sanction that wicked murder as we call it (it is only fair to say that very eminent Mahommedans utterly and indignantly denied it), and that heaven actually was opening to receive the assassin as he hung [sic] from the gallows at the Andamans, was he wrong in what he did? or if he was why should he not do wrong? That depends upon the evidence about Mahommed. I should be quite willing to leave to experience the question whether murder in general and that murder in particular is or is not an abominable crime which can lead to nothing but evil in this world or any other constructed on similar principles. That this world is not a proper place for murderers I am deeply convinced, and if there is any other world and it is at all like this it is probable that a man who enters it with such an introduction is in a very unpleasant position, and that instead of being welcomed by houries he finds reason to wish he had not committed murder. If not, so much the better for him.

perhaps less inclined than others, there being in the make of an English mind a certain gloom and eagerness which carries to the sad extreme.'[7] The remark is as true now as it was then.

A very important objection may be made to these views, to which I shall be glad to do full justice. I cannot quote any distinct expression of it, but I have frequently observed, and the same observation, I think, must have been made by others, that there are in these days a certain number of persons who regard a belief in God not merely as untrue, but as unfavourable to morality; and in a matter which does not admit of demonstration this of course inclines them to take the negative side. A being in any way responsible for such a world as ours would, they think, be a bad being, and a morality based upon the belief in such a being would be a vicious morality. Put in the plainest words, this is the upshot of much modern writing. It supplies a curious illustration of the persistency with which great moral and religious problems reproduce themselves in all sorts of shapes. The doctrine is Manicheeism without the two gods. We must have both a bad and a good god (said the Manichees), because there are in the world both good and evil. A certain class of persons in these days draw from the same premise the conclusion that no God is possible except a God who would be worse than none.

This is not a view to be passed over lightly, nor does it admit of being superficially answered. It raises the question not of the origin of evil, but of the attitude towards good and evil which is to be ascribed to God. It is idle to ask the question, How did evil originate? because it is impossible to answer it; but the question, What do you think of it now that it is here? is perfectly fair. Anyone who holds the views just stated is bound to say whether a God who is responsible for this world must not be a bad God; whether a belief in such a God will not have the effect of justifying many of the wrongs of life; whether the brotherhood which consists in a common allegiance to the laws of such a God will not be an association of enemies of the human race?

Such questions imply a belief which, though obscure, is not on that account the less influential, in some sort of transcendental system of human

7. George Berkeley, *The Works of George Berkeley, Bishop of Cloyne*, ed. T. E. Jessop, 9 vols (London: Thomas Nelson and Sons, 1949–57), vol. 3, *Alciphron: or the Minute Philosopher* (1950), p. 131 (3rd dial., sec. 12).

rights. God himself, some people seem to feel, must recognize human equality, the equal right of human creatures to happiness, and if men are not equal in fact, it is because they are the product not of will, but of blind chance. Rather than acknowledge a God who does not acknowledge the equality of men, let us, they say, acknowledge no God at all, and establish human equality as far as we can, in despite of the blind fate to which we owe our origin, and which we do not·and will not reverence. Man in the future, Man as we would have him, is the object of our reverence and love; not anything or anyone who is outside of Man, least of all anyone who is in any way responsible for what we see around us.

This is the deepest root of the revolutionary form of modern humanitarianism. Those who think it, as I do, a baseless and presumptuous dream must not shrink from the questions founded upon it. As to loving man as man, the bad as well as the good, others as well as myself, dreams about future generations as well as actual generations past or present, I have said what I had to say. 'Humanity' is as thin a shadow to me as any God can be to others. Moreover, it is a shadow of which I know the source and can measure the importance. I admit, however, that anyone who cares for it is entitled to an answer to the questions stated.

The answer goes to the very root of things, yet I think the moral difficulty of giving it is greater than the intellectual one. If the order which we observe in the physical universe and in the moral world suggests to us the existence of God, we must not shrink from the inference that the character of God, in so far as we have anything to do with it, is to be inferred from that order. To say that the Author of such a world is a purely benevolent being is, to my mind, to say something which is not true, or, at the very least, something which is highly improbable in itself, impossible to be proved, and inconsistent with many notorious facts, except upon hypotheses which it is hardly possible to state or to understand, and of which there is absolutely no evidence whatever. Therefore, to the question, 'Admitting the existence of God, do you believe him to be good?' I should reply, If by 'good' you mean 'disposed to promote the happiness of mankind absolutely,' I answer No. If by 'good' you mean virtuous, I reply, The question has no meaning. A virtuous man is a being of whom we can form an idea more or less distinct, but the ideas of virtue and vice can hardly be attached to a Being who transcends all or most of the conditions out of which virtue and vice arise. If the further question is asked, Then what moral attributes do you ascribe to this Being, if you ascribe to him any at all? I should reply, I think of him as conscious and having will, as infinitely powerful, and as one who, whatever he may be in his own nature, has so arranged the world or worlds in which I live as to let me know that virtue is the law which he has prescribed to me and to others. If still further asked, Can you love such a Being? I should answer, Love is not the word which I should choose, but awe. The law under which we live is stern, and, as far as we can judge, inflexible, but it is noble and excites a feeling of awful respect for its Author and for the constitution established in the world which it governs, and a sincere wish to act up to and carry it out as far as possible. If we believe in God at all, this, I think, is the rational and manly way of thinking of him.

This leads to the further question how belief in such a Being would affect a man's view of this present life. Would not such a belief, it may be said, justify and sanctify much of the injustice and many of the wrongs of life? To this I answer thus. The general constitution of things, by which some people are better off than others, and some very badly off in all respects, is neither just nor unjust, right nor wrong. It simply is. It affects the question of the benevolence, not the question of the justice, of its author. The idea of justice and right is subsequent to the idea of law. It is, in the etymological sense of the word, preposterous to apply those ideas to the state of things in which we live. It is simply unmeaning to assert that A is *wronged* because he is born with a predisposition to cancer, or that B *ought* to have had wings, or that C *had a right* to a certain power of self-control. As against God or fate, whichever you please, men have no rights at all, not even the right of existence. Right, wrong, and obligation begin after laws, properly so called, have been established, and the first laws, properly so called, which we have any reason to believe to exist are moral laws imposed upon beings, of whom some are far more favourably situated for keeping them than others. All moral codes and customs are so many different versions, more or less correct and more or less fully expressed, of these laws. Accounts of their administration are to be read in all human history, from Cain and Abel to today's newspapers.

The answer, then, to the question, How does a belief in God thus explained affect our view of human life? is this: Every man born into the world finds himself placed in a position in which he has a variety of wants, passions, faculties, and powers of various kinds, and in which some objects better or worse are attainable by him. The religious theory of life may be thrown into the shape of the following command or advice: Do the best you can for yourselves, but do it in a definitely prescribed manner and not otherwise, or it will be the worse for you. Some of you are happy; it is the better for them. Some are miserable; by all means let them help themselves in the appointed manner; let others help them on the appointed terms, but when all is done much will remain to bear. Bear it as you can, and whether in happiness or in misery, take with you the thought that the strange world in which you live seems not to be all, and that you yourselves who are in it are not altogether of it.

The facts are the same upon any hypothesis, and Atheism only makes the case utterly hopeless, whereas the belief in a God and a future state does throw some rays of light over the dark sea on which we are sailing.

This does not show or tend to show that there is a God, but only that the belief in God is not immoral. That belief is immoral only if the unreserved acceptance of the terms on which life is offered to us, and an honest endeavour to live upon those terms, are immoral. If some theory about human happiness and equality and fraternity makes it our duty to kick against the pricks, to live as rebels against that, whatever it is, in which we find ourselves, a belief in God is immoral, but not otherwise. To my mind the immoral and unmanly thing is revolt, impatience of inevitable evils, gratuitous indiscriminate affection for all sorts of people, whether they deserve it or not, and in particular, a weak, ill-regulated sympathy for those whose sufferings are their own fault. These are sufferings which I, for one, should not wish either to relieve or to avert. I would leave the law to take its course. Why there should be wicked people in the world is like the question, Why there should be poisonous snakes in the world? Though no men are absolutely good or absolutely bad, yet if and in so far as men are good and bad they are not brothers but enemies, or, if the expression is preferred, they are brothers at enmity whose enmity must continue till its cause is removed.

It may again be asked—and this is the last question of the kind which I shall attempt to consider—What is the relation of all this to Christianity? Has not the humanitarianism of which you think so ill a close connection, both historically and theoretically, with the Sermon on the Mount and the Parables?

To this I reply: The truth of Christianity, considered as a divine revelation, depends upon questions of fact which I certainly shall not at present discuss. Who can add much to what has been said by Grotius, Jeremy Taylor, Lardner, Paley, and their successors, on the one side, or by a variety of writers from Celsus to Strauss on the other? 'Securus judicabit orbis.' The witnesses have been examined, the counsel have made their speeches, and the jury are considering their verdict. Whatever that verdict may be, one thing is quite clear. Almost any theological system and almost any moral system is consistent with the Sermon on the Mount and the Parables. They, as has been observed a thousand times, are obviously not philosophical discourses. They are essentially popular, and no one, with few unimportant exceptions, has ever attempted to treat them as a system of moral philosophy would be treated. No doubt they express the charitable sentiment in its most earnest and passionate form, but both the theory and the practice of mankind show clearly that this has been, as no doubt it will continue to be, understood by those who believe in the supernatural authority of Christ as a pathetic overstatement of duties which everyone would acknowledge to be duties, and to be peculiarly likely to be neglected. Everyone would admit that good men ought to love many at least of their neighbours considerably more than most men actually do, and that they are not likely to be led into the error of loving them too much by the Sermon on the Mount, or by any other sermon.

It must also be borne in mind that, though Christianity expresses the tender and charitable sentiments with passionate ardour, it has also a terrible side. Christian love is only for a time and on condition. It stops short at the gates of hell, and hell is an essential part of the whole Christian scheme.* Whether we look at the formal doctrines or at the substance of that scheme, the tenderness and the terrors mutually imply each other. There would be something excessive in such an outpouring of sympathy and sorrow about mere transitory sufferings, which do not appear after all to have been specially acute or specially

*In a curious article in the *Contemporary Review* for January 1874, called 'Dogmatic Extremes,' Principal Tulloch refers to this passage with disapproval. He does not deny its truth. Two short extracts from his article will be enough to show the value of his opinion: 'True religious thought is always and in its nature indefinite. "Haze," if you choose to use the expression, is of its very nature.' Again he observes, 'Imperfection or partial error is of the very essence of Christian dogma.' According to this Augustine, Calvin, Knox, Bossuet, Bellarmine, Wesley, Whitefield, Fénélon and others had no religious thought except when they were obscure, and the

unrelieved with happiness in Judæa in the first century. The horrors of the doctrine of hell would have been too great for human endurance if the immediate manifestations of the religion had not been tender and compassionate.

Christianity must thus be considered rather as supplying varied and powerful sanctions (love, hope, and fear in various proportions and degrees) for that view of morality which particular people may be led to on other grounds than as imposing upon them any particular moral system. There have been Christian Stoics; there have been Christian Epicureans; and immense numbers of people are, or imagine themselves to be, in love with Christian charity, although they never heard of and could not understand any ethical system whatever. Christianity, in a word, in relation to morals, is a means whereby morality may be made transcendental—that is to say, by which an infinitely greater importance may be and is attached to the distinction between right and wrong (understand it as you will) than reasonable men would attach to it if they simply calculated the specific ascertainable effects of right and wrong actions, on the supposition that this present world is the whole of life. The weakest part of modern philanthropy is that, while calling itself specially Christian, it has completely set aside and practically denied the existence of that part of Christianity which it does not like. If of a system which is essentially an appeal to a variety of emotions you adopt that part only which appeals to the tender emotions, you misrepresent the whole.

As a matter of historical fact, no really considerable body of men either is, ever has been, or ever has professed to be Christian in the sense of taking the philanthropic passages of the four Gospels as the sole, exclusive, and complete guide of their lives. If they did, they would in sober earnest turn the world upside down. They would be a set of passionate Communists, breaking down every approved maxim of conduct and every human institution. In one word, if Christianity really is what much of the language which we often hear used implies, it is false and mischievous. Nothing can be more monstrous than

---

authors of the New Testment not much. 'Hazy' would be an odd word to apply to the Sermon on the Mount and the Parables. Religious thought began it would seem when Englishmen and Scotchmen took to the hopeful task of sitting on two stools and trying to put new philosophy into old dogmas. The great truth that error is of the essence of Christian dogma is a new and surprising discovery of Principal Tulloch's own, and will no doubt add greatly to the value of dogma.

a sweeping condemnation of mankind for not conforming their conduct to an ideal which they do not really acknowledge. When, for instance, we are told that it is dreadful to think that a nation pretending to believe the Sermon on the Mount should employ so many millions sterling per annum on military expenditure, the answer is that no sane nation ever did or ever will pretend to believe the Sermon on the Mount in any sense which is inconsistent with the maintenance to the very utmost by force of arms of the national independence, honour, and interest. If the Sermon on the Mount really means to forbid this, it ought to be disregarded.

I have now tried to perform the task which I originally undertook, which was to examine the doctrines hinted at rather than expressed by the phrase 'Liberty, Equality, and Fraternity,' and to assert with respect to them these two propositions: First, that in the present day even those who use those words most rationally—that is to say, as the names of elements of social life which, like others, have their advantages and disadvantages according to time, place, and circumstance—have a great disposition to exaggerate their advantages and to deny the existence, or at any rate to underrate the importance, of their disadvantages. Next, that whatever signification be attached to them, these words are ill-adapted to be the creed of a religion, that the things which they denote are not ends in themselves, and that when used collectively the words do not typify, however vaguely, any state of society which a reasonable man ought to regard with enthusiasm or self-devotion.

CHAPTER SEVEN

CONCLUSION

Thrown into a positive form, the doctrine contended for in the foregoing chapters is this:

1. The whole management and direction of human life depends upon the question whether or not there is a God and a future state of human existence. If there is a God, but no future state, God is nothing to us. If there is a future state, but no God, we can form no rational guess about the future state.

2. If there is no God and no future state, reasonable men will regulate their conduct either by inclination or by common utilitarianism (p. 167).

3. If there is a God and a future state, reasonable men will regulate their conduct by a wider kind of utilitarianism (pp. 182–83).

4. By whatever rule they regulate their conduct, no room is left for any rational enthusiasm for the order of ideas hinted at by the phrase 'Liberty, Equality, and Fraternity'; for, whichever rule is applied, there are a vast number of matters in respect of which men ought not to be free; they are fundamentally unequal, and they are not brothers at all, or only under qualifications which make the assertion of their fraternity unimportant.

It is impossible to carry on speculations which lead to such results without being led to ask oneself the question whether they are or can be of any sort of importance? The questions which I have been discussing have been debated in various forms for thousands of years. Is this consistent with the possibility that they can ever be solved, and, if not, why should they be debated by anyone who has no taste for a conflict never ending, still beginning, fighting still, and still destroying?

The answer is that though these speculations may be expected to be endless, and though their results are mainly destructive, they are nevertheless of great use, and, indeed, are absolutely necessary. They can show that particular sets of opinions are incoherent, and so, properly speaking, not opinions at all. They can cut down to their proper proportions exaggerated estimates of the probability of particular systems and expose their pretensions to attain to something more than probability. Lastly, they can show how particular opinions are related to each other. And this is a wide field. As long as men have any mental activity at all, they will speculate, as they always have speculated, about themselves, their destiny, and their nature. They will ask in different dialects the questions What? Whence? Whither? And their answers to these questions will be bold and copious, whatever else they may be. It seems to me improbable in the highest degree that any answer will ever be devised to any one of these questions which will be accepted by all mankind in all ages as final and conclusive. The facts of life are ambiguous. Different inferences may be drawn from them, and they do not present by any means the same general appearance to people who look at them from different points of view. To a scientific man society has a totally different appearance, it is, as far as he is concerned, quite a different thing, from what it is to a man whose business lies with men.

Again, the largest and by far the most important part of all our speculations about mankind is based upon our experience of ourselves, and proceeds upon the supposition that the motives and principles of action of others are substantially the same as our own. The degree to which tastes of all sorts differ is a standing proof of the truth that this assumption includes an allowance of error, though it is error of a kind from which it is impossible for any human creature to free himself. It would be easy to accumulate other observations of the same sort. It is enough for my purpose to observe in general that mankind appear to me to be in the following difficulty, from which I see no means of extrication. Either they must confine their conclusions to matters which can be verified by actual experience, in which case the questions which principally interest them must be dismissed from consideration as insoluble riddles; or they must be satisfied with probable solutions of them, in which case their solutions will always contain a certain degree of error and will require reconstruction from age to age as circumstances change. Moreover, more solutions than one will always be possible, and there will be no means of deciding conclusively which is right. Experience appears to me to show that the second branch of the alternative is the one which will be accepted by mankind, and I think it is the one which reasonable people ought to accept. I think they should accept it openly and with a distinct appreciation of its nature and consequences.

As a matter of fact this conclusion has been and is accepted, though in a strangely inverted form, by many persons whom it would startle. The whole doctrine of faith involves an admission that doubt is the proper attitude of mind about religion, if the subject is regarded from the intellectual side alone. No human creature ever yet preached upon the virtue of faith in Euclid's demonstrations. They, and many other propositions far less cogently supported, speak for themselves. People naturally believe them on the evidence, and do not require to be exhorted to believe them as a matter of religious duty. If a man actually did rise from the dead and find himself in a different world, he would no longer be told to believe in a future state; he would know it. When St. Paul contrasts seeing in a glass darkly with seeing face to face—when he says that now we know in part and believe in part—he admits that belief is not knowledge; and he would have found it impossible to distinguish (at least no one has ever yet established an intelligible distinction) between faith and acting on a probability—in other words, between faith and a kind of doubt. The difference between the two states of mind is moral, not intellectual. Faith says, Yes, I will, *though* I am not sure. Doubt says, No, I will not, *because* I am not sure; but they agree in not being sure. Both faith and doubt would be swallowed up in actual knowledge and direct experience.

It is easy to understand why men passionately eager about the propagation of their creed should persistently deny the force of this argument, and should try by every means in their power to prove that in regard to religious subjects insufficient evidence may and ought to produce an unnatural effect. Their object is obvious. If an act is to be done, it is done equally, whatever may be the motive for doing it, and a probable opinion may be an adequate motive as well as demonstration. Perfect certainty of the approach of death, or a doubt whether death may not be approaching, are states of mind either of which may cause a man to make his will, and when he dies it will be equally valid whether his death was foreseen with confidence or indistinctly apprehended.

But it is otherwise with feeling. A general knowledge of the uncertainty of life produces very different feelings from an immediate and confident expectation of death. In the same way the apprehension that the leading doctrines of religion may be true may be a motive to much the same line of conduct as the most certain conviction that they are true, but it will produce a very different state of mind and feeling. It will give life a very different colour.

This does not justify the attempt to give evidence a weight which does not belong to it. Our feelings ought to be regulated by the facts which excite them. It is a great mistake, and the source of half the errors which exist in the world, to yield to the temptation to allow our feelings to govern our estimate of facts. Rational religious feeling is that feeling, whatever it may be, which is excited in the mind by a true estimate of the facts known to us which bear upon religion. If we do not know enough to feel warmly, let us by all means feel calmly; but it is dishonest to try to convert excited feeling into evidence of facts which would justify it. To say, 'There must be a God because I love him' is just like saying, 'That man must be a rogue because I hate him,' which many people do say, but not wisely. There are in these days many speculations by very able men, or men reputed to be of great ability, which can all be resolved into attempts to increase the bulk and the weight of evidence by heating it with love. Dr. Newman's 'Grammar of Assent,'[1] with all its hair-splitting about the degrees of assent, and the changes which it rings upon certainty and certitude, is a good illustration of this, but it is like the wriggling of a worm on a hook, or like the efforts which children sometimes make to draw two straight lines so as to enclose a space, or to make a cross on a piece of paper with a single stroke of a pencil, not passing twice over any part of the cross. Turn and twist as you will, you can never really get out of the proposition that the Christian history is just as probable as the evidence makes it, and no more; and that to give a greater degree of assent to it, or, if the expression is preferred, to give an unreserved assent to the proposition that it has a greater degree of probability than the evidence warrants, is to give up its character as an historical event altogether.

1. John Henry Cardinal Newman (1801–90), *The Grammar of Assent* (Notre Dame: University of Notre Dame Press, 1979). See pp. 135–208, especially. Stephen reviewed this book of Newman's in, "On Certitude in Religious Assent," *Fraser's Magazine*, N.S. V (1872).

There is, indeed, no great difficulty in showing that we cannot get beyond probability at all in any department of human knowledge. One short proof of this is as follows: The present is a mere film melting as we look at it. Our knowledge of the past depends on memory, our knowledge of the future on anticipation, and both memory and anticipation are fallible. The firmest of all conclusions and judgments are dependent upon facts which, for aught we know, may have been otherwise in the past, may be otherwise in the future, and may at this moment present a totally different appearance to other intelligent beings from that which they present to ourselves. It is possible to suggest hypotheses which would refute what appear to us self-evident truths, even truths which transcend thought and logic. The proposition tacitly assumed by the use of the word 'I' may be false to a superior intelligence seeing in each of us, not individuals, but parts of some greater whole. The multiplication table assumes a world which will stay to be counted. 'One and one are two' is either a mere definition of the word two, or an assertion that each one is, and for some time continues to be, one. The proposition would never have occurred to a person who lived in a world where everything was in a state of constant flux. It may be doubted whether it would appear true to a being so constituted as to regard the universe as a single connected whole.

But leaving these fancies, for they are little more, it is surely obvious that all physical science is only a probability, and, what is more, one which we have no means whatever of measuring. The whole process of induction and deduction rests on the tacit assumption that the course of nature has been, is, and will continue to be uniform. Such, no doubt, is the impression which it makes on us. It is the very highest probability to which we can reach. It is the basis of all systematic thought. It has been verified with wonderful minuteness in every conceivable way, and yet no one has ever been able to give any answer at all to the question, What proof have you that the uniformities which you call laws will not cease or alter tomorrow? In regard to this, our very highest probability, we are like a man rowing one way and looking another, and steering his boat by keeping her stern in a line with an object behind him. I do not say this to undervalue science, but to show the conditions of human knowledge. Nothing can be more certain than a conclusion scientifically established. It is far more certain than an isolated present sensation or an isolated recollection of a past sensation, and yet it is but a probability. In acting upon scientific conclusions we are exposed to a risk of error which we have no means of avoiding and of which we cannot calculate the value. If our conclusions about matters of sense which we can weigh, measure, and handle are only probable, how can speculations, which refer to matters transcending sense, and which are expressed in words assuming sense, be more than probable?

If upon this it is asked whether there is no such thing as certainty? I reply that certainty or certitude (for I do not care to distinguish between words between which common usage makes no distinction) is in propriety of speech the name of a state of mind, and not the name of a quality of propositions. Certainty is the state of mind in which, as a fact, a man does not doubt. Reasonable certainty is the state of mind in which it is prudent not to doubt. It may be produced in many different ways and may relate to every sort of subject. The important thing to remember is the truism that it does not follow that a man is right because he is positive; though it may be prudent that he should be positive, and take the chance of being wrong. The conditions which make certainty reasonable or prudent in regard to particular matters are known with sufficient accuracy for most purposes, though they do not admit of being stated with complete precision; but the certainty which they warrant is in all cases contingent and liable to be disturbed, and it differs in the degree of its stability indefinitely according to circumstances. There are many matters of which we are certain upon grounds which are, and which we know to be of the most precarious kind. In these cases our certainty might be overthrown as readily as it was established. There are other cases in which our certainty is based upon foundations so broad that, though it is no doubt imaginable that it might be overthrown, no rational man would attach the smallest practical importance to the possibility. No one really doubts of a scientific conclusion if he once really understands what science means. No jury would doubt a probable story affirmed by credible witnesses whose evidence was duly tested. No reasonable man in common life doubts either his own senses or immediate inferences from them, or the grave assertions of persons well known to him to be truthful upon matters within their personal knowledge, and not in themselves improbable. Yet in each case, a modest and rational man would be ready, if he saw cause, to admit that he might be wrong. There is probably no proposition whatever which under no imaginable change of circumstances could ever appear false, or at least doubtful, to any reasonable being at any time or any place.

There is, perhaps, hardly any subject about which so many webs of sophistry have been woven as about this. I cannot notice more than one of them by way of illustration. It assumes every sort of form, and is exemplified in a thousand shapes in the writings of modern Roman Catholics and of some mystical Protestants. It may be thus stated. Whereas certainty is often produced by probable evidence, and whereas the propositions of which people are rendered certain by probable evidence are frequently true, therefore the weight of the evidence ought not to be taken as a measure of the mental effect which it ought to produce. The fallacy is exactly like the superstition of gamblers—I betted three times running on the red. I felt sure I should win, and I did win, therefore the pretence to calculate chances is idle. What more could any such calculation give anyone than a certitude? I got my certitude by an easier process, and the event justified it. To guess is often necessary. To guess right is always fortunate, but no number of lucky guesses alters the true character of the operation or decreases the insecurity of the foundation on which the person who guesses proceeds.

It may be objected to all this that I have myself referred to some subjects as lying beyond the reach both of language and even of thought, and yet as being matters with which we are intimately concerned—more intimately and more enduringly indeed than with any other matters whatever. How, it may be asked, can you admit that there are matters which transcend all language and all thought, and yet declare that we cannot get beyond probability?

I am, of course, well aware of the fact that a belief in what are sometimes called transcendental facts—facts, that is, of which sensation does not inform us—is frequently coupled with a belief that a certain set of verbal propositions about these facts are not only true, but are perceived to be true by some special faculty which takes notice of them. This has always seemed to be illogical. If there are facts of which we are conscious, and of which sensation does not inform us, and if all our language is derived from and addressed to our senses, it would seem to follow that language can only describe in a very inadequate manner, that it can only hint at and seek to express by metaphors taken from sense things which lie beyond sense. That to which the word 'I' points can neither be seen, touched, nor heard. It is an inscrutable mystery; but the image which the word 'I' raises in our minds is the image of a particular human body. Indeed, the opinion that the facts with which we are most intimately concerned transcend both language and thought, and the opinion that words, whether spoken or unspoken, can never reach to those facts, or convey anything more than sensible images of them, more or less incorrect, inadequate, and conjectural, are the opposite sides of one and the same opinion. The true inference from the inadequacy of human language to the expression of truths of this class is expressed in the words, 'He is in heaven and thou art on earth, therefore let thy words be few.' As upon these great subjects we have to express ourselves in a very imperfect way, and under great disadvantages, we shall do well to say as little as we can, and to abstain as far as possible from the process of piling inference upon inference, each inference becoming more improbable in a geometrical ratio as it becomes more remote from actual observation. As we must guess, let us make our conjectures as modest and as simple as we can. A probability upon a probability closely resembles an improbability.

It must never be forgotten that it is one thing to doubt of the possibility of exactly adjusting words to facts, and quite another to doubt of the reality and the permanence of the facts themselves. Though, as I have said, the facts which we see around us suggest several explanations, it is equally true that of those explanations one only can be true. When the oracle said to Pyrrhus, 'Aio te, Æacida, Romanos vincere posse,' it meant not that he could conquer the Romans, but that the Romans could conquer him, though to Pyrrhus the words would convey either meaning; and, however fully we may admit that the question whether men are spirits or funguses is one which cannot be conclusively determined by mere force of argument, it is perfectly clear that, if the one opinion is true, the other is false. In nearly all the important transactions of life, indeed in all transactions whatever which have relation to the future, we have to take a leap in the dark. Though life is proverbially uncertain, our whole course of life assumes that our lives will continue for a considerable, though for an indefinite, period. When we are to take any important resolution, to adopt a profession, to make an offer of marriage, to enter upon a speculation, to write a book—to do anything, in a word, which involves important consequences—we have to act for the best, and in nearly every case to act upon very imperfect evidence.

The one talent which is worth all other talents put together in all human affairs is the talent of judging right upon imperfect materials, the talent if you please of guessing right. It is a talent which no rules will ever teach and which even experience does not always give. It often coexists with a good deal of slowness and dulness and with a very slight power of expression. All that can be said about it is that to see things as they are, without exaggeration or passion, is essential to it; but how can we see things as they are? Simply by opening our eyes and looking with whatever power we may have. All really important matters are decided, not by a process of argument worked out from adequate premises to a necessary conclusion, but by making a wise choice between several possible views.

I believe it to be the same with religious belief. Several coherent views of the matter are possible, and, as they are suggested by actual facts, may be called probable. Reason, in the ordinary sense of the word, can show how many such views there are, and can throw light upon their comparative probability, by discussing the different questions of fact which they involve, and by tracing out their connection with other speculations. It is by no means improbable that the ultimate result of this process may be to reduce the views of life which are at once coherent and suggested by facts to a very small number, but when all has been done that can be done, these questions will remain— What do you think of yourself? What do you think of the world? Are you a mere machine, and is your consciousness, as has been said, a mere resultant? Is the world a mere fact suggesting nothing beyond itself worth thinking about? These are questions with which all must deal as it seems good to them. They are riddles of the Sphinx, and in some way or other we must deal with them. If we decide to leave them unanswered, that is a choice. If we waver in our answer, that too is a choice; but whatever choice we make, we make it at our peril. If a man chooses to turn his back altogether on God and the future, no one can prevent him. No one can show beyond all reasonable doubt that he is mistaken. If a man thinks otherwise, and acts as he thinks, I do not see how anyone can prove that *he* is mistaken. Each must act as he thinks best, and if he is wrong so much the worse for him. We stand on a mountain pass in the midst of whirling snow and blinding mist, through which we get glimpses now and then of paths which may be deceptive. If we stand still, we shall be frozen to death. If we take the wrong road, we shall be dashed to pieces. We do not certainly know whether there is any right one. What must we do? 'Be strong and of a good courage.'* Act for the best, hope for the best, and take what comes. Above all, let us dream no dreams, and tell no lies, but go our way, wherever it may lead, with our eyes open and our heads erect. If death ends all, we cannot meet it better. If not, let us enter whatever may be the next scene like honest men, with no sophistry in our mouths and no masks on our faces.

*Deuteronomy, xxxi. 6 and 7. 'Be strong and of a good courage, fear not nor be afraid of them.' It is the charge of Moses to Joshua.

NOTE ON UTILITARIANISM

{The following is the substance of two Articles which I published in the 'Pall Mall Gazette,' in June 1869, on the subject of 'Utilitarianism.' It was suggested by some criticisms on a work of Mr. Lecky's, which have lost their interest. I have accordingly omitted all reference to Mr. Lecky and his critics, but I reprint the substance of the Articles, because they explain systematically my views on a subject which is glanced at in several places in this work.}

All moral controversies may be reduced under four general heads. First, what is the sphere of morals, what part of human life do they cover, and of what other elements in human nature do they assume the existence? Secondly, what is the nature of the distinction between right and wrong? Thirdly, how are we to ascertain whether given actions are right or wrong? Fourthly, why should we do what is right and avoid what is wrong? Of these four questions the second, third, and fourth have been discussed in every possible way from the most remote times. The first, which is of extreme importance, has as yet been hardly touched. It is in respect to the other three questions that the points of difference and agreement between the two great schools of intuition and experience have displayed and continue to display themselves.

It is necessary, in order to appreciate this, to show first what is the meaning of the leading doctrine of the two great schools in question, and next, how each of them deals with each of the three questions above mentioned. In the first place, it is obvious that there is no contradiction between intuition and experience, for all experience assumes and presupposes intuition. All men in all ages have been and are now profoundly affected by the contemplation of the conduct of other men. There never was a time or country in which people were in the habit of observing each other's conduct with the indifference with which they might watch the ebb and flow of the tide or the motions of the heavenly bodies. However we may account for it, the feelings which we call sympathy and antipathy, praise and blame, love and hatred, are, in fact, produced by observing particular kinds of conduct, and in each particular man at any given time those sentiments are as involuntary as the pain which follows a blow, or the pleasure produced by an agreeable sound or taste. If, when it is asserted that morality is intuitive or depends upon intuition, all that is meant is that the contemplation of human conduct produces involuntary emotions of various kinds in every spectator, Austin or Bentham would have admitted the truth of those propositions as much as their most vigorous opponents. They would even have gone a step farther and have owned that there is, as a matter of fact, a broad general resemblance between the acts which are regarded with sympathy and antipathy, and which excite praise or blame, in different generations and distant parts of the world. No one ever doubted that some degree of indifference to the infliction of suffering has at all times and places been blamed as cruelty, or that a wish, under some circumstances or other, to promote the happiness of others has always and everywhere received praise under the name of benevolence. The controversy between the two schools of morals relates not to the facts but to the manner in which they are to be interpreted, and this will be best displayed by considering the way in which each school would treat each of the three questions above mentioned.

The first question is, What is the difference between right and wrong? As a fact, certain classes of actions are in popular language called right and wrong, and are regarded by the world at large with praise or blame respectively. Is this an ultimate fact beyond which we cannot go?

The analogy which exists between this inquiry and kindred questions on other subjects is often overlooked, and ought to be observed. Take, for instance, such words as 'heavy' and 'light,' 'up' and 'down,' 'wet' and 'dry.' No words can seem clearer; yet experience has shown that it is impossible to use them philosophically, or to get any but the most confused, unintelligible results from the attempt to throw them into systems, until they have been interpreted by certain broad general principles which show their true relation to each other. For instance, till it was proved that all bodies attract each other under certain conditions, and that the earth is a proximately spherical body revolving in a certain course, it was impossible to use such words as 'up' and 'down,' 'heavy' and 'light' in a really scientific manner. The utilitarian answer to the question, 'What is the difference between right and wrong?' is an attempt—successful or otherwise, as it may be—to do for ethics what those who made the great elementary discoveries in physics did for the mass of observed facts, and for the expressive but indefinite words descriptive of those facts which the unsystematic observation of ages had accumulated about the heavenly bodies and common natural objects.

Of course, if we are content to confine ourselves upon these subjects to inconclusive rhetoric, it is possible to do so. There is no course of conduct for which dyslogistic or eulogistic epithets may not be found. Any given act may be described as severity or cruelty, courage or rashness, obstinacy or firmness, gentleness or weakness, according to the sympathy or antipathy which it happens to create in the speaker; and in cases which present little difficulty, and in which the only object is to bring public opinion to bear upon some action as to the moral complexion of which there is no real question, little more is required. When, however, commonplaces can be plausibly adduced on both sides, it becomes apparent that such language is useful only as a relief to the feelings, and that it supplies no guide at all to conduct. Take such a question, for instance, as alms-giving. The beauties of charity on the one side and the beauties of independence on the other, the claims of the individual and the claims of the public, may be balanced against each other indefinitely; but the process can never lead to any definite result at all, unless some general principle is laid down which enables us to affix a precise meaning to the general words employed, into which, when we wish to bring the controversy to a definite issue, they may be translated.

The utilitarian answer to the question, What is the meaning of right and wrong? is an attempt, successful or not, to supply this precise meaning to popular language. The utilitarian says, I observe that, speaking broadly, men desire the same sorts of things, and I call the attainment of these objects of desire by the general name of happiness. I also observe that certain courses of conduct tend to promote, and that others tend to prevent or interfere with, the attainment of these objects of desire by mankind, and that the popular use of the words 'right' and 'wrong' has a marked general correspondence to these two classes of conduct. Speaking generally, the acts which are called right do promote or are supposed to promote general happiness, and the acts which are called wrong do diminish or are supposed to diminish it. I say, therefore, that this is what the words 'right' and 'wrong' mean, just as the words 'up' and 'down' mean that which points from or towards the earth's centre of gravity, though they are used by millions who have not the least notion of the fact that such is their meaning, and though they were used for centuries and millenniums before anyone was or even could be aware of it. Our language begins by being vivid and inexact. We are enabled to render it precise, and so to assign what may be conveniently called its true meaning, only when experience has informed us of the relations of the subject-matter to which it applies.

Believers in moral intuitions may answer the question, What do you mean by right and wrong? in one of two ways. They may say you cannot get beyond the fact that these words and their equivalents are, in fact, applied to certain courses of conduct. Those who give this answer are bound to go on to say that the courses of conduct to which the words in question are applied are always and everywhere the same, and that they denote a specific quality like the words red or blue, which may be immediately and distinctly perceived by everyone who considers the subject; for, if they do not, the result will be that the use of the words will denote nothing except the individual sympathy or antipathy, as the case may be, of the persons by whom they are used, and this confessedly varies from time to time and place to place. On the other hand, they may say that the words have the meaning which utilitarians assign to them, and may say nothing about their moral intuitions till they come to the second of the questions referred to.

This second question is, How am I to know right from wrong? It is independent of the first question, though they are not unconnected. The utilitarian answer is that the knowledge of right and wrong does not differ from other branches of knowledge, and must be acquired in the same way. An intuitive moralist would say that there is a special function of the mind—namely, conscience—which recognizes at once the specific difference which is alleged to exist between them, whether that difference consists in their effect upon happiness or in anything else. It is, however, to be observed that almost all utilitarians admit the existence of conscience as a fact. They admit, that is, that men do pass moral judgments on their own acts and those of other people, that these moral judgments are involuntary when the moral character is once formed, and that whether they apply to the acts of the judge himself or to the acts of other persons. They would say, for instance, that an ordinary Englishman of our own time, who shares the common opinion of his country as to monogamy and polygamy, would be as unable to regard a given act of bigamy with approval as to think that on a given day the earth did not move round the sun. They deny, however, that conscience is the ultimate test of right and wrong in the sense of being able to tell us with unerring certainty whether a given action is or is not in accordance with a rule calculated to promote the general happiness of mankind, or what in respect to a given subject-matter those rules are. They also deny that conscience recognizes specific difference between right and wrong actions, and that there is any such specific difference other than the one already stated to be recognized. It is also to be observed, on the other hand, that there is nothing inconsistent in believing that right and wrong depend upon the tendency of actions to produce happiness, and that we have in conscience a specific quality or power which enables us to recognize this tendency in any action to which we turn our attention.

The third question is, Why should I do right? Upon this several observations arise which are continually overlooked. The first is that people usually write as if every moralist were bound to supply a satisfactory answer to it; whereas, it is perfectly conceivable that there may be no answer. A man may give a full definition of health, and may point out the measures by which healthy symptoms may be distinguished from the symptoms of disease, and he may yet be quite unable to lay down rules by which health can be secured. Thus it is possible that a consistent meaning can be assigned to the words 'right' and 'wrong,' and that the appropriate means for distinguishing between them may be pointed out, but that there may be no sufficient reason why people in general should do right and avoid doing wrong.

The second observation is that the fact that there is so much wrongdoing in the world seems difficult to reconcile with the theory that right and wrong are recognized by intuition; and that as soon as the rightfulness of an action is recognized the fact is of itself a sufficient reason why it should be done.

The third observation is that the question itself cannot be put except in a form which assumes that the utilitarian answer is the only one which can possibly be given. That answer is, I ought to do right, because to do right will conduce to my greatest happiness. It is impossible to assign any other meaning than this to the words 'why should' or to any equivalent which can be devised for them. The words 'why should I' mean 'what shall I get by,' 'what motive have I for' this or that course of conduct. The instant you assign a motive of any sort whatever for doing right, whether it is the love of God, the love of man, the approval of one's own conscience, or even the pleasure of doing right itself, you admit the principle that the question relates to the weight of motives. The only acts, if acts they can be called, which do not fall under this principle are acts which cannot be helped. If upon recognizing a given course of conduct as right a man had as little choice about doing it as he has about dying of a mortal wound, it would be taken out of the utilitarian principle, otherwise not.

These remarks bring us to the question itself, which is beyond all doubt the most difficult as it is the most important of the great ethical questions. I have already given the utilitarian answer, but, before noticing the standard objection to it, it may be as well to expound it, so as to show what it implies. It implies that the reasons for doing right vary indefinitely according to the nature of the right act to be done, and the circumstances of the person by whom it is to be done. There is no one sanction which applies with precisely equal weight to every conceivable case of doing right. For instance, why should not the Lord Chancellor commit given theft? Because amongst other things by committing theft he would fall from a very high to a very low position. Why should not an habitual pickpocket commit the same theft? Because he would confirm a wicked habit and risk punishment, but as for his character and position he has none to lose. The reasons, therefore, why the two men should or ought to abstain, the elements of their respective obligations, are different. To use Jeremy Taylor's appropriate though obsolete expression, they are not 'tied by the same bands.' Obligation is simply a metaphor for tying. This of course suggests the standard difficulty upon the subject. Why should A. B. do a specific right action when it happens to be opposed to his interest?

The answer usually given is not very satisfactory. It is to the effect that the utilitarian standard is not the greatest happiness of one man, but the greatest happiness of men in general; and that the rule of conduct which the whole system supplies is that men ought to act upon those rules which are found to produce general happiness, and not that they ought in particular cases to calculate the specific consequences to themselves of their own actions. This answer is incomplete rather than untrue, for, after all, it leads to the further question, Why should a man consult the general happiness of mankind? Why should he prefer obedience to a rule to a specific calculation in a specific case, when, after all, the only reason for obeying the rule is the advantage to be got by it, which by the hypothesis is not an advantage, but a loss in the particular case? A given road may be the direct way from one place to another, but that fact is no reason for following the road when you are offered a short cut. It may be a good general rule not to seek for more than 5 per cent in investments, but if it so happens that you can invest at 10 per cent with perfect safety, would not a man who refused to do so be a fool?

The answer to the question involves an examination of the meaning of the word 'ought' and its equivalent 'should.' When they are freed from their latent ambiguities the answer becomes easy. These words always denote that which would have happened if some principle tacitly assumed by the speaker to be applied to the case in question had been acted upon. It is true that most frequently their use implies that the speaker regards with approval the application of the principle which he assumes to the facts which he assumes, but this is not always the case. The following examples illustrate this: 'Did my servant give you my message? He *ought* to have done so.' This implies that the servant was ordered to give the message, and that if he had obeyed orders he would have given it, and that the speaker would approve of the regulation of the servant's conduct by the principle of obedience to orders. 'They *ought* to be in town by this time. The train left Paris last night.' This implies that the journey from Paris to London by a certain route occupies a certain time under circumstances which the speaker assumes to apply to the case of which he speaks. 'I *ought* to have five shillings in my purse, and there are only three.' This implies that the speaker has made an arithmetical calculation as to the money which he had at a given time and the money which he had since spent, and that, applying the rules of arithmetic to the facts known to him, the result does not correspond. As no one doubts the truth of the rules of arithmetic, it is a way of saying that the facts assumed to exist are incomplete. In these cases no approval on the part of the speaker is indicated by the word 'ought.'

We can now answer the question, what is meant by such expressions as 'He ought not to lie,' or 'He ought to lie'? They mean, first, that the speaker assumes human conduct to be regulated by given principles, and that the application of those principles to some state of facts will or will not result in lying; but they may mean, secondly, that someone or other, the speaker or the person referred to, would regard with approval such a course of proceeding. Thus the word 'ought,' even when explained, is still equivocal; for it may refer either to the principles accepted by the speaker himself or to those which are accepted by the person referred to. Thus the expression, 'You, as Christians, ought to love one another,' is an argument *ad homines.* You acknowledge principles which, if applied to practice, would make you love one another. 'I cannot say that a Mahometan ought not to practise polygamy,' would not convey any approbation of polygamy on the part of the speaker. It means merely that no principle admitted by Mahometans condemns polygamy.

When, therefore, utilitarians are asked whether a man who upon the whole thinks it for his advantage to commit a gross fraud ought or ought not to commit it, the question is ambiguous. It may mean either, Would utilitarians in general blame a man who so acted? or, Would the man himself act inconsistently with any principle admitted by him to be true? To the first question the answer will be that the man ought not to act as suggested. To the second, the answer will be that he ought.

The explanation and illustration of the second answer will serve to explain the first. A man who, upon the whole and having taken into account every relevant consideration, thinks it for his interest to do an act highly injurious to the world at large, no doubt would do it. But let us consider what would be the state of mind implied by the fact that he did take this view of his interest. A man who calmly and deliberately thinks that it is upon the whole his interest to commit an assassination which can never be discovered in order that he may inherit a fortune, shows, in the first place, that he has utterly rejected every form of the religious sanction; next, that he has no conscience and no self-respect; next, that he has no benevolence. His conduct affords no evidence as to his fear of legal punishment or popular indignation, inasmuch as by the supposition he is not exposed to them. He has thus no motive for abstaining from a crime which he has a motive for committing; but motive is only another name, a neutral instead of a eulogistic name, for obligation or tie. It would, therefore, be strictly accurate to say of such a man that he—from his point of view and upon his principles—ought, or is under an obligation, or is bound by the only tie which attaches to him, to commit murder. But it is this very fact which explains the hatred and blame which the act would excite in the minds of utilitarians in general, and which justifies them in saying on all common occasions that men ought not to do wrong for their own advantage, because on all common occasions the word 'ought' refers not to the rules of conduct which abnormal individuals may recognize, but to those which are generally recognized by mankind. 'You ought not to assassinate,' means if you do assassinate God will damn you, man will hang you if he can catch you, and hate you if he cannot, and you yourself will hate yourself, and be pursued by remorse and self-contempt all the days of your life. If a man is under none of these obligations, if his state of mind is such that no one of these considerations forms a tie upon him, all that can be said is that it is exceedingly natural that the rest of the world should regard him as a public enemy to be knocked on the head like a mad dog if an opportunity offers, and that for the very reason that he is under no obligations, that he is bound by none of the ties which connect men with each other, that he ought to lie, and steal, and murder whenever his immediate interests prompt him to do so.

To regard such a conclusion as immoral is to say that to analyse morality is to destroy it; that to enumerate its sanctions specifically is to take them away; that to say that a weight is upheld by four different ropes, and to own that if each of them were cut the weight would fall, is equivalent to cutting the ropes. No doubt, if all religion, all law, all benevolence, all conscience, all regard for popular opinion were taken away, there would be no assignable reason why men should do right rather than wrong; but the possibility which is implied in these 'ifs' is too remote to require practical attention.

This brings us to the consideration of the answer which a believer in moral intuitions would return to the question, Why should not I do wrong? The answer must be, that there is in man an irreducible sense of obligation or duty—a sort of instinct—an intuitive perception of a higher and lower side to our nature which forbids it. The objection to this answer is that it is not an answer at all. Nothing is an answer which does not show that on full computation the balance of motives will be in favour of doing right. The existence of a sense of duty in most men at most times and places is not in dispute. Upon utilitarian principles it is one of the chief sanctions, in all common cases it is the chief sanction, of morality; but, like all other motives, its force varies according to circumstances, and anyone who will consider the matter for a moment must see that it often is too weak to restrain men from every sort of iniquity, even when it is backed by all the sanctions of religion, conscience, law, and public opinion.

What would it be if all these sanctions were withdrawn? It would be simply an irrational, instinctive shrinking from a particular set of acts which men are prompted to do by motives which in practice frequently prove strong enough to overpower not only that instinct, but the fear of punishment, of infamy, and of self-reproach as well. Suppose that a man neither feared God nor cared for man, but had a sensitive conscience, what reason can be assigned why he should not systematically blunt it? The admission that conscience represents the higher side of our nature, whatever that may mean, proves nothing. Conscience is, no doubt, a motive of action, but it is impossible to regard it as anything else; and if it is regarded as a motive, it must come into competition with other motives, and so the utilitarian answer to the question, 'Why should I do right?' must be given.

This review of the points at issue between believers in the principle of expediency and believers in moral intuitions shows where the real difference between them lies and how far it extends. Unless those who believe in moral intuitions go so far as to assert the existence of specific moral rules expressed in a definite form of distinctly intelligible words, capable of being applied at once to human conduct, and perceived by some specific faculty of the mind to be absolute unvarying ultimate truths, they assert nothing which utilitarians are interested in denying. Probably no one in these days would make such an assertion.

Again, as Bentham pointed out, the principle of moral intuitions, or, as he called it, the principle of sympathy and antipathy, never can, from the nature of the case, be so applied as to lead to any definite result. It proposes no external standard to which disputants can appeal, and its adoption would involve as a necessary consequence the hopeless perpetuation of all moral controversies.

It is impossible to express any proposition affecting morals in words which are perfectly perspicuous and free from metaphor, and it will be found that as soon as an attempt is made to explain the words which are inevitably em-

ployed, and so to reduce to a precise meaning the propositions which are constructed out of them, it is absolutely necessary to have recourse to the principle of utility. A moral intuition, or any other intuition which does not go so
far as to enunciate definite propositions in express words, is only a fine name
for those inarticulate feelings which utilitarians recognize like every one else,
and which their system attempts to name, to classify, and to arrange. Take an
instance. Even if our moral intuitions told us that it is wrong to commit
murder, they would be of no use unless they also told us what no moral intuition ever yet told anyone—namely, what was the meaning of the word
'murder,' and how the killings which do amount to murder are to be distinguished from those which do not. To say that the moral intuitions tell us only
that a tendency towards humanity is good and a tendency towards cruelty
bad, is only to put the difficulty one step further back; for neither a moral intuition nor anything else can enable us to define cruelty or humanity except as
that attitude of mind with respect to the causing of pain which, upon the
whole, and under given circumstances, produces a maximum of happiness;
and this varies from age to age.

It is sometimes urged as an objection to utilitarianism that happiness is a
vague and unsettled idea. No doubt it is. Happiness has a very different meaning to a fierce pastoral tribe in Central Asia; to an ignorant husbandman in
Bengal; to a cultivated modern European; to a naked savage in Central Africa,
to say nothing of the different conceptions of happiness which are formed by
different individuals similarly situated. But what does this prove? Merely that
morality is not fixed but varying, that there is no such thing as absolute, un-
changeable morality, and that it is therefore hardly possible that there should
be moral intuitions, and this is the plain truth and the ultimate result of these
speculations. Bring any considerable number of human beings into relations
with each other. Let them talk, fight, eat, drink, continue their species, make
observations, form a society, in short, however rough or however polished,
and experience proves that they will form a conception more or less definite of
what for them constitutes happiness; that they will also form a conception of
the rules of conduct by which happiness may be increased or diminished; that
they will enforce such rules upon each other by different sanctions, and that
such rules and sanctions will produce an influence upon individual conduct
varying according to circumstances. Moreover, notwithstanding the great

differences which exist between nation and nation, country and country, the substantial resemblance between one man and another is so great that it will be found upon examination that the great leading outlines of all these systems will, in fact, closely resemble each other, and the only profitable or solid way of studying morality is to consider, to understand, and to compare these different systems, and to try to discover how far the specific rules of any particular one which may be chosen for examination really contribute to the attainment of its specific ideal; how far that ideal corresponds to the existing state of knowledge in the community which entertains it; and what are the sanctions which, at a given time and place, affect the individuals who live under it.

All of this, moreover, must be taken subject to an observation of which it is impossible to overrate the importance, though much of the speculation which is in fashion at the present day studiously keeps it out of sight. It is that the conception which a given society will form of happiness—that is to say, of the general and permanent object of human life—must always depend to a very great extent upon the view which they take as to what is in fact the nature of the world in which they live and of the life which they lead in it, and that any serious change in this conception will produce corresponding changes in all moral conceptions whatever. The question whether this present life is all that we have to look to and provide for, or whether there are reasonable grounds for supposing that it is a stage in a longer and probably larger life, and the further question whether the universe in which we live is a mere dead machine, or whether it is under the guidance of a being with whom we share the attributes of consciousness and will, overshadow all moral philosophy. The notion that two men, of whom one does and the other does not believe in God and in a future state of existence, will form the same conception of happiness, of the means by which it is to be attained, and of the motives which would dispose him individually to promote the happiness of others, is a dream as wild as any that ever was contradicted both by theory and by practice. Let it be distinctly proved and universally understood that religion is a mere delusion; that whatever else we have to love, to fear, or to hate, we need take no account at all of either God or devil, and the sun at noonday is not clearer than the conclusion that every moral conception which we can form will have to be recast. Morality would, no doubt, survive in some shape or other. There was plenty of morality in Old Rome amongst men who had little or no religion, but its whole character differed from that which was founded on Christianity. The question which moral system was the best depends principally upon the question whether the heathen philosophers or the Christian preachers were right in their estimate of the facts. To suppose that Christian morals can ever survive the downfall of the great Christian doctrine of a future state of rewards and punishments is as absurd as to suppose that a yearly tenant will feel towards his property like a tenant in fee simple. To say that, apart from the question whether there is or is not a future state of rewards and punishments, it is possible to compare the merits of Christian and heathen morality, is as absurd as to maintain that it is possible to say how the occupier of land ought to treat it without reference to the nature and extent of his interest in the land. Now the questions whether we ought to believe in God and in a future state are questions of fact and evidence, and thus the truth of the utilitarian system is proved, for it is shown that the rightness of an action depends ultimately upon the conclusions at which men may arrive as to matters of fact.

PREFACE TO
THE SECOND EDITION

As this work has been fortunate enough to be very generally criticised, I take the opportunity of a new edition to make some remarks on the most important of my critics, Mr. John Morley and Mr. Frederic Harrison. The unfortunate death of Mr. Mill makes it impossible to say whether he would have considered the book deserving of notice; but an article in the 'Fortnightly Review' by Mr. Morley* may be taken as being as near an approach as can now be had to a statement of what Mr. Mill would have said by way of reply to me on the subject of Liberty, if he had thought it worth while to say anything. I have, indeed, Mr. Morley's authority for saying that some of those best qualified to know Mr. Mill's mind, and to understand his principles, accept the article in question as a just and adequate statement of the case.

Mr. Harrison's criticism is valuable partly because it is his, and partly because the point of view from which it sets out is very different from that of Mr. Morley. The one represents the Radical, the other the positivist objections to my views.

Mr. Morley's article begins with a statement of Mr. Mill's doctrine connecting it with Milton's 'Areopagitica' and Locke's letters upon toleration. Upon this I have only to observe that I do not see much difference between Mr. Morley's account of Mr. Mill's doctrine and my own. He admits, indeed, that 'two disputable points in the above doctrine are likely to reveal themselves at once to the least critical eye.' The first is that 'that doctrine would seem to check the free expression of disapproval.' He thinks, however, that

*'Mr. Mill's Doctrine of Liberty,' 'Fortnightly Review,' Aug. 1, 1873.

this objection is satisfactorily answered by a passage in Mr. Mill's Essay, which is referred to by me at length at pp. 8–11. As Mr. Morley takes no notice of my arguments in this and other passages, it is unnecessary for me to add to them.

The 'second weak point' admitted by Mr. Morley, 'lies in the extreme vagueness of the terms protective and self-regarding' employed in Mr. Mill's main proposition that 'self-regarding' acts ought not to be interfered with and that 'self-protection' is the sole end which will justify an interference with liberty of action. Upon this Mr. Morley says, 'Can any opinion or any serious part of conduct be looked upon as truly and exclusively self-regarding? This central ingredient in the discussion seems insufficiently laboured in the Essay on Liberty.'

Mr. Morley argues (pp. 252–53) upon this subject to the following effect: He complains that I neither admit nor deny the distinction between self-regarding acts and acts which regard others; that I have failed 'to state in a definite and intelligible way my conception of the analysis of conduct on which the whole doctrine of Liberty rests'; and he suggests that I have done this because 'holding that self is the centre of all things, and that we have no motives which are not self-regarding,' I fear to say that no acts can be regarded as exclusively self-regarding, which, he adds, is the doctrine of Comte.

As to the distinction itself, he admits that 'even acts which appear purely self-regarding have indirect and negative consequences to the rest of the world.' But he says, 'You must set a limit to this "indirect and at a distance argument," as Locke called a similar plea; and the setting of this limit is the natural supplement to Mr. Mill's simple principle.' The classification he describes as 'a common sense classification,' and he says, we must continue to speak of self-regarding and not self-regarding acts, although they do not form two absolutely distinct classes, just as we speak of light, heat, and motion as distinct notwithstanding the doctrine of the conservation of physical forces.

I should have thought that my own views upon this subject were expressed with sufficient distinctness and emphasis in every part of my chapter on Liberty in relation to Morals, and in particular at pages 86 and 91–97; but as I appear to have failed, I will re-state them, and in doing so I will explain more pointedly than I have done elsewhere my view of Mr. Mill's classification of actions.

First, then, I think that the attempt to distinguish between self-regarding acts and acts which regard others is like an attempt to distinguish between acts which happen in time and acts which happen in space. Every act happens at some time and in some place, and in like manner every act that we do either does or may affect both ourselves and others. I think, therefore, that the distinction (which, by the way, is not at all a common one) is altogether fallacious and unfounded.

As to what Mr. Morley says about the 'indirect and at a distance argument,' I should admit the force of his remark if he could show that the sort of acts which he regards as specially self-regarding affected others only remotely, at a distance, and under strange and unusual circumstances. There are no doubt imperfections in language which would make it impossible ever to establish any distinctions at all if they were insisted on too closely. What, however, are the great cases of 'self-regarding' acts to which Mr. Mill's doctrine of liberty mainly applies? They are the formation and publication of opinions upon matters connected with politics, morality, and religion, and the doing of acts which may, and do, and are intended to set an example upon those subjects. Now these are all acts which concern the world at large quite as much as the individual. Luther would never have justified either the publication of his theses at Wittenberg or his marriage on the ground that they were acts which concerned himself alone. Mr. Mill would hardly have written his Essay on Liberty in order to show that it would be wrong to interfere with your neighbour's hours or with his diet.

As to my 'conception of the analysis of conduct on which the whole doctrine of liberty depends,' I thought I had given it clearly enough in the passages referred to above; but I here repeat it as shortly and pointedly as I can.

There are some acts, opinions, thoughts, and feelings which for various reasons people call good, and others which for other reasons they call bad. They usually wish to promote and encourage the one and to prevent the other. In order to do this they must use promises and threats. I say that the expediency of doing this in any particular case must depend on the circumstances of the case, upon the nature of the act prevented, and the nature of the means by which it can be prevented; and that the attempt to lay down general principles like Mr. Mill's fails for the reasons which I have assigned at length in different parts of my book. How I can put the matter more clearly than this I do not know. That people often are mistaken in their judgments as to moral good and evil, and as to truth and falsehood; that different people have conflicting ideals of happiness; that conflict is unavoidable; that most people are not half sceptical enough, and far too much inclined to meddle and persecute; and that the commonplaces about liberty and toleration have been useful, notwithstanding their falsehood, I have admitted over and over again. As to the notion that I have an interest in being obscure on this matter for fear of finding myself in contradiction to my own principle that self is every man's centre and that all motives are self-regarding, I can only say that such a criticism shows that my critic has not thought my views worth study. That self is every man's centre, and that every motive must affect and come home to the man who moves, are principles perfectly consistent with the belief that men are so connected together that it is scarcely ever possible to think of oneself except in relation to other people, and that the desire to give pleasure or pain to others is one of the commonest and strongest of our motives. Love and friendship, hatred and spite, are mixed in various degrees with nearly all that we do, think, feel, and say.

This, I think, is the most important of Mr. Morley's criticisms, though he also states and re-states in various forms that I have misunderstood Mr. Mill. I have, it seems, 'failed to see that the very aim and object of Mr. Mill's Essay is to show on utilitarian principles that compulsion in a definite class of cases—the self-regarding parts of conduct, namely—and in societies of a certain degree of development, is always bad.'

That this was Mr. Mill's 'very aim and object,' I saw, I think, as distinctly as Mr. Morley himself. My book is meant to show that he did not attain his object, that the fundamental distinction (about self-regarding acts) upon which it rests is no distinction at all, and that the limitation about 'societies of a certain degree of development' is an admission inconsistent with the doctrine which it qualifies.

A few observations of Mr. Morley's deserve notice here, and I have referred to others in foot-notes. He charges me with an 'omission to recognise that the positive quality of liberty is the essence of the doctrine which' I 'so hastily take upon' myself 'to disprove.' Mr. Mill, he says, 'held that liberty was more than a mere negation, and that there is plenty of evidence in the various departments of the history of civilisation that freedom exerts a number of positively progressive influences.'

This and other passages appear to me to show that Mr. Morley has not done me the honour to read my book with any care. I do not understand what he means by liberty, and whether or not he agrees, or supposes that Mr. Mill would have agreed, with the account which I give of the meaning of the word at page 8 and elsewhere.

Yet this definition of liberty, which is in exact agreement with Mr. Mill's own views as expressed in his chapter on Liberty and Necessity, in the 2nd volume of his Logic,*[1] is the very foundation of my book. Liberty is a eulogistic word; substitute for it a neutral word—'leave,' for instance, or 'permission'—and it becomes obvious that nothing whatever can be predicated of it, unless you know who is permitted by whom to do what. I would ask Mr. Morley whether he attaches any absolute sense whatever to the word liberty, and if so, what it is? If he attaches to it only the relative sense of 'permission' or 'leave,' I ask how he can make any affirmation at all about it unless he specifies the sort of liberty to which he refers?

Of course, liberty may have positive effects. Give all men leave to steal, and no doubt some men will steal, but this does not show that liberty itself is a definite thing, with properties of its own, like coal or water.

One of my critics,† who has so far understood me as to perceive that I regard 'the free-will doctrine as not a doctrine at all, but simply an inconceivable confusion of ideas,' gives the following strange definition of freedom: 'An action is free if it proceeds from the deliberate and rational act of the

---

*Fifth edit. pp. 413–21. I may observe that at p. 536 of the same volume, Mr. Mill did me the honour to quote, with high approbation, two essays of mine on the 'Study of History,' published in 1861, in which this theory is developed at length.[2]

1. John Stuart Mill, Collected Works of John Stuart Mill, ed. J. M. Robson, 33 vols (Toronto: University of Toronto Press, 1963–1991), vol. 8, A System of Logic: Ratiocinative and Inductive (1973), pp. 836–43.

2. In Cornhill Magazine numbers 3 and 4. Mill cites the second of these essays as "in [my] judgment the soundest and most philosophical productions which the recent controversies on this subject have called forth. . . ." Ibid., p. 941.

†'The Spectator,' June 14, 1873. Of this critic I will only say that he and I write different languages so far as the fundamental terms employed are concerned.

mind itself.' So that if a man gives up his purse to a robber, he does it freely, provided only that the robber gives him time to consider deliberately the alternative—'Your money or your life.' The opinion attributed to me is that of Locke, who says that the question 'whether the will is free' is as unintelligible and 'as insignificant as to ask whether a man's virtue is square.'*

Mr. Morley makes only one other observation general enough to be noticed here. He says that Mr. Mill's Essay on Liberty is 'one of the most aristocratic books that ever was written,' and he quotes a variety of passages in which Mr. Mill expresses the utmost possible contempt for the opinions and understandings of the great majority of his fellow-creatures. He then proceeds thus: 'Mark the use which Mr. Mill makes of his proposition that ninety-nine men are incapable of judging a matter not self-evident, and only one man capable. For this reason, he argues, leave the utmost possible freedom of thought, expression, and discussion to the whole hundred, because on no other terms can you be quite sure that the hundredth, the one judgment you want, will be forthcoming, or will have a chance of making himself effectively heard over the incapable judgments.'

'Mr. Stephen says otherwise. He declares it to be an idle dream "to say that one man in a thousand really exercises much individual choice as to his religious or moral principles. I doubt whether it is not an exaggeration to say that one man in a million is capable of making any very material addition to what is already known or plausibly conjectured on these matters."'

'Argal' (it is odd that Mr. Morley should see any point in argal) 'beware of accepting any nonsensical principle of liberty which will leave this millionth man the best possible opening for making his material addition; by the whole spirit of your legislation, public opinion, and social sentiment habitually discourage, freeze, browbeat all that eccentricity which would be sure to strike all the rest of the million in the one man and his material addition. If Mr. Stephen's book does not mean this, it means nothing, and his contention with Mr. Mill's doctrine of liberty is only a joust of very cumbrous logomachy.'

The last sentence betrays a suspicion on Mr. Morley's part that my book does not mean what he says it means. But let that pass. The real difference

*Essay, Book II. ch. xxi. s. 14. [John Locke, *An Essay concerning Human Understanding,* in *The Clarendon Edition of the Works of John Locke,* ed. P. H. Nidditch (Oxford: Clarendon Press, 1975), p. 240.]

between Mr. Mill's doctrine and mine is this. We agree that the minority are wise and the majority foolish, but Mr. Mill denies that the wise minority are ever justified in coercing the foolish majority for their own good, whereas I affirm that under circumstances they may be justified in doing so. Mr. Morley says that Mr. Mill's principle would protect the minority from being coerced by the majority, whereas my principle would expose them to such coercion. My answer is that in my opinion the wise minority are the rightful masters of the foolish majority, and that it is mean and cowardly in them to deny the right to coerce altogether for fear of its being misapplied as against themselves. The horse is stronger than the rider in one sense, but a man who maintained that horses and men ought to be entirely independent of each other for fear of the horses riding the men would be a very poor creature. In many respects one wise man is stronger than a million fools. The one man in a million who possesses extraordinary intellect, force of character, and force of sympathy is more likely to coerce the rest than they are to coerce him, and I affirm his right in certain cases to do so. Mr. Mill is so timid about the coercion of the one man (who has no business to permit himself to be coerced) by the many that he lays down a principle which confines the one man to a way of acting on his fellow-creatures which is notoriously inoperative with the vast majority of them.

Mr. Frederic Harrison's criticisms turn upon points of even greater general interest than Mr. Morley's, and are specially valuable to me because they show me to some extent what parts of my book men of his way of thinking feel a difficulty in understanding. They are contained in another article which appeared in the 'Fortnightly Review,' called 'the Religion of Inhumanity.'* It is in all respects a characteristic production. I have pointed out in foot-notes some of the strange misrepresentations which it contains. In this place I shall notice only two or three of its leading points.

Mr. Harrison represents me as the author of a new and horrible form of religion which he calls 'the Religion of Inhumanity,' or 'Stephenism.' The centre of this creed would appear to be a belief in hell. He says that I am 'preaching of hell from' my 'new edition of "Bentham"'; that I draw 'a fearful picture of the soul which has lost its trust in hell'; that I appear to think

---

*'Fortnightly Review,' June 1873, pp. 677–99.

'that, so long as we have a hell, any hell will suffice'; that I seem to say, 'spare us the last hope of eternal damnation, and you may take Bible, Gospel, Creeds, and Articles'; and much more of the same sort. To all this I reply that there is not a word in my book which implies or suggests that I believe in hell—that is, in any place or state of infinite torture reserved for the wicked after death. In fact I do not hold that doctrine, for I see no sufficient evidence of it. Mr. Harrison indeed admits this in a paragraph which appears to me to stultify all the expressions which I have quoted. After saying that I insist that 'a future state' 'is the sole sanction of morality'—a statement which is entirely opposed to the fact*—he proceeds: 'Mr. Stephen appears to think that, so long as you have a hell, any hell will suffice. But surely this is the whole point. The Christian may very well say, "we have a heaven and hell revealed, certain, and part of a system of theology. . . . But your hell," he will say to Mr. Stephen, "is a vague possibility of which you tell me nothing. To you it is a probable state which as a moralist and politician you wish men to believe in, but about which you can tell them nothing." To which he (i.e., Mr. Harrison, as distinguished from 'the Christian,') adds, If there be any hell, what do you know of it? how do you know anything about it? You do not seem to believe in the harp and tabor idea of heaven, or in the gridiron theory of hell. What are the hopes and fears you appeal to? Is your heaven and hell a transcendental state of feeling, or is it intense human pleasure and acute human pain, and, if so, pleasure of what sort, and pain of what sort? For on your answer to that question the influence it will exert over different characters entirely depends.'

After much illustration to which I do not at present refer, he says, 'There is a curious sophism running through Mr. Stephen's book, as if a future life were identical with moral reward and punishment. The two ideas are perfectly distinct, and require totally different proofs.' He adds that 'to console the wretched, religion must show how suffering will be redressed in a distinct way. To control passion, religion must show how passion will be punished with specific penalties. Otherwise a future life is a doctrine which may almost

---

*To take one passage out of many, I say, at pp. 223–24, 'The existence of a sense of duty . . . is one of the chief sanctions, in all common cases it is the chief sanction, of morality.' And at p. 224 and elsewhere, I enumerate four leading sanctions of morality.

stimulate the self-will of the self-regarding. The giants of self-help will feel that brains and nerve have carried them well through this world, and they trust they may be accepted in the next.'

Though I do not make these quotations with the view of detaining my readers with anything so petty as a personal dispute between Mr. Harrison and myself, I cannot refrain from pointing out that if my book shows that I do not believe 'in the gridiron theory of hell,' it is unjust to heap abuse upon me which is pointless unless it means to say that I do believe in it. But those who have followed Mr. Harrison's career, as I have, with interest and personal regard, will be rather amused at the super-heated steam which he is continually blowing off, than scalded by it. My object in quoting these passages is to give some explanations which they show to be necessary. If a man of Mr. Harrison's ability is so completely mistaken as these passages show him to be on the scope of my book and the doctrines which it contains, I must have failed in making my meaning plain.

In the first place it is altogether unjust to describe me as the would-be author of a new religion. My book contains no religion whatever. It is not in any sense of the word a sermon or a set of sermons. It expresses no opinion of my own upon religious questions, except a conditional one, that is to say, that the character of our morality depends and must depend upon the conceptions which we may form as to the world in which we live; that upon the supposition of the existence of a God and a future state, one course of conduct will be prudent in the widest sense of the word, and that if there is no God and no future state, a different course of conduct will be prudent in the widest sense of the word. I am not trying to make men believe in a God and a future state. I have nowhere said that I, 'as a moralist and politician, wish men to believe' in these doctrines. I have made no attempt to put forward matter which will either 'console the wretched' or 'control passion.' There is a previous question, Whether in fact there is any consolation for wretchedness? and any and what reason for controlling passion? and this I say depends upon questions of fact as to a future state and the existence of God. At present I go no further. My present object is to controvert the opinion which is so commonly and so energetically preached in these days, that morality is or can be independent of our opinions upon these points, and to show both that the prudence of virtue (as commonly understood) depends upon the question whether there is a future state or not, and that the question what is the nature of virtue, understood as the course of conduct which becomes a man, also depends upon it.

Probably this is an unfamiliar doctrine. At all events I am led to suppose that it is so by the degree in which I have been misunderstood. To some extent the misunderstanding may be due to the form of my work, which, being mainly controversial and negative, affords comparatively little opportunity for the direct expression of my own views. In order to give full expression to those views it would be necessary to write upon human nature, and the influences which restrain and direct it, namely, morals, law, and religion. I am not in a position, as regards time or otherwise, to undertake so great a task, and I have therefore been obliged to content myself with the humbler one of attempting to expose popular fallacies about Liberty, Equality, and Fraternity, glancing incidentally at the positive side of the question as I go on. I am fully sensible of the consequences of this. It gives the book an incomplete and negative aspect, and lays me open to the charge of undue reticence upon subjects at which I hint without discussing them fully. These no doubt are great defects, but they could be avoided only by the opposite and far more important defect of the publication of opinions for the due statement and defence of which I am not as yet prepared, and upon subjects on which in many cases my judgment is suspended. The defect, therefore, must be endured, but I will make a few remarks which will show at all events that Mr. Harrison's estimate of my meaning is quite mistaken.

As I have already said, the common doctrines about heaven and hell do not appear to me to be supported by adequate evidence. But the opinion that this present life is not our whole life, and that our personal consciousness in some shape survives death, appears to me highly probable. As to the further question, What sort of thing will this future state be if there is one? I can only answer, like everyone else, by a confession of ignorance. I think, however, that though we have no knowledge on the subject, we have some grounds for rational conjecture. If there is a future state, it is natural to suppose that that which survives death will be that which is most permanent in life, and which is least affected by the changes of life. That is to say, mind, self-consciousness, conscience or our opinion of ourselves, and generally those powers and feelings which, as far as we can judge, are independent of the constantly flowing stream of matter which makes up our bodies. I know not why a man should fear that he will endure bodily sufferings, or hope that he will enjoy bodily pleasures, when his body has been dispersed to the elements, but so long as a man can be said to be himself in any intelligible sense of the word, he must more or less remember and pass judgment on his past existence, and the only standard which we can imagine as being used for that purpose is the one with which we are acquainted.

The next question is, What habits of mind, what feelings and powers would a rational man cultivate here, having regard to the probability or possibility that this world is not all, but part of something larger? He would cultivate those feelings and powers which are most advantageous to him upon the supposition that he is a permanent being, and that the part of his nature which remains comparatively unaffected by the different accidents of life is the part which will remain after death.

On the other hand, I see no reason why he should suppose that any future state is generically unlike this present world, in the matter of the distribution of happiness and in the rewards and punishments of virtue and vice. Why the author of this present world, assuming it to have an intelligent author, should be supposed to give a prominence to moral good and evil in any other world which he has not given to them here, I cannot see. Important as morality is in this world, it is very far from being all-important. Many of the joys and sorrows of life are independent of moral good and evil. For instance, there are few greater pleasures than the pleasure of exercising the powers of the mind and gratifying the wider forms of curiosity. 'The eye is not filled with seeing nor the ear with hearing,' but such conduct cannot be described as either virtuous or vicious except by an abuse of terms.

Hence the supposition that this life is not all, but only a part of something wider, is important, not exclusively, perhaps not even principally, because it tends to heighten the importance of moral distinctions, or because the hypothesis, if admitted, solves the moral difficulties which many persons find in what they call (I think incorrectly) the wrongs and injustices of this present world (which, for what I know, may be repeated elsewhere), but because it supplies a reason for attaching more importance than we should attach, if this life were all, to those elements of our nature which, though permanent and deep-seated, are often weak in comparison with others of a more transient kind. If a lad were perfectly certain that he would die at twenty, he would arrange his life accordingly, and would not enter upon pursuits which could be of no value to him till a later period of life. If, on the other hand, the average length of life were 1000 years, the importance of a good character, and of the acquisition of industrious habits and intellectual tastes would be enormously increased. The chances of detection in fraud or falsehood would be multiplied. The loss of life at an early age would be a far greater evil than it now is. Our whole sphere of action and of interest would be immensely widened. But notwithstanding all this the relative importance of morality and other things, and the distribution amongst mankind of the means of happiness would not be affected in principle, though they would be greatly varied in detail.

The complete renunciation of the idea of a future state appears to me to be exactly like the certainty of death at twenty. The admission of the probability in whatever degree is like the extension of our present term. How anyone can say that the doctrine is irrelevant to human conduct is to me inconceivable. I have sometimes thought that the amiable and able men who have brought themselves to believe that they do think so, are in truth only trying to console mankind under an irreparable loss by trying to persuade them that their loss is of no importance.

It is not unnatural to ask what is the value of the probability to which you attach so much importance? I cannot affect to assign its arithmetical value, but I may remark in general terms that it appears to me common in these days to underrate the importance of probabilities, and of that imperfect knowledge which gives occasion for rational conjecture. A crack through which a glimpse of sunlight enters a room lighted by a single candle is not a large thing, but it might suggest a new world to a prisoner whose experience was bounded by those four walls. Nor would its real significance be diminished, though it might attract less attention, if the room were illuminated by a lime-light instead of a single candle. Open a very small chance of life to a man who regarded himself as doomed to death absolutely, and you substitute passionate feverish energy for the stupor of despair. In the same way, as long as men can entertain a rational hope of their own permanence, the colour, the character, and, above all, the importance of their lives will differ radically from what they would be in the absence of such a hope.

The hope in question appears to me to rest principally on everyone's experience of his own individual permanence under all manner of conditions of time, place, age, health, and the like; and if this is treated as a small matter, I would ask whether the motion of a needle over a card, the adhesion of a bit of paper to amber, a twitch in the leg of a dead frog did not afford the first indications of the greatest of physical forces. It seems to me improbable to the very last degree that the one fact of which everyone is directly conscious, and which determines and is assumed in every item of human conduct, should be unmeaning, should point to nothing at all, and suggest nothing beyond itself.

Be this as it may, whenever men of science succeed in convincing us that we exist only in the present moment as it passes, that our present consciousness, whether directed backwards or forwards, is the whole of us, and that it ceases absolutely at death, when the forces of which, as M. Renan says, it is the resultant cease to act upon each other, there will be an end of what is commonly called religion, and it will be necessary to reconstruct morals from end to end. I do not at all say that in such an event reasonable people (at least in middle age) would burst into desperate sensuality or other violent forms of vice, but I think that there would be no rational justification for the type of character which attaches more importance to what is distant than to what is present or near. Whether even upon the hypothesis of a future state the devoted, self-denying, self-sacrificing character is entitled to more admiration than a self-regarding moralist who takes account of a future life in his calculations, I need not now inquire, but if there is no future state at all the man who pursues enjoyments in the present or in the near future appears to me more reasonable than either. At all events, I do not see how a man, so acting, can be shown to do wrong.

The article which suggested these remarks ends with an attempt on the part of Mr. Harrison to meet this conclusion. He is of opinion that 'a rallying point of human life may be ultimately found in the collective power of the human race; that a practical religion may be founded on grateful acceptance of that collective power and conscious co-operation with it.' He continues: 'The history of institutions, of ideas, of morality is continually deepening our sense of a vast collective development in the energies of man, ever more distinctly knitting up in one the spirit of races, and forming that dominant influence which ultimately shapes the life of societies and of men.' This, he says, is called by theologians 'the mind of God working out his purpose in the history of man'; the philosopher calls it 'the evolution of intelligence bringing contradictions to a law of higher unity'; the historian calls it 'the development of ages and the law of civilization'; the politician calls it 'human progress.' For my part I call it a bag of words which means anything, everything, or nothing, just as you choose. Mr. Harrison, however, thinks otherwise. Humanity, he says, 'has organic being, and beams with human life.' It is 'the stream of human tendency in which the good alone is incorporated, but in which is incorporated every thought or feeling or deed which has added to the sum of human good.' (I have to abridge a good deal, for Mr. Harrison's style is rather diffuse.) 'This is no hypothesis, no theory, no probability. There it stands, its work and its influence as capable of solid demonstration as the English nation or any other organic whole which is not within the range of the eye.' On the other hand, 'It contains not all that ever were, for countless lives of men have but added to its diseases or its excrescences. It contains not all that are, for thousands have organic life in no other sense than as secretions and parasites.' Language like this appears to me like that of a woman who, having lost her real child, dresses up a doll, and declares that it does a great deal better, as there is no fear of its dying. 'Humanity,' as an abstract term for the whole human race, past, present, and future, no doubt is as intelligible as other abstract terms, though, like all very wide abstractions, it has scarcely any meaning, but the humanity which excludes whatever the person using the expression regards as diseases, excrescences, parasites, and secretions, which takes up only what he regards as good, and rejects what he regards as bad, is, as I have said, simply I writ large. It is to each of its worshippers a glorified representation of himself and his own ideas. To take Mr. Harrison's own illustration, the English nation is a definite expression. It means the inhabitants of a definite portion of territory, with their various institutions and the acts done in their corporate capacity; but as soon as this intelligible idea is abandoned, as soon as we are told that there is an abstract transcendental England which represents and incorporates whatever is good in the actual England, that not everyone born in England is a true Englishman, and that 'countless lives' of so-called Englishmen have only added to the diseases and excrescences of the nation, the phrase 'the English nation' ceases to have any definite meaning at all.

Mr. Harrison insists at considerable length on the beauties of a religion of which this impalpable cloud is the God. It shows us, he says, 'the immortal nature of all true life. It shows how the man, the soul, the sum of the moral powers, live eternally, and are most really and actively continuing their task in the mighty life in which they are incorporated but not absorbed.' He observes incidentally, as if it were a matter of no great importance, 'It may be that it will not be a life of sensation or of consciousness, but it is not the less truly life for all that, since all that makes the soul great will work continually and in ever new and grander ways.' At last, after a tribute to the memory of Mr. Mill, which is an expansion of the statement that he rests from his labours and his works follow him—that is, that his influence still survives—he concludes with these remarkable words, 'We, of all others, have a right to say, "O Death, where is thy sting? O Grave, where is thy victory?"'

It would be harsh to ridicule any considerations, however empty they may appear, which really have power to console a man in the presence of the death of a friend, but I cannot understand how the fact that a man's books can be read, and that his opinions will continue to exercise an influence after he is dead, can console for his death anyone who really cares about him. If the books of the deceased were not read when he was alive, if his death in any way increased his influence, there might be some consolation in the substitution of the greater posthumous influence for the lesser living influence. The real sting of death, and victory of the grave, lies in the fact that this is not so; that if when a man dies there is an end of him, something is gone which can never be replaced. The records of his thoughts, and the effect of his acts may remain, but if he had gone on living, they would have not only been just as good, but he might have improved them. Whereas by his death they in a sense die also; they become incapable of further alteration. Besides, a man, if he is fit to be called a man, is other and more than his thoughts, words, or deeds. To tell a widow who had lost her husband that death had lost its sting because she could go and read his old letters, or his books (if he was an author), would be a cruel mockery. I do not think Mr. Harrison is capable of writing anything cruel, but his funeral oration is essentially a mockery. It could console no one who wished to be consoled. The death of a friend admits of no consolation at all. Its sting to the survivors lies in the hopeless separation which it produces, and in the destruction of a world of common interests, feelings, and recollections which nothing can replace. The amount of suffering which it inflicts depends on the temperament of the survivors, but it impoverishes them more or less for the rest of their lives, like the loss of a limb or a sense. The lapse of time no doubt accustoms and reconciles us to everything, but I do not believe anything can blunt the sting of death or qualify the victory of the grave, except a belief of some sort as to a future state; and that, for obvious reasons, does little enough. The common views upon the subject are anything but consolatory, and the more rational views are of necessity vague. Their importance lies not in creating definite posthumous fears, or in applying definite hopes or consolations to definite suffering, but in the fact that they give to life, and especially to that which is most permanent in life, a degree of dignity which could hardly attach to anything so transient and uncertain as the time which we pass upon this earth, if it is viewed as the whole of our existence.

As to Mr. Harrison's language about the soul working continually in new and grander ways, after it has ceased to have conscious existence at all, it appears to me as empty and unsatisfying as undertaker's plumes. It would be just as much to the purpose to say that our bodies do not really die because the matter which composed them is here, there, and everywhere, forming part of the water of the clouds, part of the grass of the earth, part of the cattle which feed upon it, and part of men perhaps better and wiser than ourselves who feed on the cattle. Play with these fancies as you will, death is death, and if nothing lies beyond it, it is nearly related to despair, for it is the end of all rational hopes and wishes. Wherever individual consciousness ends, existence ends. A man either is himself, or he does not exist at all.

There is one other point in Mr. Harrison's article which calls for notice. He totally misapprehends the object of my chapter on the distinction between the temporal and the spiritual power, and he naturally misrepresents what I have said on the subject. As to his misrepresentations, I have dealt with them as far as I thought it necessary in foot-notes to the passages misrepresented, and I will only say here that they may be summed up in a few words. Mr. Harrison supposes me to teach 'the paradox' of 'the essential identity of material and moral power,' in order to establish the conclusion that the 'State ought to be the Church,' that 'it is not to be a Pope-king, but only a King-pope.' If Mr. Harrison had read the chapter in question with any care, he would have seen that I said nothing of the sort.

I admit as fully as anyone can the difference between temporal and spiritual power. The one I say is the power which rests upon temporal sanctions, and the other the power which rests upon spiritual sanctions, and I think that when for this expression, Mr. Harrison substitutes the word 'hell,' he does me great injustice. I mean by spiritual sanctions all the hopes and fears, all the feelings of various kinds which may be excited by the prospect of a future state.

What I deny is the right of positivists, who do not believe in spiritual sanctions at all, and who do not accept the distinction between spirit and matter, to make use of the word 'spiritual,' and I say that their theory becomes nonsense without it.

Again I do not deny, but assert, the distinction between persuasion and force.

What I deny is that this distinction corresponds to the distinction between temporal and spiritual power. I observe indeed, in passing, that persuasion and force run into each other, as do many other dissimilar things, but the whole of my argument shows that I recognise the distinction, as, indeed, Mr. Harrison himself proves from other parts of my book, thinking to catch me in a contradiction. This, however, is unnecessary to my argument, and the passage which Mr. Harrison refers to as if it conveyed the substance of the whole chapter might have been struck out of the book without interfering with its principal positions. The whole chapter forms a carefully constructed argument, and it is difficult to answer it without an equally careful consideration of it as a whole.

I do not, however, care to insist upon these matters. It is more important to remark that Mr. Harrison has entirely failed to understand not merely the argument itself, but the object for which the argument was composed, and its place in the general discussion. He supposes me to wish to substitute 'a King-pope for a Pope-king,' and to teach that 'the State ought to take in hand the moral and religious guidance of the public.' I have not the slightest wish for either of these things. I have as little belief in the infallibility of Parliament as Mr. Harrison himself, and I should have thought that few men were less open to the charge of a blind admiration for the Statute Book. The object of the chapter in question, and indeed one main object of the whole book, is to show that every attempt to lay down theoretical limits to the power of governments must necessarily fail, and that the method of specific experience is in politics the only one from which much good can be got. Thus I have tried to show that Mr. Mill's principle about Liberty is mere rhetoric dressed out to look like logic, and that the principle which warns off the State from a whole department of life on the ground that it is 'spiritual' while the State is 'temporal,' is a juggle of words. I do not mean for a moment to say that Parliament ought to lay down a religious creed and enforce its acceptance by penalties. I should as soon think of recommending it to determine controversies about mathematics. What I do say is that the government of a great nation can never be carried on satisfactorily without reference more or less direct and frequent to moral and religious considerations, and that when such considerations come before parliaments or other civil rulers, they ought not to refuse to entertain them on the ground that they are of a spiritual nature, just as they ought not in case of need to shrink from taking a side in mathematical or scientific controversies. I should not wish to see Parliament enter upon the discussion of the Athanasian Creed, any more than I should wish to see them enter upon the discussion of the controversy between the rival theories as to the character of light, but it seems to me as absurd to blame the legislation of Henry VIII or that of the present Emperor of Germany on the ground that it trespasses on the spiritual province, as it would be to blame the authors of the Act for changing the style in 1752 on the ground that they trespassed on the province of mathematics. In short, what I have at heart is not the establishment by authority of an official creed, but the general recognition of the principle that men cannot be governed either by priests or by parliaments without reference to the most important part of human nature.

Suppose, for instance, that so simple a question as this is to be determined, Shall the law proceed on the principle of *caveat emptor,* or shall it compel the vendor to disclose to the purchaser defects in the thing to be sold? This question forms a branch of the law of contracts, and must obviously be decided by law. It is no less obvious that it has a distinct relation to morals, and that the solution of it one way or the other will produce an appreciable effect on the morals of the nation. Here then is a case in which the governing power must act with reference to morals.

I might heap up such illustrations indefinitely, but I will mention only two glaring ones—War and Capital punishment. I know not what morality is worth if it does not take notice of acts of such significance as the deliberate putting of a man to death, or a war which may devastate a nation, and change the whole course of its thoughts and the character of its institutions. It appears to me that those who have to decide upon such questions cannot hope to decide them rightly if they regard themselves as being excluded by their position from the consideration of the great principles of morals and religion, which, whether they are called spiritual or not, lie at the very root of human life. Mr. Harrison, if I understand him rightly, means (as he says Comte means) by the word 'spiritual,' 'all that concerns the intellectual, moral, and religious life of man, as distinct from the material.' Passing over Mr. Harrison's account of the distinction between the moral and material nature of man, I observe that the whole object and point of the chapter which he attacks is to show that every important part of human life, and in particular everything which deserves the name of law and government, is intimately connected with the 'intellectual, moral, and religious life of man,' and can no more be carried on without constant and habitual reference thereto than the muscles or bones can move if their connection with the brain is cut off, or if the brain itself loses that mysterious power, whatever it is, which the nerves transmit. I say in short that all the problems of government, law, and morals revolve round the questions which lie at the root of religion—What? Whence? Whither? The lay legislator, the lawyer who is not a mere tradesman, need a creed as much as the priest. Each wishes more or less to regulate, or at all events to affect artificially, every branch of human life. Each has his own means of action and his own objects. Much is to be said as to the truth of the different theories which different priests and different laymen adopt upon these points, and as to the efficiency of the means of which they dispose; but the value and the force of their respective schemes will be found to depend ultimately upon the degree of truth or probability which they contain. Their success in carrying them out will depend on the degree in which they understand the nature of the instruments of which they dispose. But it is idle to try to parcel out human life into provinces over some of which the priest, and over others of which the legislator is to preside. Both laws and sermons affect the whole of life, though in different ways.

I will try to explain this principle a little more fully, as it appears to me to be of the last importance and to be continually overlooked. The great instrument by which parliaments, kings, magistrates of every sort rule, is law. Law, as I have shown in various parts of my book, affects all human conduct directly or indirectly, and is itself connected with and affected by all the principles which lie deepest in human nature, and which would usually be called spiritual. Though in this sense law applies to things spiritual just as much as theology, its application must of necessity be limited by considerations which arise out of its nature as law. It can only forbid or command acts capable of accurate definition and specific proof, and so on. (See p. 97.)

The great instrument by which priests rule is an appeal not merely to heaven and hell, personal hope and fear, but to a variety of hopes and fears, sympathies and antipathies, which depend upon and refer to an unseen and future world. These hopes and fears, sympathies and antipathies, affect people's conduct in reference to this present life as directly as law affects them, and in this sense religion is as temporal as law. It differs from law in the circumstance that the foundations on which it ultimately rests are the sentiments of those to whom it is addressed. Those sentiments are determined by causes which lie outside both religion and law. They vary in force from person to person, place to place, and generation to generation. The instrument used by the priest differs from the instrument used by the legislator, in being on the one hand more delicate and more powerful where it acts at all, but on the other hand less definite in all cases and less general in its application. Law and religion might be compared not quite fancifully to surgery and medicine. Surgical and medical treatment each affect the same subject, namely the whole human body, and every part of it. Surgery, when required at all, may, under circumstances, be required by anyone—the strongest and most healthy, as well as the most delicate, and when applied it produces in every case closely analogous effects. A man who loses a hand loses it equally and sustains the same sort of loss whether he is old or young, strong or weak, healthy or sickly. Medical treatment on the other hand presupposes a certain state of body, and produces effects which, if in some instances more radical than those of surgery, are far less definite, and are varied in every case by individual peculiarities of constitution. Men who try to divide human life into a temporal and spiritual province appear to me to commit the mistake of a man who should say that medical treatment had no effect on the muscles and that surgery had nothing to do with the nerves. Mr. Harrison's criticism on me is about as intelligent as if he had charged me with wishing to do away with the distinction between physicians and surgeons because I had pointed out the fact that the whole of the human body is the province of each, or as if from my having (suppose) a low opinion of medicine he had drawn the inference that I thought that surgical operations ought to be performed on everyone who caught cold or was threatened with consumption.

To point the matter still more, let us assume, for the sake of argument, that the doctrine which he twits me with so lavishly, and I must add, so coarsely— the doctrine of eternal damnation—were indisputably proved to be true, and were heartily accepted as such by all mankind. Surely it would have a most direct and powerful influence both upon law and upon religion. To take one instance out of a million, it would have a direct and important bearing on the question of capital punishment in the province of law, and it would obviously determine the whole character of religious teaching.

Suppose, on the other hand, it were to be established beyond all doubt whatever that there is no life at all beyond the grave, and that this doctrine was accepted by the whole human race with absolute confidence. This would have an equally powerful and direct influence both on law and morals. The value which is set upon human life, especially upon the lives of the sick, the wretched, and superfluous children would at once appear to be exaggerated. Lawyers would have occasion to reconsider the law of murder, and especially the law of infanticide; priests would have to pass over in a body to some such creed as Mr. Harrison's, or to give up their profession altogether.

I will shortly notice in conclusion the efforts made by Mr. Harrison to explain and to show the importance of the distinction between the temporal and spiritual provinces of life. He says: 'Human nature consists of actions, thoughts, and feelings; and life has also its material, intellectual, and moral sides. When societies form, they throw up various forces which aim at giving some discipline to these material, intellectual, and moral energies of man. The force which tries to give order to the material life of man is necessarily a physical force, because the energies it undertakes to combine are at bottom muscular, and in the last resort muscle must be overcome by a superiority of combined muscles, and any combined direction of muscles involves this inferiority. This is the essential element in what we call the State, and as it is the condition of any other government, it is the first to appear. In half-civilised communities the State uses this muscular superiority to order not only the material concerns of the community, but the intellectual and moral concerns.'

He then proceeds to show that the 'ultimate appeal to muscular power' can be made only in a rather narrow class of cases. Law proper can only prohibit.

He then adds: 'The non-material energies of mankind are organised and stimulated in a very different way. Muscular force will not control them, whether it be thought or feeling, emotion or art. The powers which order feelings and thoughts may justly resort to positive appeals. They must erect ideal standards, lay down grand principles, and show uncompromising consistency.' 'Such men make the religious teachers, the moralists, the philosophers.' He adds a little further on: '*Of course society is made up of these elements together, and almost every act of life is a combination of them.* But the organs or centres of expression of these respective kinds of power are distinct, just as head and heart are distinct, though both of the body. And these organs of social authority, like the organs of the body, will act in different ways and under different conditions'; and he goes on to show the evils which follow when law-givers and philosophers encroach on each other's provinces, and employ law or preaching for purposes for which they are not adapted.

Mr. Harrison's views as to the State representing 'muscular power' appear to me very strange. I should have thought in the first place that the muscles had no power at all except through their connection with the nerves and the brain, which are also the organs of thought and feeling in so far as thought and feeling can be referred to the physical organisation, and it would be strange to learn from Mr. Harrison that they cannot. In the next place I should also have thought that the roughest and most exclusively muscular hero could no more dispense with thought or morals of some sort than an English Prime Minister. There is surely no lack either of intellect or of morality in the warriors of the Iliad, though neither their intellect nor their moral qualities are employed upon the same objects or regulated by the same principles as ours. From the first day when a savage perseveringly chipped a flint axe-head into shape, intellect, feeling, and action have gone hand in hand. We cannot even imagine the one without the other. Putting this aside, however, it will perhaps surprise Mr. Harrison to learn that I not only agree in the greater part of what he has said, but have actually said the same thing myself in the chapter which he supposes himself to have refuted. The passages quoted amount to saying that by spiritual and temporal Mr. Harrison means theory and practice, and that, in his opinion, the proper functions of practical men and philosophers differ, and cannot be confounded without mischievous results. I have said the same thing with some qualifications at p. 78, and have pointed out that if this is what positivists mean by what they say about the temporal and spiritual powers, they throw a very well-worn commonplace into most inappropriate language, and as it would appear for an indirect purpose. Mr. Harrison appears either not to have read this passage or to have forgotten it.

I have only one other remark of his to notice. It is as follows:

'In these days, when the tide sets so fiercely against State religion, it is strange to find a practical man like Mr. Stephen arguing for such a paradox as a State religion and a State morality.' I have never argued for what is usually meant by a State religion. What I have argued for is the proposition that both religion and morals have in a thousand ways direct relations to political and legal questions, which will be decided this way or that according to the views which people take on religion and morals. I think, therefore, that politicians should not be afraid, when the occasion arises, to take account of the question whether this religion or that is true, whether this moral doctrine or that is well founded. I protest, in short, against the dogma which appears to be received by so many people in these days, that statesmen, as such, are bound to treat all religions, or at least all common forms of religion, as having an equal claim to be regarded as true. In such a question, for instance, as that of Irish education, Parliament, according to this doctrine, would have no moral right to consider the question whether the Roman Catholic Church is or is not what it professes to be.

As to the question whether a State religion, in the sense of an endowed Church with more or less authority over individuals, should or should not be established or maintained in any given country, it is a question of time, place, and circumstance, on which no general proposition can, in my opinion, be laid down.

That Mr. Harrison should object to a State morality appears to me astonishing. What is international law except a branch of State morality? What is the whole volume of positivist essays called 'International policy,' published by Mr. Harrison and his friends a few years ago, except a series of awakening discourses on the many sins of this benighted country, addressed to it by zealous preachers. It is really a little hard upon a poor sinner if his clergyman says to him, Not only have you broken each and every one of the ten commandments, but you actually are presumptuous enough to believe that there are ten commandments to break. You are not only immoral, but you claim to have a conscience.

Of the other criticisms made upon my book I have nothing to say, nor should I have noticed those of Mr. Morley and Mr. Harrison if they had not been in a certain sense representative performances.

INDEX

COMPARATIVE TABLE OF SUBJECTS
IN JAMES FITZJAMES STEPHEN'S
LIBERTY, EQUALITY, FRATERNITY
AND JOHN STUART MILL'S
ON LIBERTY

We offer this table of subjects comparing Stephen's *Liberty, Equality, Fraternity* with Mill's *On Liberty* so readers can more easily examine the alternative understandings of liberty and other related moral and political matters found in these two works. Such an examination may also provide a vehicle for reassessing Stephen's place in the history of nineteenth century political thought and the history of liberty.

On some subjects, for example, utilitarianism and marriage, the reader will find more extensive discussions in Mill's *Utilitarianism* and *The Subjection of Women*; however, we have limited our comparison to *On Liberty*. Nor does this table include other subject-themes that are important to *Liberty, Equality, Fraternity*, such as "the Religion of Humanity," when they are not central to *On Liberty*.

We have tended to choose Mill's idiom rather than Stephen's for the names of the subjects. Insofar as an examination of liberty is ubiquitous throughout the two works, especially *On Liberty*, we did not think it necessary to have a separate entry for "liberty." The page references to *On Liberty* cite two different editions: *On Liberty with The Subjection of Women and Chapters on Socialism*, ed. Stefan Collini, Cambridge Texts in the History of Political Thought (Cambridge: Cambridge University Press, 1989); and *Collected Works of John Stuart Mill*, ed. J. M. Robson, 33 vols. (Toronto: University of Toronto Press, 1963–1991), vol. 18, *Essays on Politics and Society*.

Subject	Liberty, Equality, Fraternity *Liberty Fund Edition*	On Liberty *Cambridge Edition*	On Liberty *Toronto Edition*
Calvinism	29–32	62	265
Character	11, 95–96	15, 23, 28–29, 41–43, 52, 53–63	226, 232, 236, 247, 248, 256, 258–66
Coercion	6, 8, 10, 11–17, 18–20, 21, 31, 36–51, 76–78, 82, 86–87, 111–12, 128, 230	13, 15, 56–57, 75–78, 80, 83, 98, 102–5, 108	223, 225, 260, 276–78, 280, 283, 295, 299–301, 304
Democracy	120–21, 155–62	7–8, 48–49, 66	219, 253–54, 269
Diversity (variety)	32–34, 45, 91, 95	3, 45, 47, 49, 52, 57–58, 68, 72, 74, 106, 110	215, 250, 252, 254, 257, 260, 261, 270, 274, 275, 302, 306
Education	37–38, 49, 103–4, 137, 151, 152–53	46, 51, 57, 72–73, 76, 102, 105–8	251, 255, 261, 273, 274, 277, 299, 301, 302, 304
Equality	4, 120, 124–63	48, 89	254, 287
Family	82–83, 92, 108, 138	61, 81, 105, 108	264, 281, 301, 304–5
Fraternity	3–4, 120, 132, 164–203		
Freedom of the will	5, 233–34	5	217
Human nature	10, 31, 114, 240	17, 60–63, 69, 69n, 77	227, 263–66, 271n, 272, 278
Individuality	7, 24, 29–31, 33–34	8, 49, 57–61, 63–67, 69, 71, 73–77, 81, 106, 110	220, 254, 261–64, 266–69, 271, 273, 275–78, 281, 302, 306

Subject	Liberty, Equality, Fraternity *Liberty Fund Edition*	On Liberty *Cambridge Edition*	On Liberty *Toronto Edition*
Justice	87, 122, 125–33, 136, 141–42, 153, 174–75	14, 28, 63, 70, 83	224, 236, 266, 272, 282
Law	40, 46, 49, 97–108, 109–10, 248, 250	9–12, 13–14, 16, 19, 26, 31, 34, 46, 54, 61, 75, 81–82, 87–88, 90, 97, 105, 106, 114	220–23, 224, 226, 228, 234, 239, 241, 252, 258, 264, 276, 281–82, 286–87, 289, 295, 301, 303, 309
Liberalism	67	7	218–19
Liberty of thought	7, 19–20, 21–22, 24–29, 37–51, 54–57, 57–69, 82, 91	15, 17, 19–55	225, 227, 228–59
Marriage	139–143, 145, 148–50, 153–54	91–92, 103, 108	290, 300, 304
Morality	8–10, 11, 13–15, 52–53, 56–60, 63, 75, 83–110, 127–28, 145, 166–71, 174–82, 186–87, 191–203, 215–27	9–11, 14–17, 26, 41, 49–51, 56, 59, 69, 78, 81–82, 83–84, 87, 95, 98–102, 104, 108, 114	220–22, 224–27, 234, 247, 254–56, 260, 262, 271, 279, 281–82, 283–84, 286, 293, 296–98, 300–1, 304, 309
Nation	110–11, 145, 152	7, 42, 112	218, 248, 307–8
Order	116	48, 112	253, 307
Privacy	106–8	16, 51, 83, 86–88	226, 256, 283, 285–87
Progress	116–18, 136, 143–44, 146, 179–80, 183–84	5–6, 9, 13, 41, 43, 47–48, 57, 70, 92–93	217–18, 220, 224, 247, 249, 252–53, 261, 272, 291

Subject	Liberty, Equality, Fraternity *Liberty Fund Edition*	On Liberty *Cambridge Edition*	On Liberty *Toronto Edition*
Public opinion	104–9	12–13, 20, 27, 66, 69, 72–73, 84, 85–86	223, 229, 235, 268, 271, 274–75, 283, 285
Punishment	8–9, 10–13, 58, 97–99, 128–29, 246–47	19–20n, 29, 34, 56, 78–81, 94, 98, 100, 108	228n, 237, 241, 260, 278, 279–81, 292, 295, 297, 304
Religion	3–4, 8–9, 12–14, 16, 37–51, 54–56, 58–69, 73–81, 84n, 89, 93–94, 110–11, 151, 194–204, 206–7, 210, 212–13, 235–41, 251	11–12, 17, 23–24, 33–34, 33n, 37–40, 43–44, 49–53, 62, 69n, 83–87, 85n, 90–92, 107	222, 227, 236, 240–41, 240n, 244–46, 249–50, 254, 255–58, 265, 271n, 283–85, 285n, 289–90, 303
Rights	85, 128–29, 136–37, 139	6, 11, 59, 63, 73, 75, 78, 89, 102, 105	218, 222, 262, 266, 274, 276, 279, 288, 299, 301
Self-development	77	3, 8, 35, 57, 63–64, 66–68, 72, 79, 89, 109, 115	215, 220, 242, 261, 266–67, 269–70, 274, 279, 288, 305, 310
Self-regarding conduct	16–18, 85–87, 230–32	10, 13–16, 75–84, 98–99	221, 223–24, 277–85, 295–96
Socialism	120		
Utilitarianism	5, 6, 35–36, 89, 125, 129–30, 132, 136–37, 166–67, 170, 171–72, 175, 178–79, 193–94, 204, 215–27, 233	14, 27	224, 238
Virtue	93, 96–104, 108–9, 114, 187	20n, 27–28, 33, 60	228n, 235–36, 239, 264

*This book was set in Berner, Varityper's version of Sabon.
Sabon was designed by Jan Tschichold in the 1960s.
Based upon sixteenth-century French types,
it is an Old Style face and is characterized by a
flowing passage from thick to thin strokes
and by bracketed serifs.*

*Printed on paper that meets the requirements
of ANSI/NISO Z39.48-1992 (Permanence of Paper).* ∞

*Editorial services and composition by
Custom Editorial Productions, Inc., Cincinnati, Ohio
Design by Sandra Strother Hudson, Athens, Georgia
Index by Shirley Kessel, Primary Sources Research,
Chevy Chase, Maryland
Printed and bound by Sheridan Books, Inc.,
Chelsea, Michigan*